"I'm Not a Racist, But. . ."

"I'm Not a Racist, But..."

The Moral Quandary of Race

Lawrence Blum

CORNELL UNIVERSITY PRESS

Ithaca and London

First published 2002 by Cornell University Press
First printing, Cornell Paperbacks, 2002

Printed in the United States of America

Library of Congress Cataloging-in-Publication Data

Blum, Lawrence A.
    "I'm not a racist, but—": the moral quandary of race / Lawrence
Blum.
        p. cm.
    Includes bibliographical references and index.
    ISBN 0-8014-3869-1 (cloth : alk. paper)
    ISBN 0-8014-8815-X (pbk. : alk. paper)
    1. Racism—Moral and ethical aspects. 2. Race discrimination. 3.
Social ethics. I. Title.
    HT1523 .B58 2001
    305.8—dc21

                                        2001042296

Cornell University Press strives to use environmentally responsible suppliers and materials to the fullest extent possible in the publishing of its books. Such materials include vegetable-based, low-VOC inks, and acid-free papers that are recycled, totally chlorine-free, or partly composed of nonwood fibers. Books that bear the logo of the FSC (Forest Stewardship Council) use paper taken from forests that have been inspected and certified as meeting the highest standards for environmental and social responsibility. For further information, visit our website at www.cornellpress.cornell.edu.

Cloth printing   10 9 8 7 6 5 4 3 2
Paperback printing   10 9 8 7 6 5 4 3 2 1

Contents

Preface

Two years ago, the University of Massachusetts at Boston, where I teach, examined the "racial climate" on campus, and students were encouraged to air their concerns. Karen and some other African American students concluded that their department did not feel hospitable to them. They reported their findings to members of the department and Joe, a white professor, was fairly representative of his colleagues in reacting defensively. He felt he had been charged with being a racist, and found it difficult to hear what the black students had to say. Further investigation revealed that virtually all students, not just blacks, found the department generally unfriendly. Joe was relieved: "At least it isn't racial." The issue seemed to lose some of its urgency. Karen and her fellow students felt their concerns had been swept under the rug.

Joe and his colleagues missed a chance for constructive dialogue with the black students, as well as an opportunity to address a problem facing all their students. On both counts they were blinded by a concern, widely shared in the contemporary United States, especially among whites, not to be seen as "racist." Perhaps the cause of the problem in Joe's department was not racism. But it may still have been racial; the black students like Karen may be more sensitive to messages of unwelcome, as they struggle for an acceptance at the university that white students generally take for granted. At the same time, the black students had tuned into a problem of unfriendliness facing all the students in the department.

The terms "racist" and "racism" are undoubtedly conversation stoppers. Yet how many of us have asked ourselves exactly what they mean? If we agree that racism is so important, don't we need to know what it is? How can we talk intelligently, especially across racial lines, unless we do? Furthermore, in the past several decades, "racism" has come to be used so expansively as to refer to virtually anything regarded as wrong in the area of race. This "conceptual inflation," in Robert Miles's felicitous phrase, has prompted a conservative backlash. "Racism" is said to have become virtually meaningless, and those accused of it are thus encouraged not to take the charge to heart.

I suggest in these pages that moral philosophy can help us out. We need to clarify what racism is, to find a basis in history and current use for fixing a definition, one that will reveal why racism is rightly regarded as a grievous moral wrong. At the same time we need to recognize the manifold ways things can go racially wrong, without being racist. Joe and his colleagues may have been racially insensitive, failing to appreciate the concerns of their black students, without being racist. A racial anxiety not rooted in actual racial prejudice can prevent people of any racial group from reaching out to those of other groups. A morally based approach can help us retrieve a more nuanced value-laden vocabulary than "racism" and "racist" for characterizing racial wrongs and missteps.

Racism seems to presuppose that there are things called "races," and in recent years the idea of race has come to seem increasingly problematic. Again, a moral perspective helps us make sense of this confused state of things. I question whether races exist, but as long as people think there are races, there can be racism. "Race," as it has structured our thinking and our world, is a morally infused idea, and a destructive one at that. It has a reality that is partly distinct from "racism," and demands an account informed by morality.

I am indebted to the support and assistance of many friends and colleagues. For their valuable and insightful feedback, I thank Anita Allen, K. Anthony Appiah, Rene Arcilla, Benjamin Blum-Smith, John Broughton, Harry Chotiner, George Frederickson, Marilyn Friedman, Jorge L. A. Garcia, Lani Guinier, Marcia Homiak, Jennifer Hochschild, Martha Minow, Melissa Nobles, Nel Noddings, Diane Paul, Audrey Smedley, Laurence Thomas, Cally Waite, David Wilkins, and Alan Zaslavsky. I am especially grateful to Sharon Lamb, Sally Haslanger, and David Wong, who have been particularly generous with their personal and intellectual support at many crucial moments in the course of this project. This book was an outgrowth of an earlier project focused on education, and I am grateful to

Laura Black, Margaret Cronin, Angela Harris, Ronald Elson, Sharon Lamb, Eleanor Lee, and Frances Maher for their responses to that manuscript. I benefit in an ongoing way from two longstanding discussion groups—the Pentimento group and the Moral Psychology group. I thank the National Endowment for the Humanities, that vital yet underfunded source of support for those of us working in the humanities, for a fellowship in 1995–96 that allowed me to begin work in earnest on this project.

Thanks to Cornell University Press for permission to use a previously published article, "Moral Asymmetries in Racism," in *Racism and Philosophy*, ed. Susan Babbitt and Sue Campbell, as a basis for chapter 2. Writing on race and racism is a daunting task, especially from a strict disciplinary perspective. Virtually every discipline bears on the subject. Philosophers, I believe, owe a particular debt to those mostly African American philosophers—Bernard Boxill, Laurence Thomas, Adrian Piper, Lucius Outlaw, Anita Allen, Leonard Harris, Howard McGary, Albert Mosley, Tommy Lott, Bill Lawson, and others—who wrote on racial topics in the 1980s. Long before the profession could see its way clear to making sessions on race and racism a staple of American Philosophical Association meetings, they demonstrated that race is philosophically significant and showed how philosophy can make a distinctive contribution. I want to acknowledge my debt to these pioneers.

My greatest personal debt, which I happily acknowledge, is to Judith Smith. Jude has always been available to read chapter drafts and to discuss ideas with which I was struggling. Her historical and cultural-studies perspectives on race in American history have been an invaluable source of insight and wisdom. I am fortunate that my own intellectual interests have drifted close enough to hers to benefit from her expertise. For her love, friendship, everyday partnership, and intellectual comradeship I am deeply grateful.

I hope for this work to contribute to fruitful conversation about race and racism especially among persons of different racial groups. During the writing of this book, I have had the good fortune to teach at educational institutions that are a good deal more racially and ethnically mixed than the average, and thereby to explore the challenges of learning, and teaching students to learn, to listen and respond across racial boundaries. I am especially grateful to my students at the University of Massachusetts at Boston for their honest, grounded, and open-minded engagement with racial issues. I have learned much from them. UMass/Boston is a particularly hospitable environment for this sort of work, and I am grateful to my supportive and stimulating colleagues, especially those in the philosophy department and in a long-standing interracial and international faculty discussion group. I also learned a great deal from the students I taught in courses relating to race and multiculturalism at Teachers College in 1997, and especially from the engaged and open-hearted high school students (and my teaching assistants, Myriam Guerrier and Nakia Keizer) in a course on race and racism at the Cambridge Rindge and Latin public school in 1999 and 2000. Finally, I have profited from my association over the years with Facing History and Ourselves, an exemplary antiracist and civic education professional development organization for educators in grades 7–12.

I thank Ishani Maitra and Barbara Martin for utilizing internet skills far surpassing my own to track down representative uses, and frequency, of "racist" and "racism" in the news media in the 1990s; Barbara also located essential resources in the final stages of the manuscript. Sarah Blum-Smith's exceptional organizational abilities helped keep my accumulated materials from burying me alive, and Johanna Black and Laura Black helped with a similar task at earlier stages. Catherine Rice of Cornell University Press has been as supportive and constructive an editor as an academic author could hope to have. My copy editor, Joel Ray, has miraculously reworked my philosopher's prose for consumption by non-philosophers. I am grateful to both of them.

I would like to dedicate this book to my children Laura, Sarah, and Benjamin Blum-Smith. My initial interest in the intersection of racial, moral, and educational matters was prompted by reflecting on the racially mixed world of their schools and friends—so different from my own at their age. I see my children, each in her and his own way, reaching for a world more equal, more diverse, and more harmonious than the one they have inherited. I am deeply proud of them, and hope this books sheds a bit of light on their path.

LAWRENCE BLUM

Cambridge, Massachusetts

"I'm Not a Racist, But. . ."

1

"Racism": Its Core Meaning

A part from a small number of avowed white supremacists, most Americans wish very much to avoid being called "racist."[1] Yet the moral reproach carried by the term is threatened by a current tendency to overuse it. Some feel that the word is thrown around so much that anything involving "race" that someone does not like is liable to castigation as "racist." "Is television a racist institution?" asked an article concerning the National Association for the Advancement of Colored People's (NAACP) criticism of prime-time network shows for having no "minority" actors in lead roles.[2] A local newspaper called certain blacks "racist" for criticizing other blacks who supported a white over a black candidate for mayor.[3] A white girl in Virginia said that it was "racist" for an African American teacher in her school to wear African attire.[4] The Milton, Wisconsin, school board voted to retire its "Redmen" name and logo depicting a Native American wearing a headdress, because they had been criticized as "racist."[5] Merely mentioning someone's race (or racial designation),[6] using the word "Oriental" for Asians without recognizing its origins and its capacity for insult, or socializing only with members of one's own racial group are called "racist."

A few observers suspect that the word has lost all significant meaning. "Racism is . . . what black activists define it to be. . . . When words lose coherent meaning, they also lose the power to shame. 'Racism,' 'sexism,' and 'homophobia' have become such words. Labels that should horrify

1

are simply shrugged off."[7] The *Time* columnist Lance Morrow sees social damage in this development: "The words 'racism' and 'racist' are a feckless indulgence, corrosive to blacks and whites alike and to relations between them."[8]

"Racism" and "racist" should be reserved for certain especially serious moral failings and violations in the area of race. They should not be permitted to spread to include everything that someone might justifiably disapprove of. A major reason for what Robert Miles calls the "conceptual inflation"[9] of the idea of "racism" is its having become the predominant notion used to mark morally suspect behavior, attitude, and social practice regarding race. The result is that either something is racist or it is morally in the clear.

In Boston a white police officer, as a bizarre joke and apparently with no malice intended, placed a hangman's noose on the motorcycle of a black police officer. "Police Probe Sees No Racism," says the headline of an article reporting the findings of an investigation into the incident.[10] Perhaps the white officer was not "a racist", nor operating from racist motives. The victim in the incident said, however, that "you cannot hang a noose like that near any black man who knows his history and say it does not have tremendous significance."[11] If our only choices are to label such an act either "racist" or "nothing to get upset about," those who seek to call attention to any racial malfeasance will be tempted to describe it as "racist." That overuse in turn diminishes the moral force of the word and thus contributes to a lowering of concern about both racism and other racial wrongs.

Not every instance of racial conflict, insensitivity, discomfort, miscommunication, exclusion, injustice, or ignorance should be called "racist". Not all *racial* incidents are *racist* incidents. We need a more varied and nuanced moral vocabulary for talking about the domain of race. We need to articulate the range of values and disvalues implicated in race-based beliefs and attitudes, actions and interactions, institutions and practices. All forms of racial ills should elicit concern from responsible individuals. If someone displays racial insensitivity, but not racism, people should be able to see that for what it is. In a soccer game, a nine-year-old white boy said to one of his black teammates, "Boy, pass the ball over here," and "was virtually accused of being a racist by the father of one of his teammates," according to an article on the incident. (The word "virtually" itself suggests the loss of an evaluative vocabulary other than "racist" and "racism.") The white boy was almost surely not "a racist," and the article itself goes on to express more accurately the racial ill involved in his remark: "The word 'boy' is a tripwire attached to so much charged racial baggage that it is no longer safely used as a term for a prepubescent male."[12]

If a policy has a racially unjust effect, or unequally affects already unequally positioned racial groups, it should be reason for concern even if there is no suspicion that it arises from racist motives or is part of an entrenched pattern strongly rooted in historical racism. For example, school lunch programs have been criticized for relying too strongly on milk, in light of African Americans' substantial propensity toward lactose intolerance; but no untoward motives or failures of sensitivity need have prompted this policy for it to be of moral concern. Similarly, it is troubling if prime-time TV fails adequately to reflect its viewers' ethnoracial diversity; but the failure is not necessarily "racist."[13] Someone who exhibits a culpable ignorance about racial matters that bear on an interaction with an acquaintance or co-worker should feel a degree of shame, and resolve to correct that ignorance, without having to think she has been "racist." We should not be faced with the choice of "racism or nothing."

Conceptual inflation and moral overload arise from another source as well—designating as "racism" any prejudice, injustice, inferiorizing, or bigotry against human groups defined, say, by gender, disability, sexual orientation, or nationality. In *The Decent Society*, Avishai Margalit, an Israeli philosopher, discusses racism as the denying of dignity to *any human group*, and he uses as a particular test case "retarded" persons.[14] This inflated use of "racism" does, certainly, pay indirect tribute to racial oppression and denial of dignity as the central form of such mistreatment in contemporary Western consciousness; and that centrality is reflected also in coinages such as "sexism," "ableism" (discrimination against the disabled), "classism," and "heterosexism."[15] This proliferation of other "isms" at least avoids the confusion wrought by Margalit's conflating all of them with "racism" itself and encourages us to explore both the similarities and the differences between discrimination, exploitation, and denials of dignity based on race and those based on gender, sexual orientation, disability, national membership, and the like. But Margalit's subsuming all these moral ills under "racism" cuts off such inquiry at the starting line, and, in so doing, contributes to a counterproductive inflation of the term "racism."

"Racism": A History

The term "racism" was first used by European social scientists in the 1930s to characterize and condemn the Nazi belief system, which posited the superiority of the "Aryan" race over an elaborate ranking of allegedly lesser races.[16] The Nazis were not the first to make use of ideas of a hierarchy of human groups distinguished by inherent characteristics and generally distinguishable by physical appearance. As I observe in more detail in chapter 6, the idea of racial hierarchy had become firmly entrenched in American and, to a lesser extent, European thought in the nineteenth and early twentieth century. (Indeed, the Nazis were distinctly influenced by American racial thought.[17])

Although many persons had opposed previous race-based ideas and the systems of social domination they rationalized, it was not until the Nazi period that the term "racism" came to express moral revulsion at such systems. The rejection of racism was fed, in addition, by developments within the sciences that, independently, had begun to throw into question the idea of a hierarchy of discrete human populations or "races".[18]

Postwar revelation of the extent of Nazi atrocities helped intensify the revulsion attached to the concept of racism. At the same time, the word's central locus of reference shifted to still-existing systems of domination, exclusion, and oppression—segregation in the United States, racialized colonialism among the European powers (in Asia, Africa, Latin America), and apartheid in South Africa.[19] Retrospectively, American slavery contributed to the strongly negative moral valence of the term, especially, though not only, in the United States.

George Mosse, a historian of European racism, notes that originally the term "racism" referred not merely to an "articulation of prejudice" or a "metaphor for suppression" but to "a fully blown system of thought, an ideology like Conservatism, Liberalism, or Socialism."[20] What was rejected in the ideology or doctrine of racism was the idea that so-called racial groups, however identified, possessed inherent and inescapable characteristics and could be ranked on a scale from inferior to superior. That is, "racism" was defined as biological or quasi-biological determinism, plus inegalitarianism. What was being condemned was a system of thought; but the moral revulsion carried by the term was intimately bound up with the dehumanizing and sometimes murderous *social* systems the ideology was used to rationalize.

Although "racist" phenomena predated the invention of the concept itself, not every system of belief that led to the rationalization of human inequality or subordination could be called "racist." The social system in question must have developed a conception of "race" in terms of which subordination was justified. The acceptance for centuries in Europe and North Africa of Christians enslaving Muslims, and Muslims enslaving Christians, was not premised on race and racial inferiority; and the idea that it was morally permissible to subjugate conquered people culturally distinct from the conquerors was long unrelated to any racial ideas. Slavery or subjugation, whether founded on religion or conquest, is morally repulsive, but they are not intrinsically "racist" unless enslaved groups are seen as races distinct from the race of the enslavers.

Racist doctrines were not fully utilized to justify slavery in the Americas until the nineteenth century (though proto-racist ideas were so employed in the previous two centuries), in part because slavery was not thought to require a moral justification, and in part because the concept of "race" had not been fully developed. As we shall see also, the American "racial worldview," to use Audrey Smedley's expression, did not reach full development until the post-slavery period.

Many current authoritative definitions of "racism" preserve the original focus on a doctrine, ideology, theory, or cohesive set of beliefs. The *Oxford English Dictionary* of 1982, for example, says, "Racism is the theory that distinctive human characteristics and abilities are determined by race." Blackwell's 1993 *Dictionary of Twentieth-Century Social Thought* begins its entry on "racism" thus: "Any set of beliefs which classifies humanity into distinct collectivities, defined in terms of natural and/or cultural attributes, and ranks these attributes in a hierarchy of superiority and inferiority, can be described as 'racist'."[21] Charles Taylor, in his influential philosophical work *Sources of the Self*, says, "Racists have to claim that certain of the crucial moral properties of human beings are genetically determined: that some races are less intelligent, less capable of high moral consciousness, and the like."[22]

But established contemporary use does not confine "racism" as a term of moral reproach to doctrines of biological superiority. In the past several decades, we have come to criticize as "racist" not only beliefs but actions, motives, attitudes, statements, symbols, images, practices, societies, and persons. Nor do we require that racist manifestations involve such doctrines. (At most they may presuppose that the targeted group had historically been the subject of such beliefs.) If it is racist to steer blacks away from buying homes in a particular neighborhood because they are seen as "undesirable," rather than because they are seen as biologically inferior, then "racism" is not limited to a system of belief in racial inferiority.

The Native American logo mentioned at the outset of this chapter is racist because it demeans a group that has been seen in racial terms, not because anyone displaying the logo necessarily holds racist beliefs about them presently. In the summer of 1999, a young white man, Benjamin Nathaniel Smith, murdered a Korean American man and a black man and shot at several Jews and other Asian Americans, evidently out of racial hatred for these groups. These actions, and the motives that prompted them, were uniformly regarded as racist in the major media, prior to knowing whether Smith also believed in explicitly racist doctrines.[23] Use of the epithets "racist" and "racism" is widely accepted regardless of knowledge about whether those so characterized believe in "races," in the sense meant in the original definition of racism.[24] For example, though the use of epithets such as "wetback," "greaser," and "nigger" are unproblematically referred to as "racist," their usage does not require belief in a hierarchy of biologically based "races" (on the part of the user, hearer, or anyone else).

Even when racial bigotry or hatred do involve racist beliefs, such views of the group in question are often a product of the hatred rather than a consequence of adhering to a racist ideology. As hatred and antipathy, especially of a racial nature, are socially proscribed, the hater may be tempted to rationalize them by casting the target of her antipathy as evil, criminal, menacing, "taking over," or the like. Here the belief is secondary to the emotion or attitude, not its basis.

The sense of wrongfulness evoked by the term "racism," originally attached to a system of beliefs, drew its moral force from the evils of the social systems in which those beliefs were embedded. (A belief unconnected to horrible practices would be unlikely to garner such strong moral opprobrium.) Hence it was natural to extend the reach of the term to the acts, attitudes, emotions, and symbols that were integral to systems of oppression. Segregation, for example, functioned not only through the *belief* that blacks were racially inferior to whites, but through *attitudes* of contempt, scorn, prejudice, and hatred; through *acts* expressing such attitudes; and through particular *institutions* or *practices* (for example, blacks being referred to by their first names but being compelled to address whites of any age as "Mr." and "Mrs.").

The historical process by which "racism" expanded its reference from doctrines to systems, acts, and persons, and became the central term of moral condemnation, was neither simple nor inevitable. For example, in the 1930s and before, the word "racialism" was also employed to refer to the doctrine of hierarchically arrayed, biologically defined racial groups, as in Jacques Barzun's influential 1938 book, *Race, A Study in Modern Superstition*.[25] However, if someone tried to condemn the array of phenomena we *currently* call racist with the epithet "racialist," she would be unsuccessful. It remains a term used primarily by specialists, with little popular moral cachet.[26] In the postwar period, especially in the United States, attention turned to the psychological underpinnings of racist structures and behavior, and the idea of "racial prejudice" took center stage as the concept that best described those underpinnings. Gordon Allport's magisterial *The Nature of Prejudice* in 1954 helped to promote this notion of prejudice as the central factor in racial ills; the idea became a prime mode by which social scientists attempted to come to grips with the moral legacy of the Holocaust and with racial segregation in the United States.[27]

Allport did not refer to racial prejudice as "racism,"[28] perhaps in part because he was concerned with all forms of prejudice (racial, religious, ethnic, and others), and believed there to be a psychic unity among them, involving a distinction between "in-groups" and "out-groups." Still, his work helped to prompt a focus of moral (and research) concern on various attitudes that underlay the operation of racist systems.

The Kerner Commission's report on civil disorders in 1968, following the urban riots and uprisings in black areas in the mid-1960s, made "white racism" a central organizing idea, blaming it for the unsatisfactory conditions of life in Detroit, Los Angeles, Brooklyn, and other cities that led to the "disturbances."[29] The prestige and wide circulation of that report helped to bring the terminology of racism to a broader popular audience. The Black Power movement of the same era also tended to employ "racism" as a primary means of conceptualizing the state of black America. *Black Power*, an influential work of that time by Kwame Ture (then Stokely Carmichael) and Charles Hamilton, was critical of the Allportian focus on individual prejudice and bigotry, and shifted the locus of "racism" from the individual to broader social structures of inequity and to socially pervasive antiblack stereotypes and prejudices.[30] They referred to this phenomenon as "institutional racism" (further discussed below), arguing that progress in reducing individual prejudice had by no means erased pervasive inequities in the life chances of blacks and whites. Both their specific analysis and the increasingly general use of "racism" further served to embed that term in the moral vocabulary that referred to objectionable phenomena of a racial nature.

As segregation and colonialism (and, more recently, apartheid in South Africa) were dismantled, it became evident that racist attitudes, actions, and statements could also occur outside of such systems. They could be directed by members of any racial group toward any other, independent of the social and economic position of either of the parties, and they seemed deserving of condemnation in their own right.

As concepts of moral disapprobation, "racism" and "racist" have definitively broadened their reach beyond doctrines of biologically based hierarchy. At the same time, current use is not sufficiently unified or stable to allow us to point to one definition as the "true meaning" of "racism." Nevertheless, I will suggest a core meaning, rooted in the history of its use, that secures "racism" as referring to phenomena deserving of the severest moral condemnation, and that encourages us to make use of the considerable other resources our language offers us for describing and criticizing race-related ills that do *not* characteristically rise to the level of racism—racial insensitivity, racial conflict, racial injustice, racial ignorance, racial discomfort, and others. An agreed-upon meaning that avoids conceptual inflation and moral overload would facilitate interracial communication, and it should diminish an inhibiting fear of the dreaded charge of "racism" while also encouraging a more morally nuanced vocabulary for discussing race-related phenomena. My suggested definition of "racism" should stanch its threatened loss of moral impact, which discourages moral concern about racism and other race-related ills.

Defining "Racism"

I want to suggest that all forms of racism can be related to one of two general themes or "paradigms": *inferiorization,* and *antipathy.*

Inferiorization is linked to historical racist doctrine and racist social systems. Slavery, segregation, imperialism, apartheid, and Nazism all treated certain groups as inferior to other groups (mostly the dominant group, although sometimes other non-dominant racial groups) by reason of their biological nature.

Though race-based antipathy is less related to the original concept of "racism," today the term unequivocally encompasses racial bigotry, hostility, and hatred. Indeed, the racial bigot is many people's paradigm image of "a racist." A disturbing but illuminating example of contemporary antipathy racism occurred in Washington state in 1999. The Makah tribe of the Olympic Peninsula announced its intention to hunt for whales as a way of instilling pride and tradition in the tribe's youth. The hunt was permitted by the government, and the tribe killed a whale in May of that year. Many non–Native American residents of the state were outraged by this act. Amidst some arguably reasonable objections were expressions of outright antipathy racism toward the Makah, and toward Native Americans more generally. One letter to the *Seattle Times,* for example, said, "I have a very real hatred for Native Americans now. It's embarrassing, but I would be lying if I said it wasn't the truth."[31]

Historical systems of racism did of course inevitably involve racial antipathy as well as inferiorization. Hatred of Jews was central to Nazi philosophy; and it is impossible to understand American racism without seeing hostility to blacks and Native Americans as integral to the nexus of attitudes and emotions that shored up slavery and segregation.[32]

I suggest that all the various forms of racism are related to inferiorization or antipathy, and will illustrate this in the next several chapters. To simplify that discussion, I want to introduce three other general categories. *Personal racism* consists in racist acts, beliefs, attitudes, and behavior on the part of individual persons. *Social* (or sociocultural) *racism* comprises racist beliefs, attitudes, and stereotypes widely shared within a given population and expressed in cultural and social modes such as religion, popular entertainment, advertisements, and other media. *Institutional racism* refers to racial inferiorizing or antipathy perpetrated by specific social institutions such as schools, corporations, hospitals, or the criminal justice system as a totality.[33]

Each of the three operates in complex interaction with the others. Persistent institutional racism encourages personal belief in, or suspicion of, racial inferiority. Personal racism reflects already existing social racism, and also sustains it. Personal racism slows or blocks society's moral impetus to change racist institutions. Some contemporary writing has attempted to reduce one of these forms to another, or to demote it in importance. For instance, in some influential writing on racism, the Ture-Hamilton notion of racism as a *system* of injustice and unequal advantage or power has almost entirely eclipsed the earlier Allportian focus on individual attitude and behavior.[34]

The view of racism as solely systemic substitutes one partial conception of racism for another. For instance, suppose a white person hates black people, but the white person is relatively isolated and powerless, does not come into contact with blacks, and generally does not even express his or her feelings to others. This hatred is unquestionably racist, yet it contributes virtually nothing to a system of unjust advantage based on race. If racism were only systemic, then such an individual would not be racist and, indeed, individuals could never be racist. It is revealing, however, that adherents of the view in question seldom follow that logic exclusively. Generally they at least implicitly acknowledge that individual actions and persons may be "racist." They imply, however, that when an individual acts in what would ordinarily be called a racist manner, the action is to be condemned as racist only insofar as it contributes to a system of unjust racial advantage.[35]

This institutional conception unnecessarily narrows the reasons to condemn racism. We do better to accept the plurality of items that can be racist (beliefs, institutions, systems, attitudes, acts, and so on), without thinking that one of these need be the foundation of all the others. Personal, social, and institutional racism are each morally problematic, in at least partially distinct ways.

Inferiority and Antipathy Racism

Inferiorizing personal racism is expressed in various attitudes and behavior—disrespect, contempt, derision, derogation, demeaning. It can also involve a developed set of beliefs about a biologically based hierarchy of races, but it need not do so. For one thing, an individual may be racist against only one racial group and have no views about others. An individual can be contemptuous toward another racial group without really believing that it and its members are inferior. A white or black person, for example, may grow up in an environment in which Mexicans and Mexican-Americans are routinely treated and regarded with contempt. On reflection she may realize that she does not really believe Mexicans to be inferior or otherwise worthy of contempt, yet her manifestations of contempt toward Mexicans will still be racist in character.[36]

An inferiorizing racist generally thinks that the racial other is inferior to her own group, but sometimes people believe their own group to be inferior. The film *A Soldier's Story* depicts this internalized racism very powerfully.[37] The film focuses on a black company at an army base during World War II, whose sergeant, Waters, hates another black soldier as representing all that is deficient in blacks. As the story unfolds, Waters reveals an extreme desire for the approval of whites. Ultimately he acknowledges a racial self-hatred that has fueled his attempts to purge his company of forms of black behavior (and types of black persons) that he regards as making "the race" look bad to whites. The film powerfully illustrates that internalized racism is the product of a society in which the group in question is devalued.[38]

Inferiorizing and antipathy racism are distinct. Some inferiorizing racists do not hate the target of their beliefs; they may have a paternalistic concern and feelings of kindness for persons they regard as their inferiors. This form of racism characterized some slave owners and many whites' views of blacks during segregation. (Joel Kovel has called this form of racism "dominative."[39]) The concern and kindness are misdirected, and demeaning, because the other is not seen as an equal, or even as a full human being; it is a racist form of concern, yet is distinct from antipathy and hatred.

Conversely, not every race hater regards the target of her hatred as inferior. In the United States, antipathy toward Asians and Jews often accompanies, and is in part driven by, a kind of resentment of those seen as in some ways superior (for example, more economically successful). And some whites who hate blacks do not really regard blacks as inferior; they may fear and be hostile to them, but fear and hostility are not the same as contempt and other forms of inferiorizing (though they may accompany one another). Survey research suggests that pure inferiorizing racism toward blacks has substantially decreased since segregation, more so than antipathy racism.[40] Still, the great and persistent racial inequalities in our society provide a standing encouragement to advantaged groups to see disadvantaged groups as deserving their lower status.

The two forms of personal racism are not entirely separate either. Mexican Americans are often seen as inferior and also hated as a "foreign element" allegedly usurping jobs that whites regard as their prerogative. (African Americans can also have racial hostility toward Mexican Americans for the latter reason, but are much less likely to regard them as racially inferior.) The paternalistic inferiorizing racist, such as a white segregationist, often hates those members of the racial group who do not maintain what he regards as "their place"—for example, blacks who do not engage in the deference behavior the paternalistic racist expects. Emmett Till was lynched in 1955 out of hatred directed toward a young black man who had transgressed the rules of racial deference and constraint defining him as an inferior being. Hatred characteristically surfaces toward those members of the inferiorized group who act in a manner implying they do not regard themselves as inferior to the racist.

Racial Prejudice

The idea of *racial prejudice* will help clarify the antipathy paradigm for personal racism. The word "prejudice" can be confusing, since its linguistic form suggests that it simply means "prejudging" something before you have a chance to really know it. Certainly prejudging can be part of racial prejudice, but as generally understood the term implies something more—a general antipathy, or animus, toward another racial group, or toward an individual because he or she is a member of that group. Gordon Allport's classic definition of prejudice states that the antipathy is "based upon a faulty and inflexible generalization."[41] This is an important point. An individual is not prejudiced if she has good reason for antipathy toward a group—for example if she is hostile toward a family plotting to undermine her business. As Allport notes, antipathy toward Nazis is not prejudice.[42]

Not all antipathy is prejudice, but all antipathy toward a racial group is prejudice, as such groups are too large for anyone to have valid personal grounds for antipathy toward the entire group. Blacks or Latinos do not have grounds for antipathy toward all whites (although some people think they do). Neither blacks, Latinos, nor whites who have been personally victimized by members of the other groups have grounds for hostility toward the entire group. They are prejudiced if they have such hostility.

Prejudice need not be conscious. (The same may be said of bigotry, though stronger forms of animus may be less liable to stay hidden from consciousness.) A white individual may feel hostility toward African Americans or Asian Americans without realizing she does. Although the increasing social disapproval of racial prejudice (and other comparable group prejudices) in the past forty years or so is a positive development, it has had the effect of providing some people with an incentive to suppress acknowledgment of their prejudice.

Prejudice may be nonconscious in another sense as well. An individual may be hostile toward a certain group but not realize the racial basis for her hostility. For example, she may dislike a certain style of personal interaction no matter who exhibits it, without recognizing that her reason for doing so is that she generally associates that style with black people, and dislikes black people.[43]

Moreover, as Allport suggests, prejudice generally involves not only dislike of a group but a faulty view of it as well. Someone who is prejudiced against Mexicans, or Mexican Americans, generally both dislikes members of that group and regards them as having negative characteristics that justify her dislike—being lazy, dirty, dangerous, or unfairly taking "her people's" jobs.[44] Classic understandings of prejudice assumed that these faulty conceptions always stem from ignorance of the group, arising from lack of contact with it. Allport himself did not make this error; he realized that contact with another group does not always lead to understanding. Research on school desegregation suggests that some whites become *more* prejudiced when they are put in schools with blacks than they were before they knew any blacks.[45] In any case, what it means to "know" another group well enough to avoid faulty generalizations about it is a very complex matter. At the least, it involves getting to know some members of the group both as individuals and as members of the group. It always means having a lived understanding of the great diversity within any racial group. For true "knowing," other conditions must no doubt be met as well.[46]

Yet Allport is not correct to build into the definition of prejudice "based upon a faulty and inflexible generalization." For one thing, generalizations about the group could be after-the-fact rationalizations of prejudice, rather than the actual basis of the prejudice. In addition, someone could be hostile toward a group, but when asked why would say "I don't know; I just don't like them." Such a person may be suppressing some conception of the group that he is reluctant to state. Or he may just have an irrational antipathy. We would still call that person "prejudiced". He may have some rudimentary negative images of the group that accompany his antipathy, but these do not rise to the cognitive status of Allport's "generalization."[47]

Thus prejudice is a kind of antipathy, toward a race-defined group, and would by my definition appear to count as a form of "racism". Indeed racial prejudice is often called "racism."[48] But, "prejudice" often implies dislike or antipathy, but not necessarily hatred or strong antipathy. Intensely negative affects are *beyond* prejudice—for example the hatred shown by some Serbs in driving Kosovar Albanians from their homes and territory in the spring of 1999. It seems absurdly understated to say that the Serbs "were prejudiced against the Albanians."

Because prejudice is, in general, a less malevolent attitude than hatred and intense hostility, it is less morally evil. It is not clear whether we should call weaker forms of racial prejudice "racism." These forms should, in any case, evoke opprobrium in their own right.

Categorial Drift

We have looked at two ways that "racism" and "racist" have been conceptually inflated and morally overloaded, diminishing their usefulness and force as concepts expressing moral reproach: the tendency to apply them to every malfeasance in the racial area, and to use them as general concepts for all forms of group discrimination, oppression, or denial of dignity. We are now in a position to discuss a third such devaluation of these words, which results from their undifferentiated use in regard to very different entities: beliefs, acts, attitudes, statements, symbols, feelings, motives, and persons. I call this confusion "categorial drift." For instance, a person commits one racist act and is called "a racist," or makes a racist statement and is assumed to be doing so from a racist motive. Here we have drift from one category of racism to a second, generally more objectionable one.

A discussion of categorial drift will enable us to clarify how personal racism in the different categories (acts, statements, persons, and so on) relates to the antipathy and inferiorization themes. Let us begin with an example.

> Ms. Verano is a white fourth grade teacher. She feels comfortable with all the children in her very racially-mixed class. She holds all students to equally high standards of performance. But, though she has never admitted this to herself, she is not really comfortable with most of the black parents. She does not dislike blacks, nor does she think they are inferior. She is not particularly familiar with African American culture, however, knows very few blacks other than her students, and is not confident about her ability to communicate with blacks. As a result Ms. Verano is somewhat defensive when speaking with black parents in conferences, and is not able to listen to their concerns and viewpoints about their children as well as she does with parents in other racial groups. Because she does not glean as much information from the black parents about their children as she does from the other parents, she is not able to do as much for these children as for the others in her class. Ms. Verano does not recognize any of this, however.

Is Ms. Verano a racist? Is she prompted by racist motives?

Motives, Acts, and People

Racist *motives* are those based in antipathy toward or inferiorizing of a racial group, the latter category including contempt, derision, disrespect, and the like. Racist *acts* are diverse, and one type is an act prompted by a racist motive. Acts that make use of racist statements, jokes, symbols, or images, even if the person performing the act is not motivated by antipathy or an inferiorizing attitude, may be called "racist". For example, an individual may tell a racist joke in order to go along with a group, in order to feel accepted, or merely to get into the spirit of an occasion, without holding the inferiorizing or hostile attitude expressed in the joke. Yet acts whose motives are racist seem to me more definitively racist than those whose motives are not, even if the latter in some other way do involve racism.

A racist *person* is not merely someone who commits one racist act or acts on a racist motive on a small number of occasions. Motives and attitudes such as bigotry, antipathy, and contempt must be embedded in the person's psychological makeup as traits of character. In this sense, being racist is like being hateful, dishonest, or cruel, in implying an ingrained pattern of thought and feeling, as well as action.

Just as someone can act cruelly or dishonestly on one or several occasions without being a cruel or dishonest person, so someone can act in a racist manner on some occasions without being "a racist." It is a much stronger condemnation to say that a person is "a racist" than to say that some of her actions are racist. Unfortunately, current public discourse frequently conflates these two things, as if everyone who engaged in some racist behavior were a full-fledged racist. People confusedly and inadequately defend themselves against the charge that they have committed a racist act by saying "I'm not a racist."

The *New York Times* ran a long article on Al Jolson, the entertainer of the 1920s and 1930s who was best known for performing in blackface. "Was Jolson a racist?" the *Times* asked, and answered by saying, "Although he was guilty of many faults, Jolson showed no sign of ethnic hatred."[49] But the racial issue in Jolson's performances has little or nothing to do with whether Jolson was a racial bigot, or even with whether he intended to demean blacks by utilizing the demeaning black stereotypes that were the staple of blackface minstrelsy. The article goes on to pinpoint the real issue, which is independent of Jolson's own character or motives: "Blackface evokes memories of . . . an age in which white entertainers used the makeup to ridicule black Americans while brazenly borrowing from the rich black musical traditions that were rarely allowed direct expression in mainstream [that is, white] society."[50]

It is true, and fortunate, that some people who are racist in their character can learn not to be, if they disavow their racism and go through a process of personal struggle. An inspiring example of such a transformation is C. P. Ellis, a former Klansman who became antiracist, largely through being forced to work on a school board with a black woman from his town.[51] Of course, a person who merely commits a racist act is a much better candidate for avoiding racism in the future than is an ingrained racist. The former may just be thoughtless or ignorant about the nature or effects of her racist acts, or her antipathy may not run deep nor be securely lodged in her psychological makeup. Without being overly sanguine about the prospects of reducing attitudinal and motivational racial prejudice, I would suggest that racial animus rooted in someone's character is more difficult to erase than that which is not.[52]

In her uncomfortable reactions to black parents, Ms. Verano, the white fourth grade teacher, is neither a racist nor does she act from racist motives. She holds no antipathy toward blacks. She is not an inferiorizing racist. Though uncomfortable with black adults, she is not racially prejudiced against them.

Symbols, Jokes, and Remarks

Symbols, jokes, images, epithets, and remarks can be racist in their own right, apart from people's motives in using them. What makes them racist is that they either directly or indirectly portray a racial group in an inferiorized manner (for example, as stupid or otherwise worthy of contempt, disrespect, or derision), or in a manner rendering them appropriate targets of hatred, antipathy, or dislike. An example of direct symbolic racism is the logo of the Cleveland Indians baseball team—a grinning, moroniclooking Native American. As nonrepresentational symbols often involve no explicit portrayal of a group, a symbol can be indirectly racist—the swastika, for example—when its origin and cultural meaning are associated with racist portrayals, hostility, or inferiorizing. A racist epithet may involve no distinct portrayal of a racial group, and attribute no specific characteristics to the group; epithets such as "spic," "kike," "nigger" are racist, however, because they are generally understood to be derogatory and insulting.

Many symbols are racist whether those who display them are aware of this or not. Like the swastika, the Confederate battle flag is such a racist symbol.[53] The flag symbolizes the Confederacy as a defender of the "Southern way of life" that involved slavery as an essential component. The contemporary history of the flag's presence in official venues and incorporation within some official southern state flags is a further manifestation of its racist meaning. In 1956, for example, Georgia incorporated the "stars and bars" into its state flag as a sign of defiance of the *Brown v. Board of Education* school integration ruling two years previous. Mississippi has done so as well. In 1961 and 1962, in the midst of controversy over segregation, Alabama and South Carolina, respectively, raised the Confederate flag over their state capitols (beneath the American flag) for a similar reason. In the summer of 2000, partly in response to a national boycott called by the NAACP, the South Carolina legislature voted to remove the flag from the dome atop the statehouse, and Georgia has demoted the Confederate emblem to a much smaller place within its state flag.

Some white Southerners, perhaps entirely sincerely, purport to regard the Confederate flag as a merely regional symbol, or a symbol of the heritage of that region. In a widely publicized incident in the early 1990s, a white Harvard University student hung a Confederate flag from her dormitory window, saying that it symbolized warmth and community associated with her southern home and heritage.[54] Unquestionably the Confederate flag is a regional symbol, and, moreover, it may well not convey a racism-infused message to all who display or value it. But a symbol can be both regional *and* racist. One who understands the history of the Confederacy and the use of its flag, as well as the flag's recent historical use as a sign of defiance against federally-enforced desegregation, can not pretend the flag does not symbolize slavery, segregation, or black subordination more generally.[55] Southerners who wish to distance themselves from nostalgia for a way of life built on slavery or segregation must find a different regional symbol, as, indeed, some southerners are attempting to do.[56]

The public meanings of flags, monuments, and other symbols can be multiple or contested. Symbols can mean different things in different contexts and to different groups, and the meanings can change over time.[57] The shamrock is a traditional Irish and Irish American ethnic symbol. But in Boston, some African Americans see its current display in traditionally Irish areas such as South Boston, which have been compelled, against the wishes of many of its white residents, to undergo residential integration in the past two decades, as a sign of exclusion.[58] Although these blacks might attach a meaning to a particular display of the shamrock, they do not thereby deny that it is an Irish American ethnic symbol. In the Confederate flag dispute, by contrast, some whites wish to deny the racist meanings of the flag.[59]

The making of a racist joke or the displaying of a racist symbol does not make someone "a racist." It does not even necessarily signify a racist attitude or belief. One may use a racist symbol, make a racist remark, or tell a racist joke without realizing it, though such ignorance is more generally found in children than adults. For example, a child may wear his brother's hat with a Confederate flag symbol, without knowing what that symbol means, because he likes the way it looks or admires his brother. As mentioned earlier, someone may retell a racially offensive joke she has heard just to get a laugh, without recognizing that the joke is racist.

Lack of such knowledge generally has no bearing on whether the symbol or joke is *itself* racist. However, it does bear on the user's moral responsibility for using or telling it. Again, there is likely to be an asymmetry between adults and children in this regard. Adults generally know that a joke or symbol is racist. An adult who uses what he knows is charged racial language but then acts surprised that someone in the targeted group is offended often appears disingenuous.[60] We continually hear of radio and television announcers, and politicians too, excusing their use of offensive and racist language, symbols, jokes, and remarks on the grounds that they did not intend for them to be racist, or to offend. The California state assemblyman William Knight distributed to his fellow Republican legislators a poem, written in a style that demeaned native Spanish-speakers' way of speaking English and implied that Mexican immigrants are mostly illegal, have too many children, come to the United States to exploit a generous welfare system, are contemptuous of white people, and intend to take over the United States. When the Latino legislative caucus complained that the poem was "racist," Knight declined to apologize but said he thought the poem clever and funny, and that it was not intended to offend anyone.[61] It is impossible to believe that Mr. Knight failed to recognize that the poem was offensive, although he may well have believed that none of the persons whom he intended to see it would be offended. Be that as it may, since the poem is so patently racist and offensive, Assemblyman Knight is morally at fault for distributing it, even if he did not realize that it was. In general, people beyond a certain age should recognize what is racist; their moral responsibility for perpetrating racism when they do not recognize it is analogous to the fault of citizens who cause injury through negligence rather than direct intent. They *could be reasonably expected* to recognize or anticipate the moral damage. Except for people with extraordinarily sheltered lives and upbringings, ignorance of racism does not absolve one from responsibility, although, everything else being equal, intentionally demeaning a racial group is morally more blameworthy than unintentionally doing so.

So not intending to be racist does not absolve a speaker from having made a racist remark, nor, generally, of moral responsibility for doing so. If a racist remark is made, it is entirely appropriate and understandable for a member of the targeted group to be offended, whether the user meant it as racist or not.

Symbols and Offense

Often racist symbols, remarks, and jokes are discussed as if they were objectionable *only* because they cause offense to some group. This puts the cart before the horse. Their inherent racism is generally *why* members of the group targeted by the racism are offended.[62]

Moreover, those in the targeted group are not the only persons who have reason to object to racist expressions. Every person has reason to object to racism, just as we all have reason to object to cruelty, dishonesty, and the violation of human rights, no matter who suffers from them. Students often think it is "weird" or in some way pretentious or inauthentic— merely trying to be "politically correct"—if someone objects to a racist remark that demeans a group other than his own. They expect someone from the targeted group to object, but no one else. Moral outrage and offense should not be racially balkanized in this way.

Racism is not the only valid grounds for offense, either. Mike Royko, the tough-talking columnist for the *Chicago Tribune*, displays an instructive array of confusions on this point in a column, "Time to Be Color Blind to All Words of Hatred." Royko defends a cartoon intended to make the valid point that the use of words (not only actions) can be racist. Louis Farrakhan's attacks on Jews were the intended example. The cartoon showed a Ku Klux Klan member holding a paper with Farrakhan's remark, "You can't be racist by talking—only by acting." The Klan member says, "That nigger makes a lot of sense."[63]

Many readers took offense at the cartoon—at Farrakhan being labeled a "nigger"—and Royko appears to have regarded these readers as morons who can not understand that the context and intent of a word's use affects its moral standing. Obviously there is an important moral difference between mentioning the "n"-word in the course of criticizing it, and actually using the word as a racial insult. But Royko should understand that any use of this word by a white person in application to a black person, even if satiric and ironic, is offensive to most blacks and is generally inappropriate. As used by whites, "nigger" is a unique word in its congealing the set of attitudes embedded in white supremacy that expressed contempt, hatred, derision, and exclusion toward blacks.[64] The legacy of white supremacy, has not been sufficiently transcended for whites simply to appropriate the term to make valid points through satire. The word is still hurtful and offensive, even if Royko is certainly correct that it has different significances in different contexts. (The use of the word by young blacks as a term of affection and bonding is a context-bound use that has confused many whites, and is objected to by many, especially older, blacks.[65]) Its use in the cartoon is not itself *racist*; but it is objectionable.

Certainly not every time someone feels offended by a racial term is the offense warranted. Meanings and intentions can be misinterpreted, and people can be oversensitive. Nor is it possible to draw a sharp line between warranted and unwarranted offense; sometimes potential offense should be avoided even when unwarranted. Perhaps a white Washington, D.C., official should not have used the word "niggardly" in the presence of blacks, even though that word has no historical or linguistic relation to "nigger," apart from sounding like it. Still, it is not the causing of offense only that can be the source of moral objection, but the racially offensive remark itself.

Finally, people frequently fail to realize that it is wrong to tell a racist joke even though no member of the target group is present, because such jokes cause harm by contributing to hurtful, false, and degrading views of particular groups.

At the same time, not all remarks, jokes, and symbols that have a *racial* significance are necessarily *racist.* Jokes that depend on a stereotype of Italians as loving pizza or whites as a bit uptight may offend; but they are not racist. They do not portray their targets in a degraded or seriously deficient light. The characterization of something as racist must be done with care, partly to avoid emotionally and morally overloading a situation that does not warrant it, partly to assure that other ills and missteps in the racial arena garner their appropriate claim on our consciences, and partly to protect the severe opprobrium that currently attaches to the epithet "racist."

Racist Beliefs and Racist Believings

As we have seen, the original definition of "racism" referred to a system of belief, regarding the biological inferiority of certain races to others, but current understandings of racism are not confined to and do not depend on such belief. What does it mean, then, for a belief to be racist? There are two distinct questions here: (1) when is it racist for an individual to believe something? (call this "racist believing,"); (2) what makes a proposition—the content of a belief—racist? (call this "a racist proposition [or belief]").[66]

Racist believing is a state of belief to which one is led because of a racist attitude or sentiment. For example, some white people who espouse strong adherence to grades and test scores as the sole legitimate basis for selecting students for admission to college do so because they are prejudiced against blacks or Latinos, rather than because they have arrived at their belief through a dispassionate assessment of its pros and cons. In such cases it would be accurate to say that the individuals are racist in holding the belief. One test of the psychic basis of an individual's espoused belief in test scores is whether she accepts the large number of Asian students who will be and have been admitted to top colleges when test scores are the major basis for admissions. If she shows hesitation on this matter—saying for example that the Asian students are "grinds" and are not sufficiently "well-rounded"—her inconsistency is grounds for suspicion of a racist motivation underlying her resistance to race-sensitive admission plans. (Even here, however, plain self-interest rather than personal racism may be operating in the resistance to admitting blacks and Latinos with lower test scores and to admitting Asian Americans with high scores.)

This is a case of a "racist believing" in a nonracist proposition. A racist proposition is one whose content is of a racial group characterized as deserving of racial antipathy or inferiorization: Examples are "Jews are evil and scheming," "Blacks are intellectually inferior," "Mexicans are lazy."

An individual may hold a racist belief or proposition without recognizing this. Because beliefs are not necessarily consciously endorsed thoughts, a person may unthinkingly adopt a racist view of a particular group from her family, or from the society around her, without ever consciously endorsing it, being committed to it, or even contemplating it. Suppose, for example, that a friend of such an individual points out that she seems to be making the assumption that blacks are prone to violence and Mexicans lazy, and challenges her on her basis for holding these beliefs. The friend draws her attention to many nonviolent blacks and hardworking Mexicans. She realizes that she has held these racist beliefs without any basis, and she gives them up. In such a case, I think we want to say that the individual is not a racist and was not a racist even when she held the beliefs. The beliefs themselves were genuinely racist, but belief in them had not been deeply enough rooted in her psychological makeup to make her "a racist."[67] She must be genuinely committed to and invested in racist beliefs in order to be a racist.[68] I do not mean to imply, however, that it is typical of someone holding a racist belief to be so minimally invested in it that she abandons it immediately in the face of valid counterargument; indeed it is not typical.

If one can hold racist beliefs without recognizing them and without being psychically invested in them, it is also possible to be *unconsciously* invested in such beliefs. An individual may believe blacks to be, as a group, intellectually deficient, and he may manifest this belief in his low expectations of blacks, in surprise that certain blacks achieve at a high level, and the like—all the while being entirely unaware that he holds this belief. Unfortunately this is true of many teachers (not only white teachers) in regard to black and Latino students. Psychic investment in a destructively racist belief is reason to call an individual "a racist"; but his unawareness of this investment seems to me to be a reason not to do so. However we resolve this matter, the commitment to a racist belief, and the discriminatory acts that flow therefrom, are cause for moral concern.

Some accounts of racist beliefs or propositions define the racism of a belief not by the content of the belief but by its *effects*. David Wellman, for example, defines racist beliefs as "culturally sanctioned beliefs which, regardless of the intentions involved, defend the advantages whites have because of the subordinated position of racial minorities."[69] Wellman may be conflating the racism of believing these propositions with the racism of the propositions themselves, but his view does have the virtue of highlighting the fact that beliefs without explicit racial content may nevertheless, when acted on, affect the relative economic or social position of racial groups. For example, the belief that college admission should be based solely or predominantly on grades and test scores has generally had the effect, when translated into policy, of decreasing Latino and African-American admission to elite schools. Thus the belief as put into practice contributes to racial inequality and racial injustice.[70] This important fact about the belief and its corresponding policy may provide a basis for objecting to the policy.

But this does not make the belief itself a racist belief. Certainly the proposition that admissions decisions should be based on grades and test scores is not racist in itself. Nor is it necessarily racist to believe it. Perhaps admission policies based solely on test scores and grades do intensify educational and social inequality.[71] This does not clinch the argument as to whether they are advisable or not, all things considered. One has to weigh the values and disvalues on both sides. Some argue that the gain from the use of "color blind" admissions criteria outweighs further harm to already disadvantaged populations.[72] I disagree with this argument. However, calling the belief in question, or the believing of it, "racist" emotionally overloads a discussion of the validity or worthiness of the belief and leads us to think that because a view may have undesirable racial implications, it should be dismissed prior to discussion.

The charge of racism can be made only after determining that the motives of those espousing the belief are racist (not always an easy matter). Wellman's definition could be taken to imply that *everyone* who holds such nonracist (but inequality-intensifying) belief does so for racist reasons.

"Institutional Racism"

"Institutional racism" is often understood to refer to a practice that is itself free of racial bias but in its implementation has a disproportionately negative effect on subordinate racial groups.[73] The seniority system in the work place is often cited as an example: since previous employment discrimination has allowed whites to accumulate much more seniority than blacks and Latinos, a system of greater job protection and rewards for seniority has disproportionately negative impact on these racial groups. With less seniority, black and Latino workers are those most vulnerable to layoffs due to recession or downsizing. Yet the principle of seniority itself is entirely race-neutral; it simply favors workers with the greatest longevity in the company. (Nor was seniority originally adopted as a covert way to exclude or oppress blacks or Latinos.)

The seniority system does indeed hinder the progress of disadvantaged minorities. It perpetuates an existing racial injustice (unequal employment opportunity) caused by past practices of racial discrimination (excluding blacks and Latinos from workplaces and unions, providing them with inferior education, and so on). Seniority also places a limit on the effectiveness of affirmative action hiring programs. Even if a special attempt is made to hire blacks and Latinos, seniority renders the newer hirees most vulnerable to layoffs.

All these are valid and useful ways to express what is morally troubling about the practice of seniority. But seniority is a valuable institution in many ways, providing job security and a bulwark against management arbitrariness, discouraging destructive competitiveness among workers, and the like.[74] (And to the extent that black and Latino workers attain seniority, they share in its benefits as well.) In an overall assessment of seniority, its benefits must be weighed against its race-related costs. Some modification of seniority to protect racial minority jobs would seem a reasonable compromise, honoring the moral pull on both sides.[75] Calling seniority "institutional racism," however, both implies that the practice was, or is, driven by racist motives (despite that implication's being disclaimed in the definition), and tars it with an opprobrium that implies that it could never be morally acceptable.

Another practice that is often called "institutional racism" is employers' recruiting by word of mouth among current workers in the company rather than advertising in job listings. There is a nonracial business rationale for doing so: it saves publicity costs, and it garners job applicants for whom a reliable worker has vouched, thus saving on the costs of assessing job suitability in a larger group of unknown applicants. Nevertheless, such recruiting has a disparate racial impact similar to that of seniority; in many occupations blacks and Latinos constitute a smaller proportion of the workforce than their percentage in the population, and workers' networks are generally race-specific. Thus word-of-mouth recruiting perpetuates racial injustice and sustains the legacy of racial discrimination. Unlike seniority, however, it has less going for it ethically; it merely reduces business costs. Hence, in the service of racial justice, it should generally be abandoned; employers should seek qualified black and Latino applicants, or at least not employ practices that discourage them. But, again, "institutional racism" does not seem a helpful description, either in implying that racist motivations infect the working of processes that are in fact free of racial bias or in generating a judgment of overall moral opprobrium prior to examining the ethical pros and cons.[76]

It might be argued that word-of-mouth recruiting is sometimes employed with the intent to screen out potential black employees (even if that intent is not acknowledged).[77] In this case such recruiting *would* be a racist practice; it would amount to racial discrimination (see chapter 4).[78] The effects may be the same as when the practice is not intentionally discriminatory, but I suggest that this commonality is best expressed by saying that both practices equally sustain racial injustice, or have a deleterious impact on black job seekers, not by saying they are both examples of "institutional racism." The second practice is (arguably) racist; the first is not.

The concept of institutional racism was invented as a way of recognizing that inequalities can be sustained, or intensified, independent of racist attitudes and motives, and even in accordance with "normal operating procedures" in the society. This is indeed an important racial and ethical insight. But it is better expressed, I suggest, by recognizing that some otherwise perhaps ethically sound practices can have the effect of sustaining racial injustice, rather than collapsing this distinction by implying that the processes are themselves necessarily morally illegitimate due to their being infected with racist intentions.

I would suggest confining the concept of "institutional racism" to what might more accurately be called "racist institutions"—specific schools or workplaces, systems, such as health care, criminal justice, and education, and the practices and processes therein which perpetrate racial inferiorization or antipathy.[79]

Specific institutions can be racist in two importantly distinct ways. First, their policies or practices can be intentionally racist. A clear case of such institutional racism was the subject of a 1969 Supreme Court case, *Gaston County v. United States*.[80] Prior to 1965, Gaston County, South Carolina (like most southern voting districts) employed literacy tests as a condition for entitlement to vote. The tests were employed in an explicitly racially discriminatory manner, with blacks given lower scores than whites regardless of their actual performance on the tests. The 1965 Voting Rights Act struck down the use of literacy tests in most contexts, but a clause in the Act allowed a county to reinstate the tests if they administered them in a fair and unbiased manner. Gaston County attempted to conform to this requirement by restructuring its tests to be rid of racial bias in both content and administration. But because blacks had been systematically subjected to an inferior education under the segregated school systems, which still existed, they failed the literacy tests at a higher rate than whites. The Supreme Court ruled that this situation constituted depriving blacks of the equal right to vote that the Voting Rights Act was meant to ensure.

It is plausible to suppose that Gaston County sought that very result—that many blacks would be deprived of a vote (although the Court's ruling did not depend on this implication). If so, Gaston County's voting system was a racist institution both before and after the adjustment in the literacy tests, and intentional injustice was committed against blacks in both contexts and by both procedures. The means by which this injustice was perpetrated differed in the two contexts, but in the latter instance the county officials intended a racially discriminatory result, while using a race-neutral and facially unbiased means to achieve it. (One can imagine an unusually clueless but nonracist individual taking a job related to administering the tests without realizing this intent. Such an individual would then participate in institutional racism without herself being racist in her motives, attitudes, or beliefs.)

Intentionally racist institutions are of course not only a thing of the past. In June 2000, American General Life and Accident Insurance Co., one of the nation's largest life insurance companies, agreed to pay $206 million to settle allegations that it had overcharged millions of mostly poor, black customers for burial insurance because of their race.[81] In November 2000, Coca-Cola agreed to pay more than $156 million to current and former employees of color alleging racial discrimination and, in an unusual concession in employment discrimination cases, agreed to grant broad discrimination-monitoring powers to a panel of outsiders.[82]

A second way in which a specific institution or institutional practice can be racist is quite different, although the difference is one of degree. Here the institution has no official or intentional policy of racism or racial discrimination, yet the actual functioning of the institution involves racism or racial discrimination. A high school whose staff manifest contempt toward their black or Latino students would be a racist institution, as would a school whose staff are not actually contemptuous but nevertheless have low expectations of the students, essentially regarding them as racially inferior, and, as a result, providing them with inadequate education. Both such schools may well intend, as a matter of official policy, to do well by, and be nonracist in their treatment of, their students. Indeed, the principal and various staff members may even genuinely believe that they are doing as well as can be expected. These well-intentioned people may be sincere, and sincerely self-deceived. Racist institutions of this sort do not merely reflect the previously existing racist attitudes of their staff. Institutions possess an internal dynamic—an "institutional culture"—that can push not yet determinate attitudes in a more or less racist direction. In this sense the racism of institutions is not merely derivative from the preexisting racism of its individual members.

Institutions or practices that commit unwitting injustices against a racial group because of its race are institutionally racist in the unintentional sense. The direct committing of an injustice (even if unwitting) is morally different from employing a racially unbiased policy that has the effect of perpetuating a prior injustice. Not every employee of racist institutions (intentional or unintentional) must manifest racism, in order for an institution to be racist; some teachers in such schools, for instance, may treat students well and have appropriate expectations of them as learners. No precise line can be drawn as to the extent or pervasiveness of racist attitudes and behaviors within an institution in order for it to be appropriately called a "racist institution."

A final caveat about the central insight underlying the origination of the concept of "institutional racism"—that processes not driven by racial considerations can have racially deleterious effects. In many cases, such processes are economic in character. For example, the disappearance of fairly well-paying and secure blue-collar jobs for minimally-educated workers has had a deleterious impact on the job prospects of poorly-schooled black workers living in urban centers.[83] But if we view this development *only* in relation to its racial impact, we overlook its effect on *all* low-skilled poorly educated workers of any race. The ever-widening earnings gap between high-skilled and low-skilled workers of all races through the 1990s and beyond is a deeply troubling and pervasive form of class-based injustice plaguing the American polity. Its racial injustice (that is, its disproportionate impact on blacks and, to a lesser extent, Latinos) is only one part of the problem. It is true that the term "racial injustice" has largely disappeared from public discourse in the United States; but adequate language for class-based injustice has attenuated even more. Social-welfare policies serving all poor and working-class people have weakened since the 1980s,[84] and general, race-independent inequalities in virtually every domain of life—access to health care, income, wealth, education, housing—reached record levels in the 1990s. As William Julius Wilson said in 1996, "The emphasis is on personal responsibility, not inequities in the larger society."[85] The moral importance of these injustices against people of all races should not get lost in a focus on their disproportionate impact on blacks and Latinos, a development encouraged by the more familiar use of "institutional racism."

Why Is Racism a Moral Evil?

Different vices have different moral valences. It is worse to be cruel than to be inconsiderate, to be dishonest than to be thoughtless. Why is this? It may have something to do with the social or interpersonal damage done. Dishonesty is more corrosive to both interpersonal relations and social trust than is inconsiderateness. Why does "racism" connote the strong moral opprobrium I am concerned to preserve, against conceptual inflation, in its meaning and use? In its inferiorizing forms, it violates fundamental moral norms of respect, equality, and recognition of the dignity of other persons. This violation is exemplified both in attitudes that regard others as inferior beings, as well as in social systems that deny dignity. In its antipathy forms, it exemplifies unworthy and destructive sentiments and attitudes—bigotry, antipathy, hatred, malevolence.

But the moral wrong of race-based violations can not lie *solely* in their violating general moral norms, that is, violations that carry the same force for any victim. Otherwise, showing contempt for someone based on her race would have the same moral status as doing so because she has bad taste. What is it about racially-based violations of these human norms that intensifies the moral wrong involved.[86]

The additional opprobrium is racism's integral tie to the social and systematic horrors of slavery, apartheid, Nazism, colonialism, segregation, imperialism, and the shameful treatment of Native Americans in the United States—all race-based systems of oppression.[87] U.S. law recognizes that racially based wrongs are more serious than other similar wrongs by calling race a particularly "invidious" distinction. Because racial distinctions have been the source of the most heinous forms of systemic mistreatment, American law requires any policy that makes racial distinctions to pass the most stringent level of scrutiny as to whether its likely benefits outweigh its presumed wrongs. (The legal status of race as a basis of discrimination will be further discussed in chapter 4.)

"Racism" draws its moral valence from this historical context in two ways. First, the mere fact that these historical systems were based on race provides some of that opprobrium, even if current instances of racism no longer take place in the direct context of, for example, segregation, apartheid, or slavery. Because no historical systems have degraded whole groups of people because they were thought to have bad taste, scorning someone on these grounds, while certainly wrong, does not carry that historically-weighted moral opprobrium.

The second connection between the strong negative valence of "racism" and historical systems of subjugation is that we continue to live with the

legacy of those systems. Dismantling the legal and other structural underpinnings of apartheid, slavery, and segregation did not automatically lead
to justice for the subordinated groups. Racial injustice remains characteristic of Western society as a whole, and of some nations more profoundly
than others. Were this injustice to be overcome, the epithet "racism"
would lose some of its force (though not all, since racial prejudice and antipathy survives even in contexts of economic and civic equality). But current relations between racial groups continue to reflect past history.

Consider anti-Irish prejudice. At one point in American history, especially in the early years of substantial Irish immigration (1820–60), the
Irish were seen as a degraded type of human being, almost as low on the
scale of social esteem as blacks.[88] Nor have prejudice and demeaning images of Irish people fully disappeared; the stereotype of Irish people as
drunks still lives on in mainstream culture.

The Irish, however, are now entirely integrated into the fabric of American life as full equals; no general exclusion or stigma attached to being
Irish exists in the general culture. Blacks' and Native Americans' situation
is quite different. They are both still stigmatized and inferiorized groups.
(With exceptions in certain parts of the nation, Native Americans are
more marginalized but less stigmatized than blacks). Thus the accusation
of being "anti-Irish" rightly carries much less moral force than being "antiblack" or "anti–Native American." The stereotype of Irish as drunkards
carries much less social power than does that of blacks and Native Americans as lazy, because the latter is a cultural representation still very much
interwoven with the current unequal socioeconomic status of blacks and
Native Americans as groups.[89]

Still, stereotyping of Irish people is damaging to individuals and the
Irish as a group, leading to demeaning portrayals and even to corrosive
internalizing of the stereotypes. That it is not morally equivalent to racism
does not mean that it is not a serious moral ill. To think otherwise is to be
blinded by the "racism or nothing" outlook.

Degrees of Racism

My account of racism, rooting it in its history, is meant to help us distinguish genuine racism from lesser racial ills and infractions. The critique
of "categorial drift" turns on acknowledging moral degree also. It is a
more serious moral reproach to call a person a racist than to call one of

his acts racist. It is generally less morally serious to use a racist symbol in-
nocently than to do so with explicit intent to demean, harm, or insult.
And so on. And some acts, persons, and participants are more racist than
others. People sometimes treat "racist," as a concept, like "pregnant"—either you are or you aren't. But there can be degrees of racism, just as
there can be degrees of dishonesty and cruelty. A film can be mildly racist,
or viciously racist—for instance, in its portrayal of Arabs, or blacks, as well
as in some overall sense. An individual can be somewhat hostile or intensely hostile toward Mexicans. Some disputes about racism founder on
a felt need to make racism an "all or nothing" matter. But, like most vices,
racism comes in degrees, and it is worse to be more rather than less racist,
even if it is bad to be racist in whatever degree.

The all-or-nothing approach prevents us from seeing the complexities
in an individual's overall view of a racial other. Some whites may harbor
distinctly racist prejudices and feelings toward some blacks, or blacks in
general, yet also genuinely admire, appreciate, and be attracted to other
blacks, or to characteristics they perceive in blacks. Though racism sometimes *does* function in an all-or-nothing way, in which the racial other is
seen wholly and unambivalently through the negative lens of racism,[90]
often it does not. In the interest of accuracy and of facilitating communication about these vexing matters, we would do well to recognize such
complexity. As with all moralism, simplistic judgments in the racial domain lead to polarized positions, rendering fruitful communication difficult.

Once one moves away from the *general* idea of "racism" as a kind of
large undifferentiated thing, an "impersonal force," as Bob Blauner once
referred to it,[91] it is obvious that not all forms and instances of racism are
equally heinous. An act of racist violence is worse than telling a racist joke.
Believing in the human inferiority of a racial group is not as morally evil
as acting on that belief in order to deprive the group of its rights. Harboring racist feelings that one never expresses is not as morally bad as expressing them whenever one has the chance.

But if the term "racism" carries such different moral valences in its
many manifestations, what remains of the idea that it is *always* a term of
strong moral opprobrium, for the reasons mentioned earlier? The answer, I think, is that the opprobrium operates *within* categories of racist
manifestations. Thus racist beliefs are particularly vile types of beliefs:
racist symbols, particularly vile symbols, and so forth. But the comparative
vileness does not operate *across* categories. Racist belief is not necessarily
more objectionable morally than harmful nonracist behavior.[92]

Selective Racism

Our dominant concept of personal racism and prejudice is the targeting of an entire racial group, where animus or disrespect directed toward one member is grounded in animus or disrespect toward the group itself.[93] Much of what we call "racism" or "racial prejudice," however, does not actually work this way. In contemporary America, for example, nonblacks direct much stronger animus toward black men than toward black women, toward poor blacks than toward well-to-do blacks.[94] Asian women tend to be the object of more demeaning stereotypes than Asian men—as passive, compliant sex objects, for example. Ms. Verano, the white fourth-grade teacher, exhibits an analogous attitude of selectiveness in her discomfort with black adults but not black children. So let us call personal racism that is differentially directed toward distinct subgroups within a given racial group "selective racism."

An individual can be a target of demeaning or hostility by reason of membership in more than one group. That Asian women are subject to greater demeaning than Asian men may reflect both racism *and* sexism; the "compliant sex object" stereotype is clearly a combination of the two. Black women, too, suffer from sexism as well as racism. But this dual prejudice is not selective racism, for it involves a uniform negative view of a racially defined group, combined with a gender prejudice. Selective racism is involved when one subgroup is stigmatized *more* than another— black men more than black women, for example.

How can there be such a thing as selective racism? If we have as our model of racism that the entire group must be targeted, then what I am calling "selective racism" might seem not to be racism. Suppose, for example, that a white person feels positively toward older black persons of either sex and negative only toward young black men. She might say, "I'm not prejudiced against blacks themselves, so I'm not racist. I just don't like young black men. This might be some kind of prejudice, but it is not racial."[95]

But some forms of, or explanations for, this individual's type of animus does involve animus toward the entire group. She may harbor mild prejudice toward all blacks, yet feel positively toward the elderly; so, on balance, she feels positively toward elderly blacks. Yet, in order for this form of differential racial antipathy to be present, the subject must feel *less* positively toward elderly blacks than toward elderly nonblacks, even if her feelings toward elderly blacks are, taken as a whole, positive. Otherwise how could she have a negative affect toward blacks in general?

This explanation can not, however, apply to all forms of selective antipathy to young black males, for it is not plausible to postulate a characteristic that every black who is *not* a young black male possesses, toward which the subject in question feels favorably. Rather, what seems much more common is that the category "young black males" evokes a distinctively negative prejudice. Two explanations suggest themselves. First, the subject may think of this group as quintessentially black, the archetype of blackness. That she regards other black subgroups as not fully black shows that her prejudice is directed against blackness.[96] The subject only accepts blacks whom she does not take to be fully black.[97] A second explanation is that the prejudice is triggered only by the confluence of characteristics, not by any of them in isolation. The racial dimension "kicks in" only when youth and maleness are also present. The prejudice is not merely a sum of the prejudices against those characteristics singly.[98]

The first explanation of selectivity more clearly involves a form of racism or racial prejudice, as blackness per se is the target of hostility. The second is racism in the sense that the target's race is a necessary feature of the prejudice; but it differs from familiar understandings of racism or racial prejudice because the entire group (or blackness in general) is not a target of prejudice. Hence "selective racism," or "selective prejudice," may express this form.

To name an act or a person "racism" or "racist" is particularly severe condemnation. But the terms are in danger of losing their moral force, for they have been subject to conceptual inflation (overexpansive usage) and moral overload (covering morally too diverse phenomena), thus inhibiting honest interracial exchange.

The conceptual inflation arises from three sources. First, "racism" and "racist" have come to be applied to virtually anything that goes wrong in the domain of race, leaving us with an apparent choice between calling something "racist" or seeing it as of no moral concern at all. This development is both a cause and a product of an attenuation of other ways to describe problematic racial phenomena (racial discomfort, racial ignorance, racial insensitivity, racial injustice). I suggest that we breathe new life into those linguistic resources. Second, "racism" has begun to be used for all forms of group discrimination, denials of dignity, and stigmatization (on the basis of sex, disability, sexual orientation, and religion). Third, people have become sloppy about the category of item they name as "racist." This "categorial drift" tends to up the moral ante.

Despite their current ubiquity, the terms "racism" and "racist" are of relatively recent vintage. Their history (since their coinage in the 1930s) suggests that two distinct themes should be considered the core of racism:

antipathy toward, and inferiorization of, a racial group. The moral force of the terms lies in both the violation of fundamental moral norms and in their relation to the evils of historical systems of oppression within which racist phenomena have been embedded.

The all-or-nothing way of thinking about racial malfeasance distorts our understanding of racism itself. Racism admits of degrees. Persons, motives, portrayals, and statements can be more and less racist (than others). And racist attitudes and prejudices can be targeted to some subpopulations of a racial group more than others.[99]

2

Can Blacks Be Racist?

The idea of "racism" arose from systems of race-based degradation, persecution, and suffering. In all these systems the perpetrating group were white and, with the partial exception of Nazism,[1] the subordinated groups were people of color—Indians, American blacks, Africans. So in the original meaning of "racism" the assumption was that it was something that white people felt, believed, and practiced toward people of color.

The liberation of colonies from the European yoke, the end of legal segregation in the United States, and the recent ending of South African apartheid have heightened awareness that racism, at least in its *personal* mode, is no longer confined solely to whites. (Institutional racism is a different matter.) Contemporary use of the vocabulary of racism no longer confines it to whites; Chinese, blacks, Japanese, Latinos, and other people of color are recognized to include in their ranks racially bigoted persons and, more broadly, to be subject to racial prejudices. These attitudes can be directed toward other groups of color, toward whites, or toward members of one's own group. People of color are also capable of developing belief systems based on racial superiority, in which some groups of color are superior and whites or other groups of color are inferior.

In my view, these attitudes and beliefs are all racist, and current usage generally so refers to them. A substantial body of literature, however, challenges the idea that people of color can be racist. The dispute about who can be racist could be primarily semantic. If racial hatred and prejudice were regarded with appropriate horror and condemnation, it would not much matter whether they are called "racist" or not. But, as we have seen, who and what gets labeled "racist" or "racism" is no mere semantic issue. Those words are currently the single most powerful weapon in the arsenal of moral condemnation in the racial arena. As generally understood, to be exempt from being "racist" is to escape severe moral censure.

Differences between white and black attitudes about racial matters in the United States have been well documented. Jennifer Hochschild, Donald Kinder and Lynn Sanders, and Howard Schuman et al. have all found striking gaps between whites and blacks[2]—in beliefs about the degree of social progress made by blacks and the extent of opportunities open to blacks; on the causes of continuing racial inequality; in support for government initiatives to enforce equal opportunity; in attitudes toward affirmative action; and on general optimism and pessimism about race relations.[3] The "racial perception gap" was brought startlingly into the public eye in the widely divergent reactions to the verdict in the 1995 O. J. Simpson trial.

By themselves, these divergences are not equivalent to differences in the *meaning* of the concept of "racism." They might just be disagreement about the *extent* of racism. Bob Blauner, however, has claimed that since the 1960s the two races have developed almost distinctive racial worldviews, that are intertwined with different understandings of the term "racism" itself.[4] As Blauner describes it, blacks define "racism" as patterns of racial inequality (for example, in schooling and criminal justice), whereas whites define it as departing from color blindness (to favor one racial group over another, for whatever reason).

In chapter 1 I argued against what Blauner sees as "the black view"— that it misleadingly omits personal forms of racism (or denies them significance) in favor of a purely systemic or institutional understanding of racism; I suggested that both personal and institutional forms of racism were significant. In chapters 3 and 4 I will argue, against Blauner's "white view", that departure from color blindness is not racist, much less a paradigm of racism (and that it can sometimes be a bad thing and sometimes a good thing).

Blauner also takes note of differing views of whether only whites can be racist. Anyone who has had extensive contact with college students will recognize that the divide here produces interracial tension, anger, bafflement, and lack of respectful communication. At the same time it is wrong and counterproductive to overstate the degree to which person's racial identity correlates with her stand on whether only whites can be racist. Many whites hold that only whites can be racist and, conversely, many people of color reject it and believe that blacks, Asians, and other people of color can be racist.

The overracialization of opinions and viewpoints is an ever-present danger in interpreting statistical differences in racial groups' views. For instance, 60 percent of whites think that blacks have equal or greater job opportunity than whites, while only 33 percent of blacks believe this.[5] This is a huge and important difference, but it is still true from these figures that millions of whites (40 percent) do *not* think blacks have equal opportunity, and 33 percent of blacks do. Yet such a statistic is often popularly understood as "Whites believe blacks have equal opportunity; blacks do not." Careful researchers like the ones mentioned above (Hochschild, Schuman) generally avoid licensing such distortion of their findings. But Blauner, for example, occasionally succumbs, as with the following unqualified remark: "Whites locate racism in color consciousness and its absence in color blindness."[6]

One danger in overstating the differences is that it suggests that if you are white, then you *should* hold the view attributed to your group; and if you already *do* hold "the white view," you are closed to arguments that might persuade you otherwise. Overstating the differences also discourages racially different persons from thinking it possible to reach a common understanding through respectful and rational conversation.

My goal of an adequate account of racism is entirely antithetical to race-based attachment to definitions of "racism." I am seeking an account that will facilitate communication between groups about the character, forms, and extent of racism (and other race-related ills). For that we need some agreement on what racism is, and from there we can attempt to settle differences about its *extent*. But if the meanings of "racism" differ between groups, and if each is interested only in its own meaning, empirical inquiries about the extent of racism would produce little illumination.

Let us turn, then, to the charged issue of whether blacks and other people of color can be racist.

All Colors of Racists

Ruben Navarrette notes some Mexican American prejudice against blacks, shown in much stronger disapproval of Mexican-black than Mexican-white dating.[7] Lyrics expressing racial hatred and glorifying violence against whites can be found in many popular songs, some by Grammy award winners who are black or Latino. (One example, by the group Apache: "Kill the white people; we gonna make them hurt; kill the white people; but buy my record first; ha, ha, ha."[8]) Outside the United States, many Japanese have historically practiced a form of racism against Koreans (including ethnic Koreans in Japan), and against a subgroup of Japanese known as *burakumin*.[9] Ethnic hatreds that make use of a racialized conception of ethnicity—Tutsi and Hutu in Rwanda and Burundi, Serb and Croat, Serb and Albanian—have intensified since the end of the Cold War. Arab migrants to Australia have viewed white Australians as having low moral standards, leaving their houses dirty, being inclined to drunkenness, and being uncommitted to their families.[10] These stereotypes are at least close to being racist.

Some people of color employ the term "racism" to express race-based hatred and attitudes of racial superiority against whites. Lamond Godwin, a black man growing up in the South in the 1950s, says of the Catholic school he attended, "The nuns and priests kept us from being racists. The best people we knew were white—people we spent the whole day with . . . We had the Klan bombing churches, but we had these people on our side."[11] Forthrightly racist beliefs about whites are attributed to blacks by Orlando Patterson, who says that whites' denying black peoples' humanity "left most blacks persuaded that whites were less than human."[12] Students discussing prejudices and hatreds on the part of Asians against blacks, blacks against Puerto Ricans, and any similar combination frequently refer to these sentiments as "racist."

Most of what has been called "racism" on the part of people of color is racial bigotry, hatred, and prejudice. Inferiorizing forms of racism are rarer among groups lower in the racial status order. Such forms are much more closely tied to social standing than are bigotry and hatred; it is difficult for members of subordinate groups to truly believe in their own superiority,[13] as the dominant culture's view of them is as inferiors who deserve their subordinate place. Nevertheless, as the quote from Patterson suggests, it is possible for blacks to regard whites as morally evil precisely because they regard and treat blacks inhumanly. In addition, whether it is genuinely believed or not, blacks can purvey what Bernard Boxill calls "the racism of black racial superiority."[14]

In light of these instances of racial hatred and inferiorizing on the part of people of color, let us look at the arguments for not calling them "racism."

Is Racism Prejudice Plus Power?

One common argument is that racism requires the possession of social power; in a white-dominated society like the United States, only whites have that power, and hence are the only group that can be racist. Joseph Barndt, a white antiracist pastor, puts this view well:

> Racism is clearly more than simple prejudice or bigotry. Everyone is prejudiced, but not everyone is racist . . . To be racially prejudiced means to have distorted opinions about people of other races. Racism goes beyond prejudice. Racism is the power to enforce one's prejudices. More simply stated, racism is prejudice plus power.[15]

Studs Terkel reports a similar view from a black student:

> I can be prejudiced but not racist. To be a racist, you have to be able to oppress another race. To do that, you have to have economic and political power. Blacks don't have that; whites do. Being prejudiced is something else. You have to prejudge. Many blacks may prejudge whites, because of all their past experiences.[16]

Yet, even if power were the arbiter of racism, people of color could still be racist. In nations in which people of color are in power, they can be racist against other ethno-racial groups. Idi Amin, Uganda's ruler in the early 1970's, stirred up ethno-racial hatred among Ugandan blacks against the ethnic Indian population of Uganda (some native-born), and many were driven from the country. Japanese prejudice against and inferiorization of ethnic Koreans in Japan is another example (even if Koreans and Japanese are seen in the West as being of the same "race").

Such considerations might not be considered relevant, however, since arguments about whether only whites can be racist tend to focus only on the West, where whites are the group in power; so I will confine further discussion to that context. In the United States blacks or other people of color hold power over other ethnoracial groups in some municipalities and in institutions such as schools and hospitals. They can therefore exclude other racial groups on the basis of race. Thus if racism is prejudice plus power, people of color in power can be racist against those not in power. Consider a largely black school and a class within it that is black except for one white student. Several black students socially exclude the white student and intentionally make him feel uncomfortable in the class, calling him a "honky" and "white bread." Let us assume that these students are genuinely bigoted against whites.[17] In this particular context, blacks do have power, and are prejudiced against and discriminatory toward whites. Hence if racism is prejudice plus power, these students are racist toward the white student.

Although whites are the dominant racial group in U.S. society as a whole, the key point on which the "racism = prejudice + power" view draws, restricting the operation of power pertinent to a definition of racism to the overall structure of society seems arbitrary. If power to put one's prejudices into action is the key factor in racism, what is the basis for ruling out any context in which people of color hold power over other racial groups, including whites?[18] In the few, but increasing, cases in which people of color hold power in subinstitutions, this power should allow their racial prejudices to count as racism, on the account in question.[19]

One form of the argument that blacks can not be racist implies that the only kind of power relevant to racism is institutionalized power. Spike Lee says, "Black people can't be racist. Racism is an institution."[20] This remark could be taken to mean that, strictly speaking, there is no individual racism, only institutional racism; in chapter 1 I rejected this view. But it could also be taken to mean that only individuals with institutional power can be (individually) racist.

The counter-examples I have provided to the argument that racism equals prejudice plus power have in fact generally involved such institutional power—controlling hiring in municipal institutions, being the ruler of a country, and the like. But in Barndt's and Terkel's student's views, the relevant power is the power to put one's prejudicial views and feelings into action, to harm or deprive of benefit the member of the racial group against whom one is prejudiced. Such power does not require institutional form. A statement (cited by Andrew Hacker) from Coleman Young, a former mayor of Detroit, is illuminating in this regard. He said that blacks in the United States "cannot be called racist, for the simple reason that they are an oppressed people. Racism, he has said, should be attributed only to those who have the power to cause suffering . . . Racism takes its full form only when it has an impact on the real world."[21] But people of color can cause suffering to whites out of racial antipathy, as Nathan McCall's graphic depiction of his regretted youthful victimization of whites illustrates.[22] The Southern Poverty Law Center's periodic compilation of hate-based incidents always includes a small number of cases of blacks and Latinos attacking whites or other racial groups.[23] The power to harm others through action motivated by racial prejudice goes far beyond institutional forms of harm. (The focus on institutional power may well arise from the influence of "institutional racism" as a general definition of "racism.")

Perhaps under segregation many blacks nursed hatred of whites and wished they could harm them; but the costs of doing so were generally prohibitively high. The contemporary scene of racial interaction is very different. In many situations individuals or groups are in a position to harm members of other ethnoracial groups against whom they harbor prejudices or hatred. The harm need not be directly physical, but can also occur through exclusion, insult, or demeaning treatment. The ability of individuals to perpetrate such harm will often depend on the majority/minority configuration in the immediate context, as in the example of the black students in a majority black school excluding the white student. In this context there is strength in numbers. But any individual can use fists or weapons to cause hate-driven harm outside such contexts. The power to harm others through racially prejudicial action is not limited to any racial group.

My argument may appear to have conceded that power *is* in fact central to racism. But I have not conceded that. My argument has been more limited. Definitions that build power into "racism" cannot also claim that blacks and other people of color cannot be racist. In my view, a lonely and isolated bigot, with no influence on anyone, is still a racist in a meaningful sense, and certainly possesses racist attitudes.[24] It is the content of attitudes and beliefs that makes them racist, not whether their possessors have the power to put them into practice. I will argue below, however, that we should indeed be concerned about whether someone does have the power to implement her prejudices. Power does play a role in the moral seriousness of instances of racism, but not in its existence.

Who Cares about Prejudice?

Those who argue that blacks can not be racist appear to make a concession when they say (as Barndt's and Terkel's student do) that blacks can be prejudiced. From a moral point of view, however, this concession does not amount to much if "prejudice" is implied to be of negligible moral concern.

Barndt says that prejudice is "hav[ing] distorted opinions about people of other races." He thereby omits the affective dimension of prejudice that involves racial antipathy and other negative sentiments, which are integral to the moral wrong of racial prejudice. Nor does Barndt focus on "distorted opinions" of an inferiorizing sort, such as that blacks are intellectually deficient, or subhuman. Terkel's student, in calling prejudice "prejudging", also omits the dimension of racial prejudice that involves morally objectionable sentiments. In addition her actual example of "prejudgment" is at best normatively ambiguous; she may partly be thinking that blacks' experience of whites actually justifies them in prejudice against whites.

Spike Lee, in the interview in which he says that "racism is an institution," echoes Barndt in dismissing prejudice: "Now black people can be prejudiced. Shit, everybody's prejudiced about something. I don't think there will ever be an end to prejudice. But racism, that's a different thing entirely."[25] Both Lee and Barndt imply that because prejudice is universal, it is either not a matter of great concern or is something one can do little about, so why get too worked up over it.[26] (By contrast, they imply that one *should* get worked up over racism.)

One could, of course, take the alleged universality of prejudice in the opposite moral direction: "We're all in the same boat, so, together, let us try to do what we can to diminish prejudice in all of us." But this is not the direction the blacks-can't-be-racist adherents ever seem to go. This is no doubt due in part to the tendency, discussed in chapter 1, of racism to imperialize the moral/racial domain, rendering everything other than racism unworthy of serious moral attention. It is morally dangerous to dismiss racial prejudice as unworthy of such consideration. To do so is to invite persons of color to avoid facing up to the moral odiousness of whatever racial prejudices they may have.

Is Racism Confined to Ideology?

As we saw in chapter 1, "racism" was originally used specifically in reference to a certain type of ideology, in which human groups identified by inescapable biological natures (and generally revealing these group natures in phenotypic differences) were ranked on a scale of superior and inferior. This history can be used as an argument for confining "racism" to whites, for it was only Europeans who developed such an ideology. Even the forms of ethnic inferiorizing found in Japan, for example, do not rest on such an elaborated ideology.

This argument deserves to be taken seriously.[27] A version of it is put forth by Robert Miles in *Racism*, an indispensable text in understanding racism. As noted in chapter 1, Miles is concerned with the "conceptual inflation" that has afflicted the term "racism." His target is primarily the concept of "institutional racism" (discussed in chapter 1), and his solution to the inflation problem is to confine racism to ideologies, although he allows these "ideologies" to be less fully developed and propositional than, say, segregationist or Nazi racist ideologies were. They can include images and less systematic beliefs. Although Miles does not directly say so, his confinement of "racism" to ideology is meant partly to return the term to an agreed-upon meaning deriving from its universally-recognized history.[28]

Using "racism as ideology" to support the view that only whites (or Europeans) can be racist is open to several objections. First, some ideologies developed by people of color would have to be accounted racist. The Nation of Islam, for example, has put forth the view that Europeans' emergence from the Ice Age has condemned them to an inherent nature as "ice people" who cannot avoid attempting to dominate other peoples.[29] This is indeed a racist ideology, and someone who believes it is an inferiorizing racist; but it would be a counter-example to the view that blacks could not be racist, even in Miles's view.[30]

Second, if racism required racist ideology, some white racists would escape the charge of racism, as I argued in chapter 1. Some whites might hate Mexicans or Native Americans without believing in, much less being aware of the existence of, a full-scale ideology involving beliefs about biology, genetics, and hierarchy.

It is true that the racist must view the racial other in a negative light. But such a vague, general attitude is very different from a fully developed racial ideology. In the "racism as ideology" view, then, not only will some blacks or other people of color end up as "racist," but some white racists will not.

Reactive Racism

Another reason sometimes offered for confining racism to whites is that when blacks manifest racial antipathy, it is generally either reactive to or compensatory for white racism toward them. To assess this view, we must first distinguish between being racist and being blameworthy for racism. Someone whose racist attitudes developed as a result of racist victimization may well be less blameworthy than someone whose racism stems from other sources.[31] Nevertheless, this explanation does not mean that she is not racist, nor that she escapes responsibility for her racist attitudes and actions. Also there is a difference between reacting to one's own victimization, or that of one's loved ones, and reacting to the racial victimization of unknown members of one's racial group. The former much more strongly mitigates responsibility for racism than the latter.

Moreover, hating persons who have victimized you and hating others who simply belong to the same racial group as your victimizers are very different. Only the second is racist. I once saw a documentary in which a white man had been beaten and robbed in his house by two black men. He said that he now hated all blacks and appeared to regard this as an entirely reasonable reaction to his victimization. This appears to be a case of "reactive racism." But it is certainly morally wrong. It is even misleading to think of it as reasonable. The same applies to blacks or Latinos victimized by whites, even where there has been (as there often is) a pattern of such racial victimization, discrimination, and ill-treatment. It is still wrong to generate from such treatment animosity or antipathy to the entire group of whites. Perhaps during the segregation era it was reasonable for blacks, especially those who had very limited contacts with whites, to assume that every white person was "in on" the oppression of blacks. This would not have been true, but some blacks may not have been in a position to recognize this. In the contemporary United States, however, such a generalized racial antipathy—reactive racism—has no basis and is never justified.

It should not be thought, in any case, that all racism on the part of persons of color is reactive racism, even if, especially in the case of African-Americans, it takes place in the context of stigmatization and inequality. Elaborated racist philosophies, such as the black supremacist views of Elijah Muhammad as described by James Baldwin in *The Fire Next Time*, can not be regarded as mere reactions to white racism.[32] They involve a degree of commitment that is not merely reactive but proactive. In addition, some racist thinking on the part of any group is a product of stereotyping, scapegoating, projection of personal failure onto external sources, and the like, not prompted by reactions to personal racial victimization. Finally, immigrant groups of color may bring indigenous racist ideas with them, in addition to whatever ones they pick up here in the United States.

Reactive racism, then, is still racism. It may in some cases be less blameworthy than nonreactive racism; but it is always a very bad thing and is never justified. In addition, not all racism on the part of persons of color is reactive racism.[33]

Moral Asymmetries in Racism

Accepting my argument that racism can be manifested in any racial group should reduce the sense of mutual anger and bafflement—or at least "talking past one another"—that so often attends conversations about race, especially across racial lines. Some who accept this argument take it a step further than I wish to, however, and cloud the issue from the other direction. In a discussion among junior high school students about racist name-calling toward Haitian students, one white student said that whites were targets of racial slurs by Haitian students as well. Her point may have been merely what I have been arguing—that racism does not go in only one direction. But the student seemed to imply something further; that the slurring of whites was *morally equivalent* to the slurring of the Haitians. One might call this the "all racism is equal" view. I have not seen this view argued for explicitly; still, the idea is implicit in much discussion of racism, where the logic seems to be thus: "If blacks can be racist against whites, and whites against blacks, and both are morally reprehensible, then they are *equally* morally reprehensible."

All racism is not equal, however. There are what I will call "moral asymmetries" between racism against whites and racism against people of color.

A racist murder is worse than a racist joke. Some stereotypes are more racist than others. An intentionally threatening and demeaning display of a racist symbol is morally worse than an unwitting one. So obviously not every instance of racism is of equal moral concern.

In order to pin down the race-related asymmetries that the "all racism is equal" view denies, let us construe that view to be that "the moral seriousness of a racist act (attitude, belief, and the like) is not affected by the racial identity of the parties to it."[34] That is, racist acts of the same type, which are morally equivalent in all other respects, are also morally equivalent independent of racial identity. A black calling a white person "honky" or "white bread" is morally equivalent to a white calling a black "nigger." A white person excluding a Mexican American from a business-related social gathering out of racial prejudice is morally equivalent to a Mexican American doing the same to a white person.

Against this view, I contend that the racial identity of the victim (and, to a lesser extent, the perpetrator) is indeed morally pertinent. Hatred of blacks against whites is not a primary form of racism; hatred of whites against blacks is. Some forms of racism are central and paradigmatic, others secondary. The former have defined for us what racism is. They are more directly tied to the rationale, discussed in chapter 1, for the intense moral opprobrium carried by the term "racism." That rationale involved oppression, hatred, and discrimination against people of color, and most especially blacks and Native Americans, by whites, not the reverse. Everything else being equal, greater moral opprobrium rightly attaches to racism by whites against people of color than the reverse. This is the most important moral asymmetry in racism.[35]

There are four sources of moral asymmetry among forms of racism differentiated by perpetrator and target groups: *historical legacy; positional inferiority; patterns and prevalence;* and *contribution to racial injustice.* By and large these asymmetries correspond to racial groupings, and they reveal why racism of whites against people of color is of greater moral concern than that of people of color against whites.

Historical Legacy

A racist act against a member of a group that has suffered a strong historical legacy of racism carries the weight of that history and brings it down upon those who are the targets. In 1990 a young black man was killed in the white Bensonhurst section of New York, and blacks mounted demonstrations of protest. They were met by a large group of white residents, some of whom brandished watermelons in a contemptuous gesture toward the blacks. The force of the racial contempt was intensified by the whites' use of this historical symbol of black slavery and subordination, which invokes an image of the happy, slow-witted, agreeable slave.

Similarly, display of the swastika evokes for Jews the Holocaust and its legacy of terror and genocide. Such display operates in part by eliciting fear and the psychic pain connected with those historical events. But the effect in both cases does not depend on the target's believing that there is a real danger of slavery or the Holocaust actually recurring; it certainly does not require that the target think that the perpetrator is attempting to reinstitute that historical oppression. (Though the fear and sense of threat evoked are likely to be greater when the perpetrator *is* attempting this, as some white supremacist groups currently advocate.)

The historical legacy effect operates by way of the identity of the target group, insofar as that identity is bound up with the memory of oppression. Any manifestation of racism that carries such historical resonance renders it more morally offensive than an analogous one against a group without such a history. White people, considered as a racial group, have not suffered a history of such racial oppression, and acts of racism against them, morally offensive as they are, do not carry this historical resonance. A group of blacks waving loaves of white bread at some white people to express contempt, hatred, and exclusion can not carry the psychic force involved in invoking historical oppression. Acts of racism that partake of the historical legacy effect involve a more intense psychic harm and attack on group dignity.

The historical legacy effect makes for a clear asymmetry in otherwise similar acts. But the invoking of this effect can be subject to misuse; members of a group can "make too much of" their historical oppression—permitting it to play too central a role in their group-based identity (a fault akin to what I call racialism in chapter 3). African Americans frequently, understandably, and appropriately refer current manifestations of racism to slavery, but this connection can be overplayed and become counterproductive, as when slavery is invoked in a simplistic way to explain various ills affecting African Americans. Many Jews do something similar with regard to the Holocaust, claiming a victim status belied by their circumstances in the contemporary United States.

It is by no means easy to know where to draw the line. In 1995 the Library of Congress housed an exhibition on slavery, including material based on interviews with former slaves in the 1930's and pictures from the Library's archives. The exhibition aimed to show slavery from the slaves' point of view, highlighting the texture of their lives and culture, and including slave resistance. Black staff, who had been involved in a long-running labor discrimination suit against the Library, objected to a large photo in the exhibit of a white overseer on horseback looking down on black cotton pickers. A staffer said, "It reminded me of the the white overseers here at the Library of Congress looking down over us to make sure we're in the fields doing our work." The protest caused the Library to dismantle the display, and the exhibition was taken up by a black-run institution, the Martin Luther King Jr. Memorial Library, where it was popular and appreciated among African American viewers.[36]

For some whites especially, this incident would confirm the danger of what is sometimes called "hypersensitivity" to the historical legacy effect. The exhibit was very much meant to honor slaves and to be a strong statement against slavery; and however blacks were treated at the Library, it could not have been very much like the experience of slavery.

But a different lesson can more appropriately be drawn. Slavery remains an understandable metaphor to which current African American experience is referred—the most striking feature of African American historical experience in the United States. No doubt those who objected to the picture were quite aware of the differences between forms of discrimination suffered at the Library and working under a white overseer's power to physically harm or kill. But the black-run library was a better venue for the exhibit than the Library of Congress, given the discrimination suit. Ideally the venue should not matter; the exhibit seemed to be of real merit, and to carry a lesson rightly welcomed by those inheriting the legacy of slavery. But black subordination is undeniably a part of the legacy of slavery and segregation, and until it no longer exists, these incidents point to a need to take it into account in public portrayals of African Americans.

The complaints of the employees, with their slavery-infused sense of grievance, can not be dismissed simply on the ground that the exhibit was itself critical of slavery—any more than that the use in schools of *The Adventures of Huckleberry Finn* can be conclusively defended against many African American parents' concern about the frequent use of the term "nigger" and the servile portrayal of the slave Jim *solely* by asserting that the book is clearly meant to be critical, rather than supportive, of slavery. The historical legacy argument helps us see the complexity here.

Positional Inferiority

Moral asymmetries also arise from some racial groups' unjust "positional" (as opposed to inherent) superiority to others, economically, socially, and politically. Obviously such an arrangement in its own right constitutes a type of moral asymmetry. Blacks, Mexican Americans, Native Americans, and others are the victims of this injustice, while whites are the beneficiaries. We are concerned here, however, not with this systemic aspect of racism in itself but only as an asymmetric context for *personal* racism.

The asymmetry here concerns primarily the intentionally inferiorizing form of personal racism. To declare or portray another racial group as humanly deficient always involves racism, and is an extreme failure to respect human dignity. The claim discussed earlier that whites are humanly and morally deficient because of the lack of melanin in their skin, for example, is racist and repulsive. But when an inferiorizing racist message is directed toward a group or member that occupies an unjustly disadvantaged position in the society, the message acquires a greater power to shame than when it is directed toward a positionally superior group or member. It shames by reminding the target that the inferiority declared in the message is reflected in the social order itself. Regarding black, anti-white views, no societal inferiority corresponds to the inferiority declared in the racist message, and thus it is less able psychically to wound the target, whose situation serves as a buffer against the attack. Again, however, though the message is less hurtful, it is still racist.

In some situations, the power relations between two groups are such that it would be virtually impossible for an inferiorizing remark to succeed in scorning or insulting a member of a positionally superior group. It is not hard to imagine whites so imbued with a sense of their own superiority that any racist inferiorizing such as is involved in The Nation of Islam's outlook would seem ludicrous to them. Such an attack, though it would not carry the moral force of a successful racial insult (only an attempted one), would not, however, render the attacker less than blameworthy, if the source was racial contempt.

Subordinate vs. Vulnerable Groups

Before introducing the third type of moral asymmetry we must distinguish between two different categories of targets of racism. A "subordinate" group is "positionally inferior," as just discussed. Such a group, which in the United States comprises blacks, Native Americans, Mexican Americans, and Puerto Ricans, and others, includes those most frequently thought of as victims of racism.

Other ethnoracial groups, however, are "vulnerable" to racism yet are not subordinate. Japanese Americans, Jews, Indian Americans, and Arab Americans are examples. By general measures of economic, social, and civic well-being, these groups are doing better than average. Yet these groups are frequent targets of racial hatred, prejudice, and offensive stereotyping. This hatred sometimes breaks out into violence, even murder.[37]

Vulnerable groups are much less likely than subordinate groups to be targets of inferiorizing racism, except that they are sometimes thought of as *morally* inferior, or (especially in the case of Jews) positively evil. Arab-Americans are often stereotyped as terrorists, also an example of an evil-based stereotype. In part the difference exists because inferiorizing racism gets much more of a grip when the group being attached is positionally inferior. Vulnerable, nonsubordinate groups are more often targets of antipathy racism.

Patterns and Prevalence of Racist Acts

Both vulnerable and subordinate groups are targets of personal racism more often than are nonvulnerable, nonsubordinate groups. Asians, Jews, African Americans, Latinos, and Hispanics experience much more personal racism than do Irish Americans, Norwegian Americans, and Polish Americans. Groups that experience a greater prevalence and more pervasive patterns of racism are morally asymmetrical, with regard to personal racism, to those which do not. This is obviously so in regard to the *degree* of racism; groups that experience more racism are worse victims of racism than those that experience less. But that is not the only source of asymmetry, and is not what I mean here.

The "patterns and prevalence" asymmetry applies to individual racist acts. When patterns of racism exist, any individual act will tend to evoke them in the mind of the target individual or group. Hatred directed toward a group that is often attacked is more likely to result in fear, self-doubt, and concern about acceptance and equal treatment. One whose group is an infrequent target, such as Norwegian Americans, is much more likely to be able to slough off the psychic impact of a racial slur as an isolated incident than is the frequently targeted group member, who is more likely to be scarred and ground down by it. For the African American or Native American, the slur invokes the whole pattern of racial insults and humiliation that he, or his people, suffer. It is thus much more difficult for him to slough off the effect of the individual incident as bizarre, a fluke, or as not likely to be repeated.

But might not the psychological effect of repeated put-downs be precisely the opposite of what I have said? Might not the black individual become inured, precisely because she experiences it more frequently; while the Norwegian might be thrown for a loop, just because it is so unexpected? Certainly this can happen. Victims of repeated racism do talk about trying to rise above it, not letting it get to them, continuing to go about their business. But this is not so easy to accomplish, and we should not assume that there is no psychic cost to the black individual, for example, who maintains a calm exterior in the face of such slights.

One way of attempting to protect oneself against repeated racial attacks involves psychic withdrawal from "white society." This maneuver comes at a high price. One no longer aspires to a full, equal, and shared ownership of the major institutions, public spaces, and social milieus of one's society. One trades off social and civic engagement in the multiracial society for psychic equilibrium. Moreover, such attempts at psychic protection may well not be successful even on their own terms.

When there is a pattern of racism against a group, individual instances of it are of greater moral weight than when such a pattern is lacking. This asymmetry is related to the "historical legacy" phenomenon, as groups with current patterns of racism against them generally also have a historical legacy of racism (whose effect continues into the present). But the overlap is by no means exact. Blacks and Native Americans suffer from the historical legacy effect much more than any other groups; newer immigrant groups, such as Southeast Asians, might have strong patterns of racism against them without the intense historical legacy. (There have been outbreaks of racism against Asians since the first Chinese immigrants in the post-Civil War period; and Asians have been excluded from naturalized citizenship since the beginning of the Republic. Still, the intensity of victimization is not comparable to that of blacks and Native Americans.) Arab Americans too, are the target of often vicious stereotypes (as terrorists, or fabulously rich foreigners taking over "our" economy), yet they inherit little of an entrenched historical legacy of racism. In any case, the historical legacy effect works differently from the "patterns and prevalence" effect; the former invokes historical oppression, the latter pervasive racism or racial insensitivity in the present.

Both of these sources of moral asymmetry differ from the "positional inferiority" effect, which applies to subordinated groups only—not to vulnerable ones such as Jews, Arab Americans, and Japanese Americans. The latter groups are not positionally subordinated;[38] but they can suffer from patterns of racism and, in some cases, a historical legacy as well. The latter, for example, applies to Jews in Europe to a much greater degree than Jews in the United States. The history of anti-Semitism is much stronger in Europe than in the United States, and the memory of the Holocaust and the forces that led to it are much more salient in the European consciousness. French and German laws criminalizing the public denial or minimizing of the Holocaust—laws unthinkable in the United States—reflect this difference, and they testify to the strong presence of the historical legacy effect in current instances of anti-Semitic racism against Jews.[39]

Contribution to Racial Injustice

A final source of racial asymmetry is the contribution of the racist action to the maintenance of systemic racial injustice. Racist acts, especially those involving exclusions and deprivations of social benefit (that is, acts of racial discrimination), contribute to such maintenance when their targets are members of disadvantaged groups, but not when they are members of advantaged groups. In sustaining injustice, antisubordinate racism is much more morally objectionable than the analogous act against a member of a dominant group. In a sense, an exclusion of, say, blacks—for example, black secondary school students being placed in low-track classes—affects blacks as an entire group, reinforcing their disadvantaged position. But an analogous exclusion of whites—being excluded from a science program for minority students, for example—does not have a similar impact on all whites, or on whites as a group.

The "contribution to injustice" effect is related to the "positional inferiority" effect in that both depend on structural relations of injustice between groups. They differ in that the former concerns the impact of an individual act on those structures, while the latter concerns the impact of those structures on the individual group member's psyche.

The four forms of moral asymmetry—historical legacy, positional inferiority, patterns and prevalence of racism, and contribution to racial injustice—suggest that all racism is not equal. More specifically, racism of whites against people of color is, everything else being equal, of greater moral concern than the reverse. It is closer to the historical systems of racial oppression and injustice that provide the defining context of "racism."[40]

Moral Asymmetry and Individual Responsibility

The asymmetry of moral concern does not translate neatly into race-based asymmetries of moral responsibility. It does not follow, for example, that a white racist is more morally evil than a black racist, nor that a Puerto Rican's prejudice against white people is morally worse than the reverse, nor that a white individual is any more blameworthy or morally responsible for her racist attitudes or behavior than is a black individual (although the earlier discussion of "reactive racism" is pertinent here).

The asymmetry does mean, however, that (everything else being equal) white prejudice is laden with weightier, morally more significant meanings than are black prejudices. These meanings, as expressed in the four forms of moral asymmetry, should become part of a taken-for-granted discourse about racial issues. Their existence implies that whites should recognize that their prejudices carry these meanings, and, for that reason, can do greater psychic damage. Failure to acknowledge these asymmetrical moral meanings can constitute a kind of moral negligence.

Conversation about racial matters often omits the historical and social contexts behind these four asymmetries. Americans in general, and whites in particular, are often strikingly unattuned to their own history, and to that history's impact on the present. They fail to appreciate the significance of slavery, segregation, racial restrictions on citizenship and immigration, and the like. Related to this ignorance or indifference, though partly independent of it, many whites also do not appreciate the current structural and systemic dimensions of the situations of different racial groups. Polls consistently show that many whites think that the passing of antidiscrimination laws means that people of color face no significant barriers, relative to whites, in their aspirations to a good life; or they nominally acknowledge these barriers but do not follow the logic through to a recognition that equal opportunity does not exist and can only be created through public action.[41]

The four forms of moral asymmetry work the same way. Though a white individual is not more racist or more morally evil in harboring racial prejudice than is a black individual, the moral asymmetry makes the *consequences* of her prejudices, and of the acts expressing them, worse than those of the black individual. In this sense they are worthy of greater concern.

I have argued that people of color can be racist, and their targets of racism can be whites, groups of color other than their own, and even their own group (in the form of internalized racism). The *extent* of racism then becomes a matter for empirical investigation. It is quite conceivable that, at some particular point in time, blacks on the average might be *more* racially prejudiced against Latinos than are whites. Racial hostility, hatred, and prejudice has many sources—personal pathologies, socialization, economic competition, cultural attitudes, the dominant society's attitudes. So the prejudices of people of color may in some cases stem from different sources than whites' prejudices. Nevertheless, they are all instances of racism, and are all morally objectionable.

Apart from the philosophical arguments I have presented, from a pragmatic point of view I think we in the United States would do well to regard bigotry and (the less frequent) inferiorization on the part of people of color as forms of "racism." The racial order of our nation is changing in deeply important and structural ways. The central role of blacks in defining what racism is all about is being weakened. Latinos are essentially equal to blacks as the largest ethnoracial minority. The ranks of Native Americans doubled between the 1990 and 2000 Census, in part because more people are claiming that identity. Asian Americans, though still a relatively small minority, are the most rapidly growing one. The "white/black" paradigm for understanding racism must give way. That fact in itself is causing resentment among some African Americans; as Harlon Dalton reports, some blacks resent ceding victim-of-racism status to other nonwhite groups, and even to African immigrants.[42] Hostilities among different groups, stemming from various forms of competition, reflections of age-old white American prejudices, prejudices indigenous to the immigrant groups, inevitable scapegoating, and other factors, will continue to generate racial antipathies among some persons of color.

Ascribing "racism" to whites only seriously exacerbates problems of interracial dialogue. It feels to many whites that the onus of racial problems is placed entirely on them, and that people of color are absolved from responsibility. As long as "racism" remains the designator of the most grievous racial wrongdoing, to say that some groups are automatically exempt from that charge is deleterious to the sense that we are all responsible for and prone to racial ills, and that we need to work together to address them. Breathing life into a wider vocabulary of moral malfeasance in the racial domain—racial prejudice, racial injustice, racial insensitivity—and according the phenomena in question appropriate moral concern would help. It would render the dispute over the meaning and reach of "racism"—serious as it is—less fraught with moral overload.

At the same time, although members of all groups are capable of racism, not all racism is equal. It matters, morally, whether the perpetrator is white and the victim nonwhite, or the reverse. Racism against the vulnerable and subordinated is of especial moral concern, and a failure of whites to acknowledge the fundamental asymmetries rooted in our racialized history is equally deleterious to racial understanding.

3

Varieties of Racial Ills

We can best understand the boundaries I am suggesting that we draw around personal racism by exploring phenomena that are often called "racist" but that, on the understanding I have been developing, are something else. Doing so will help to stem the conceptual inflation of the term and help us develop the richer vocabulary that recognizes a range of racial ills distinct from racism.

Racial Insensitivity or Ignorance

There is much insensitivity and ignorance about race in people's lives. Here are some examples, the first two of which are types frequently cited as causes for resentment, irritation, and anger: (1) in a high school class, a Haitian American girl is asked to give "the black point of view" on an issue relating to race;[1] (2) a non-Asian student thinks that a Korean name is Chinese or Japanese; (3) white high school students do not understand why their African American friend cares so much that Martin Luther King Jr.'s birthday be honored publicly in their school.[2] Such behaviors are sometimes, misleadingly, referred to as "racism." Let us look at why each is objectionable.

Recognizing Ethnicity and Acknowledging Identity

By asking a Haitian American to represent a black point of view, the teacher in example 1 fails to recognize the student's distinctive ethnic identity in relation to other black groups, especially African Americans. There are two parts to this failure. One concerns Haitian Americans as an ethnic group. Charles Taylor famously argues that ethnocultural groups, especially minorities, desire recognition from authoritative institutions in the societies of which they are a part.[3] Although it is not always clear what forms such recognition should take, the teacher in this example, as an authority figure in a school, is surely denying it. A second aspect is failure to recognize the individual as having a distinctive group identity that is personally important. Whether every individual owes such recognition to every other individual, as Taylor sometimes seems to imply, it is at least reasonable to suppose that teachers owe it to students.[4] The identity feature might concern race, religion, a neighborhood, a personal interest of some sort, a family heritage—not only ethnicity. Not all identity features are equally pertinent to the educational enterprise, but if a teacher knows that a student is attached to some group, activity, or tradition, it is appropriate for her to recognize this in some way.

A similar dual failure of recognition afflicts the student in example 2 who confuses Korean with Chinese or Japanese names. If she is insufficiently aware of the existence of nationally, culturally, and linguistically distinct Asian and Asian American groups, she shares a serious form of ignorance in American society today. Furthermore, names, and especially their ethnic character, are not a trivial dimension of individual identity. In the film *Skin Deep*, a Vietnamese American student speaks with great emotion about the disrespect and nonrecognition he feels when other students mispronounce or fail to remember his name (Khanh).[5] How culpable the student who confuses Asian names is for her ignorance depends on how sheltered her background has been and, more generally, on her degree of exposure to information about Asian Americans.

Let us contrast this student with another who is perfectly aware that Koreans, Chinese, Japanese, Vietnamese, Cambodians, and so on are distinct Asian groups, that they have different languages, and that generally it is possible to discern the ethnicity from the name. She realizes, however, and regrets that she is not sufficiently knowledgeable to match names with ethnicity or country of origin. Here there is no failure to appreciate ethnic distinctiveness, and thus no failure of recognition of the Asian American groups as ethnic groups. But her lack of knowledge might result in lack of recognition at an individual level.

In each case the failure of ethnic group and individual recognition does not necessarily concern race as such. The teacher treats the Haitian American student as representing all blacks, but the failure is in not recognizing her ethnic distinctiveness within that racial group. In the Asian case, the failure of recognition may resonate with the racist depiction of all Asians as inscrutable and "alien," which has plagued Asians throughout American history. It might for that reason be a more damaging form of nonrecognition.

A more distinctly racial case is the white friends in example 3 who fail to recognize the importance to their black friend of publicly recognizing Martin Luther King's birthday. This case does not involve a failure to recognize the *existence* of the identity in question (the white friends are perfectly aware that their friend is black, in a way that the teacher is not aware, or not fully aware, that the student is Haitian).

However, the moral fault in this case is entirely analogous to the individual-level failure of recognition in the Asian and the Haitian cases; it is a failure to grant adequate recognition to an identity that is important to a given individual.[6] For the black student, not recognizing the importance to him of honoring King's birthday is a way of not appreciating the significance of his racial identity to him.[7]

Neither failure of individual identity-recognition (whether racial or ethnic), nor failure of ethnic group recognition is helpfully called "racism." Neither involves an inferiorization of or antipathy toward a racial group.

Recognizing Internal Diversity in Racial Groups

A second wrong committed by the teacher in example 1 is failure to recognize the internal diversity of racial groups. By speaking of "the black point of view" as if she believes that any black person can represent it, the teacher fails to recognize that, like any large group of persons not defined by ideology, blacks have a wide range of opinions on any issue; the fault would be no different were the student African American rather than Haitian American. There can be no single viewpoint of a group containing millions of people. This diversity of opinion can be related to age, gender, religion, region, occupation, family background, and other factors including ethnicity, and it can be inferred that the teacher is insufficiently attuned to or aware of these differences.

This failure is a form of misrecognition or inadequate recognition which may stem from ignorance; the teacher may simply not know enough about blacks to see the group's internal diversity. Such ignorance would be culpable, both because blacks are such a central group in American life that everyone (especially a teacher) should possess a lived recognition of its internal diversity, and also because a teacher has a responsibility to know something about her students' primary group affiliations. As we shall see in more detail in chapters 6–8, race as a form of group identity especially lends itself to such homogenizing. The very idea of "race" implies a false commonality among members of racial groups that tends to mask internal diversity.

The failure of recognition here is race-related although ethnic, gender, regional, and other groups can suffer similar misrecognition. But this is not personal racism, as it does not necessarily imply on the teacher's part an inferiorizing view of or animus toward blacks.

Appreciating Individuality

A distinct, though related, wrong is the teacher's failure to appreciate the Haitian American student's individuality. The student is there to learn and speak for herself, not for a group. This recognition of individuality is a form of human respect to which any participant in an educational (or other) setting is due. Nor is this recognition inconsistent with recognizing the importance of the student's ethnic, racial, and other group-based identities. A person is always more than the sum of such identities, while at the same time her sense of her own individual identity is not separable from those group affiliations.[8]

The failure to recognize individuality is encouraged by the racial homogenization that also tends to mask internal diversity. But, similarly, this failure is not in itself racist, as it need not involve seeing the individual as racially inferior nor stem from race-based animus.

Honoring the values of recognizing individual and ethnic group identity, internal group diversity, and individuality does not prevent a teacher from exploring the opinions and experiences of groups as groups. After all, statistical generalizations can be made about the opinions and experiences of a group, though they are generally made with much less basis than they require. A teacher might ask the class, "How do you think most Latinos feel about X, and do you think different groups of Latinos feel differently?" This question allows for the possibility that a non-Latino student may know as much or more about that issue than does a Latino student. This way of asking it does not treat any Latino student as an epistemological representative of his group. The open-ended question to the group allows the minority group member, should he desire to do so, to attempt to contribute the views of his ethnoracial community as he sees it, with whatever degree of qualification he sees fit, and to call explicit attention to whatever internal diversity he sees.

Sensitivity to Vulnerable Groups

A final wrong committed by the teacher in example 1 concerns the moral asymmetry discussed in chapter 2. All the forms of identity-recognition discussed here are especially important to vulnerable minority groups. Such groups are more at risk for being marginalized in important social institutions like schools and workplaces than are whites. Hence failure to accord them adequate forms of recognition is likely to contribute to such marginalizing. Suppose, for example, that a student in the same class as the Haitian American student is a Polish immigrant, and wishes this aspect of his identity to be acknowledged, but the teacher does not do so. The harm is not likely to be as great as the harm to the Haitian student, whose group is much more subject to demeaning views and stereotypes.

Thus we have considered five different forms of racial, ethnic, or cultural insensitivity or ignorance: (1) not recognizing distinctive ethnicities; (2) not recognizing personally important group-based identity components; (3) not recognizing the internal diversity within any racial group; (4) not appreciating individuality; (5) not being sensitive to vulnerability. None of these, in themselves, involve racism as either inferiorization or racial animus. Nevertheless, they are, or at least in certain situations can be, serious moral failings.

Judging Persons on the Basis of Race: Jim Sleeper's *Liberal Racism*

It has become increasingly common to hear racism identified with the idea of judging persons—and especially conferring benefits and burdens on persons—on the basis of race or skin color.[9] A famous sentence from Martin Luther King Jr.'s "I Have a Dream" speech expresses this point: "I have a dream my four little children will one day live in a nation where they will not be judged by the color of their skin but by the content of their character."[10] Popular expressions of this idea abound in many forms. The director of an organization that militantly opposed busing for integration in South Boston in the 1970s writes, "To give preference to one group over another because of the color of their skin is racist."[11] In response to an article about black students protesting the teaching of black studies courses by white faculty, a letter to the *Chronicle of Higher Education* objects that these students have forgotten the important fact that "it's racist to judge another person by her skin color."[12]

This view has been given intentionally provocative expression in the title of Jim Sleeper's popular 1997 book, *Liberal Racism*. That title, and some of the book's actual argument, suggests that liberals who favor racial preferences and more generally, believe it sometimes appropriate to take account of racial identities in public policy have abandoned their own historical allegiance to the struggle against racial discrimination and injustice. At one point Sleeper compares liberals to aristocratic southern racists who "condescend sweetly to blacks while projecting contempt for inferiors onto poor whites."[13]

To his credit, Sleeper does not sustain the implication that liberals in general have become racists. In contrast to the two letter writers cited above, Sleeper knows that King's remark about character can be understood only in the context of the struggle for black civic equality. King maintained an integrationist ideal, but he was very race-conscious. He was leading a struggle not for contextless color blindness but for justice and equality *for blacks*, in the context of a wider vision of racial harmony. As David Hollinger remarks about the Civil Rights movement, it "affirmed a national American 'we' and the solidarity of black people at the same time."[14] King's eloquent remark about his children meant primarily that they not be judged as inferiors because of their race, but be accorded equal respect as human beings. Moreover, Sleeper does not reject color-conscious policies entirely. He approvingly cites Justice Harry Blackmun's "wise dictum" in the 1978 *Bakke* affirmative action case: "In order to get beyond racism, we must first take account of race. There is no other way. And in order to treat some persons equally, we must treat them differently."[15]

I will focus on what is of genuine interest in Sleeper's argument in a moment. But first let us be clear why "judging persons on the basis of race" is not in itself "racist." It is true that an integral part of racist social systems, such as the one King was fighting, did involve judging people on the basis of their race. But the moral force carried by the idea of "racism" can not be totally severed from the particular form and purpose of such judging, which was to maintain blacks, as an inferior group, in a subordinate status. Though the meaning of the term "racism" may have undergone some change from its origins in the 1930s, if it strays too far from its context of either race hatred or racial subordination or inferiorization, it loses the moral force it has inherited.

To say this is not in itself to defend affirmative action, or any other race-preference policy, but to insist rather that the moral strengths and draw-backs of affirmative action be expressed in terms other than "racism."[16] It is also to say that what makes a particular instance of judging someone on the basis of his race "racist" is either the judgment being made (was the individual judged as inferior or humanly defective?), or its purpose (was she being selected for a degraded or inferior status in society, or in some institution?). And of course, as I have been emphasizing all along, even if the judging was not racist the act might well have been morally faulty in some other way. Perhaps taking race into account was simply inappropri-ate, irrelevant to any of the purposes at hand, or unfair for some other reason.

So we come to an interesting remark in Sleeper's book: "Liberal racism also assumes that racial differences are so profound that they are almost primordial. The term 'racialism' is sometimes used to denote this belief that racial differences are essential to our understanding of ourselves and society, and at times I will use it to refer to such thinking."[17] The concept of "racialism" is indeed a useful one. (Its meaning here is much more dis-tinct from "racism" than even Sleeper recognizes, and he slides too read-ily back and forth between the two.) I would define "racialism" somewhat differently than Sleeper—though I think my definition captures much of what he has in mind—as "conferring too much, or inappropriate, impor-tance on people's racial identity, either in general or in a particular case."[18] This definition leaves many questions unanswered, but it will do for the moment.

To understand the difference between racism and racialism, let us con-sider Asian and Asian American students protesting a white faculty mem-ber's teaching of a Asian studies course. It is racialist to assume that racial identity in itself should be a decisive criterion, or even play a large role, in whether a given instructor gets to teach a particular course (that is, con-ferring too much importance on racial identity). It is racialist to assume that a white person could not have sufficient knowledge, empathy, or ex-pertise to competently teach a subject concerning Asian Americans or any other nonwhite ethnoracial group.

Would it be racialist for the students to assume that, if the instructor were white, they would not be sufficiently comfortable in an Asian studies class to reveal their true feelings and opinions? In fact, this might well be true of at least some of the Asian and Asian American students, thereby detracting from the educational value of the course. This lack of comfort (no matter how skillful the white instructor was in trying to create a com-fortable and trusting atmosphere) might be a product of a deeply racialist sensibility on the part of the students; they might have a blanket distrust of all whites. But the discomfort need not be racialist. It might be that the racial divisions in society, and in a particular student's experience up to that point, have caused her not to feel comfortable being open with a white instructor (hardly a bizarre occurrence—the same can happen with instructors and students of different genders). This student might even be a distinct nonracialist, trying to keep race and racial identity from playing an overinflated role in her own life. But she might also know that her sentiments have not yet caught up with her convictions, and that she will in fact be uncomfortable.

The Asian and Asian American students who do reject the white instructor out of racialism are not, thereby, necessarily racist, unless their point of view stems from racial bigotry or prejudice against whites in general. The mere making of a racial distinction ("judging another person by her skin color") is not in itself racist; what determines whether it is racist is why or for what purpose the distinction is being made.

It would *not* be racialist for a member of a disadvantaged racial group to make his racial identity the centerpiece of his personal identity—for example, by dedicating his life to the welfare of his people. This would be a justifiable, and indeed a worthy and admirable, personal choice. (The African American concept of a "race man" or "race woman" expresses this idea of identity.) It *would* be racialist, however, for this individual to be unable to recognize that his goal can sometimes be accomplished only through alliances with people not of his racial group; or for him to be totally indifferent to the welfare of persons not of his group.

It is not racialist to recognize that racial divisions exist, that racial identities do matter, and that it might be sometimes appropriate to reflect that reality by giving race an importance in one's thinking and actions that, in an ideal world, it would not have. And thus in the world we live in, taking into account the likely reactions of students, it might be appropriate to select an Asian instructor over a white one for an Asian studies course.[19]

Such consideration allow us to see what is faulty about Sleeper's particular definition of "racialism," which involves "the belief that racial differences are essential to our understanding of ourselves and our society." Indeed they *are* essential, if Sleeper is talking about our actual current society and its particular history. Anyone who failed to recognize the salience of race in our history and current social arrangements would be deeply out of touch with reality, and possibly deluded about his own place in it. *Some* degree of racial consciousness is indeed appropriate. So racialism on Sleeper's definition is not something to avoid. Racialism on my understanding is the conferring of a too great, or inappropriate, importance to racial identity.[20]

My definition of "racialism" obviously leaves many questions unanswered. How much is "too much"? Who is to say what is "inappropriate"? The value of the conception, even in this vague and schematic form, is that is provides a concept distinct from "racism," invoking a different set of values or disvalues in the racial domain and thus providing another tool of moral criticism.

So judging someone on the basis of race is not, in itself, racist. But such judging can stem from a moral, cognitive, or interpersonal failing, and that is "racialism". Racialism, unlike racism, does not necessarily involve racial hatred or a belief in the inferiority of the racial other. It need not involve actual racial prejudice.

Same-Race Socializing

African Americans, Latinos, and Asian Americans sitting together in same-race groupings in student cafeterias and socializing primarily with members of their own group has produced criticism and consternation. White students who might have wanted to join these groups have sometimes felt discouraged from doing so. Such situations have led to charges of racism.[21]

Unless the black, Latino, or Asian American students believe the white students unworthy to sit with them, or unless they exclude out of racial animus, there is no racism here. Even if the students of color were hostile toward white students sitting with them, because they wanted to preserve an enclave of their own members but not out of a prejudice against whites, it would not be racist.

If we clear the charge of "racism" out of the way, we can examine the values and disvalues of same-race socializing. Some white opposition to or discomfort with such socializing stems from its implicit but publicly visible rejection of an unworthy and outdated "assimilationist" norm. A dean at Harvard once approached a group of African American students having a good time together in a dining hall and said, "Now, we didn't bring you all the way out here for you to sit off by yourselves."[22] The condescending assumptions that the institution belongs to its traditional white constituency and that groups of color are acceptable as long as they do not challenge this conception are inconsistent with a sense of equal inclusion, a norm that should govern all educational institutions. (The dean's condescension does border on racism.) Especially when all-white tables in the dining halls are not themselves a comparable target of concern, such assimilationist assumptions are likely to be operating.

Even referring to same-race socializing as "racial self-segregation," as is traditionally done, smacks of an inappropriate assimilationism. It is a biased way of characterizing the issue, blurring at least the difference between *exclusive* and *partial* in-group socializing (see below). In addition, such language misleadingly invokes the officially sanctioned exclusions of the era of state-sponsored segregation. The neutral term "same-race socializing" is more appropriate.

Nevertheless, same-race socializing is by no means always a good thing, and not all criticism of it stems from unworthy sources. To assess its value, we must view it in its wider institutional and societal context. It is not possible to look at one table of, say, only Latino students and determine whether this is a good or a bad thing. Do the students at the table always socialize only with fellow Latinos, or do they also socialize outside of their group? It is perfectly reasonable for *any* group of students, however constituted (for example, racially mixed or same race) who feel comfortable with one another to hang out as a distinct group. At the same time, it is also constricting to a student's social experience to make that group her sole source of social contact.

When the groups in question are of only one race the constriction is greater than when the group is racially diverse. Race is a major divide in the nation, and an inability to interact comfortably with members of groups other than one's own is a serious social deficiency. Though its material consequences may be worse for groups of color—since being comfortable with whites, or making whites comfortable with oneself, is generally a requirement of professional success—it is nevertheless a serious disability for whites as well, and will become more so as whites continue to become a smaller majority in the population.

Benefits of Single-Race Groups and Activities

In predominantly white educational institutions, single-race groups, organizations, programs, and activities can serve important purposes. For many students of color, especially those who come to residential colleges from same-race environments, they provide a safe and comfortable environment the students may not otherwise find. Same-race groups provide a space for students to discuss race-based experiences—of stereotyping, ignorance, unwarranted assumptions, exclusions, and perhaps stigmatizing, harassment, and discrimination—that many of them will experience. (It is also a comfortable venue in which to help sort out whether certain experiences have a racial dimension or not.) Same-race groups provide a space where many students of color will feel valued in a way they do not in the larger institution.[23]

Same-race groups and organizations can also provide natural forums for cultural expression, where the racial group (as a panethnic group—see chapter 8) encompasses distinctive cultural groups. Of course some students may seek ethnically based rather than racially based groups for this purpose—Korean American rather than Asian American, Caribbean American rather than black.

Those who advocate abolishing programs that cater to students of a given ethnoracial group or discouraging single-race socializing fail to recognize that the playing field of social and academic comfort, acceptance, and valuing is not level at most white-majority institutions. While factors other than racial identity per se, especially socioeconomic background, affect this sense of acceptance, these factors often correlate with racial identity (especially among blacks, Latinos, Native Americans, and southeast Asian groups). In any case, racial identity affects the sense of belonging at institutions partly independent of socioeconomic factors.

Single-race groupings can also provide an essential context for seeking recognition, within the wider institution, of the group's racial or ethnoracial distinctiveness. They reflect a desire to be included as equal partners and members in the institution, but recognized *as* Latino or Hispanic, black, Asian American, Native American—as a distinct group with a distinct racial or ethnoracial identity. Equality and distinctiveness are by no means at odds with one another. A group may have equal standing yet be recognized in its distinctiveness (though a misunderstanding of equality might read it as "sameness" and thus give it an unwarranted assimilationist slant). Equality and distinctiveness are different values and must be addressed separately by institutions endeavoring to honor both of them.[24]

White students are sometimes genuinely confused about why it is regarded as legitimate for students of color to have their own organizations and activities, but not them; other white students perhaps recognize that there is a difference but are unsure how to articulate it. The above analysis explains the asymmetry (other forms of which were discussed in chapter 2) between students of color and white students. Within a white-dominated institution, white students do not need special support for their identity. They are much less likely to experience objectionable stereotyping and racial discrimination. (Individual white students may, however, experience objectionable stereotyping—as being racist, clueless, wealthy, for example—and it would be appropriate for an institution to provide peer counseling and an occasional white-only setting for the explicit purpose of discussing such experiences.) Individual whites may, of course, require academic support; but they do not require race-based academic support. Where white students wish venues for cultural expression, ethnic groupings themselves (Polish American, Irish American) will serve that purpose.

Not all minority students require or desire same-race groups; it is insulting to assume that they do. Here it is important to keep in mind recognition of the internal diversity of racial groups. Single-race social and programmatic opportunities should be viewed and presented as resources for students voluntarily to avail themselves of, not as imposed race-based expectations.

Drawbacks of Single-Race Groups and Activities

Though same-race groupings can serve valuable purposes, they may be unhealthy in some respects also. Some in-group socializing can be driven by racialism—in this context, the view that racial identification *should* determine one's primary social group. It is constricting to individual members of a given group to impose on them "a kind of moral code that dictates solidarity and cohesiveness, and punishes those who stray into white circles of friendship."[25] (Whites can be victims of such racialist thinking as well.) It is not in any case inconsistent with an appropriate black solidarity and loyalty for a black student also to have white, Asian, Latino, and other friends.[26]

Bi-racial persons—those with parents from two different major ethnoracial groups—are particularly harmed by racialist ways of thinking and of organizing social life. Nonracialist ways of viewing group membership would embrace half-Mexican, half-Asian students in both the Mexican group and the Asian group, should they wish to be so identified. Adoptive students from a different group than their parents can also suffer from racialist ways of judging them as insufficiently "Asian," "black," and the like.

Even apart from racialism, the benefits of the same-race comfort zone have corresponding drawbacks. Some personal and educational growth requires risking discomfort, reaching beyond settings in which one is sure of oneself.[27] This is one reason for institutions to put in place various opportunities, incentives, and pressures for students not to remain in the cocoon of their same-race groups—in classes, extracurricular activities, racially mixed residence activities, and so on. It is a reason for the institution to empower members of same-race groups to resist the exclusivist tendencies within those groups, though it is not a reason to discourage the groupings themselves.

Another pitfall of same-race groupings appears where acceptable "modes of racial being" are too narrowly defined. A healthy mode of same-race grouping embraces the diversity, likely to be found in any sizable racial group on a campus, of backgrounds, cultural styles, and self-definitions of "being black" (or Asian, or Native American). But campus groups may instead tilt toward certain styles, sub-groups, and modes of racial being as norms against which others are found wanting; this tilt may be implicit rather than consciously adopted—as, for example, when the upper-middle-class majority (increasing at elite institutions) in such groups has the effect of making those from more modest backgrounds feel uncomfortable. (An opposite example is the adoption of urban "street" styles as the normative mode by a black group with predominantly suburban backgrounds). The idea of "not black (or Chicano, or Native American) enough" should play as little role as possible in acceptance into a same-race group.

Interracial Community

Apart from these drawbacks, exclusive same-race socializing is detrimental to interracial communication and community in any institution. It is also harmful to the development of the interpersonal skills necessary for functioning in an ethnoracially plural democracy. Interracial community is a value in its own right. Any bridging of the profound divide of race is to be especially welcomed. The value of interracial community resides not merely in recognition, or even respect, but in an embracing of the racial diversity within a community of shared purposes. Creating interpersonal community requires settings that encourage students to form cross-racial friendships and other bonds, to acquire skills of cross-racial and cross-cultural communication, and to be committed to interracial community as a distinct value.

Interracial community is not entirely at odds with same-race socializing. Some of the values of same-race socializing may even support the goal of interracial community. For example, some students of color may need the support of a same-race community in order to gain a sense of confidence, place, and security in the wider institution that enables them to connect with students of other races. The wider community morever, should not be conceived in a purely color- (or race-, or culture-) blind fashion, but the particularistic ethoracial identities of its members should instead be recognized and welcomed.

Even in the best of circumstances, there will be some tension between the pulls of interracial community and those of same-race groupings. But educational institutions should strive to realize the values of both, recognizing that some balancing will likely be required.

Is Gaertner and Dovidio's "Aversive Racism" Always Racism?

In the past forty years, social scientists have attempted to come to grips with changes in the forms of racism and other race-related ills brought about by the end of legally sanctioned segregation, the changes in moral culture spurred by the Civil Rights movement's challenge to racial inequality, and the scientific delegitimizing of classic racist beliefs. Some have adopted an inflated use of "racism" that has damaged public discourse on race-related matters. Others, alert to this problem, have fallen prey to its moral counterpart—implying that whatever falls outside the scope of "racism" is of little moral concern, or is not subject to moral criticism.

Samuel Gaertner and John Dovidio's discussion of racism among the well-intentioned was a milestone in understanding unacknowledged or unconscious racism. Their analysis derived from an elegant and striking experiment conducted by Gaertner and reported in 1973. White political liberals and conservatives received phone calls from researchers pretending to be stranded motorists attempting to call a service station and getting the number wrong.[28] The callers had culturally identifiable "black" or "white" voices. If allowed to complete their message, the callers asked the subjects if they would call the service station for them, explaining that the call to the subject had taken their last bit of change.

While the white liberal subjects offered the requested help equivalently to those white and black callers whom they permitted to present their full story, the liberals were much more likely to hang up "prematurely" (as Gaertner put it) on the black caller, before he got to present his full story.[29]

Gaertner and Dovidio coined the expression "aversive racism" to describe this behavior. The liberals thought of themselves as unprejudiced racial egalitarians. If they regarded a situation as governed by norms calling for non-discrimination, they would be likely not to discriminate. (This was less true of the conservatives.) Gaertner and Dovidio plausibly hypothesized that the stranded motorists' full story would elicit a norm of social responsibility that the liberals would not want to, and would try not to, implement in a discriminatory manner.

Prior to hearing the caller's plight, however, no norm requiring assistance (or even staying on the line) kicked in for the liberal subject; there is no socially recognized norm to hear out every phone caller. Gaertner and Dovidio hypothesized that an antiblack animus on the part of the liberals accounted for their hanging up more frequently on the black than the white callers. This "aversive racism" was unconscious; the liberal subject did not think of himself as doing something discriminatory and presumably was not aware that he had hung up on the caller because he or she was black. Such an awareness would be inconsistent with the liberal's egalitarian self-image. Later experiments revealed similar behavior and were similarly explained.[30]

The experiments do seem clearly to suggest differential feelings on the part of liberal whites toward whites and blacks. My quarrel is with the theoretical superstructure the authors erect around their findings. The term "aversive racism" suggests that behavior such as hanging up, or other "race-avoidance," is *always* a form of racism—that it always involves dislike of blacks, suggested by the term "aversive."[31] I agree of course that sometimes such unconscious racial animus might be operating, and is likely to be operating often in the motorist experiment. But other possibilities suggest themselves. The liberal might be someone like Ms. Verano, the fourth-grade teacher discussed in chapter 1. She does not dislike black parents or think ill of them, but she is not comfortable with them either. Her discomfort or anxiety could easily lead her to hang up on a black caller or to other forms of avoidance behavior (such as avoiding potential interactions with blacks) that Gaertner and Dovidio's theory would, misleadingly, call "aversive racism."

In fact, Gaertner and Dovidio say explicitly that "the negative affect that aversive racists have for blacks is not hostility or hate. Instead, this negativity involves discomfort, uneasiness, disgust, and sometimes fear, which tend to motivate avoidance rather than intentionally destructive behaviors."[32] Discomfort and uneasiness should not be placed in the same moral category as disgust, which portrays its object in a negative light; one need not actually feel negatively toward someone with whom one feels discomfort. By acknowledging that aversive racism may be discomfort and not hostility or hate, Gaertner and Dovidio should have been led to question whether it should be regarded as "racism" at all.

As far as I know Gaertner and Dovidio did not perform comparable experiments with the races reversed. People of different racial groups in our society often feel uncomfortable with members of at least some other racial group. One can easily imagine some black subjects hanging up on a caller identified by their voice as white, or Asian, or Hispanic out of the discomfort of not being confident that one could manage the interaction adequately. Would Gaertner and Dovidio want to call these actions evidence of aversive racism? Race-related discomfort should not be conflated with an actual aversion to members of other racial groups, as the term of art "aversive racism" encourages us to do.[33]

Racial Discomfort or Anxiety

We see the difference between discomfort and genuine race-based aversion among schoolchildren, say of fifth grade or above. Children recognize differing groups among their classmates. Some of the groups are defined according to racial criteria, and children of this age know that race is a socially salient category before they fully grasp what it means. They may know enough to make them feel uncomfortable with this perceived and experienced difference from another group of children. Race might be associated with somewhat different ways of behaving, in addition to visual, phenotypic differences. These ways of behaving may have a class, linguistic, or cultural dimension as well, and the children may associate these with the racial designation. (Sometimes they grasp the cultural difference as a distinct component, for example seeing Haitian, Laotian, Central American, or Mexican children as both racially and culturally or linguistically different from themselves). Some of these children will experience discomfort, though not dislike, in regard to some other group, and it would be very misleading to call them aversive racists.[34]

We can realize that a group of persons is different from us in some socially important way, and we can feel that we are just not knowledgeable enough to feel comfortable with them. We can be anxious that we will embarrass ourselves by saying or doing the wrong thing. We may worry that the group will dislike and reject us if we attempt to approach it. This social anxiety is perfectly familiar in regard to cultural differences; the individual is anxious approaching a culture about which she lacks knowledge. It might be thought that similar considerations do not apply in the case of race, since members of different races live in the same communities. But members of different racial groups are often quite ignorant of one anothers' modes of life, even if they interact in schools and workplaces. In a sense racial anxiety is even more likely than cultural anxiety, since differences in "race" are more socially charged than are cultural differences. (We will discuss this further in chapters 5–8.) If one is equally ignorant of a racial and a cultural group, there may be more reason to be anxious about violating some unknown norm with regard to the racially different group than with regard to the culturally different one.[35]

Racial anxiety or discomfort is not necessarily racist.[36] Nor is racial discomfort the sort of thing for which its possessor is subject to moral criticism. It is not morally bad to be racially anxious, as it is morally bad to be racially prejudiced.

But an individual who recognizes her racial anxiety should not rest content with it just because it is not a moral blot on her character, in part because, as in Ms. Verano's case, it can lead to discriminatory behavior. In addition, racial discomfort invites stereotyping—an especially acute problem with regard to race. Racial anxiety reinforces a sense of separateness from other racial groups. It makes it difficult to recognize internal diversity in such groups, and to appreciate the individuality of members of the group. Racial anxiety feeds into (in addition to drawing on) the homogenizing of racial groups that is a particular pitfall in the racial arena.

Racial discomfort is also inimical to the development of interracial community, reinforcing a sense that interracial groupings are somehow not "natural" (this seems particularly true among high school and some college students). Racial comfort not only makes social existence more pleasant, varied, and interesting for members of all groups, but serves the purposes of civic attachment and civic engagement as well.[37] Teachers in particular would do well to try to decrease racial discomfort and anxiety in their classes, for example by forming interracial groups for various tasks.[38]

That it is often difficult to tell whether reluctance to engage with racial others is a product of animus or mere discomfort takes a toll on racial minorities who have to worry and wonder. " 'In waiting rooms or lobbies . . . I've tried to initiate a conversation [with whites], and I could tell they don't want to talk,' says Sharon Walter, an African American. 'But when a white person walks in, conversation begins. I don't want to think it's racism . . . The better part of me wants to think otherwise.' "[39] Merely having such thoughts is itself a psychic cost.

Racial Prejudice and Racial Equality: Sniderman and Piazza's *Scar of Race*

In *The Scar of Race*, Paul Sniderman and Thomas Piazza present an argument, drawing largely on sophisticated opinion survey data and carefully crafted experiments, about the relations among racial prejudice, stereotyping, and people's stances on public policies bearing on race. They concur with my contention that the use of "racist" is frequently corrosive to honest and fruitful discussion, and that its current conceptual inflation has backfired into a diminishing of moral concern for racism and racial prejudice.[40] The authors are particularly concerned to demonstrate that attitudes and feelings toward blacks are much less determinative of white people's stances on policy-related matters concerning race than one might think; opinions on affirmative action, especially, they argue, are minimally correlated with significant prejudice against blacks. (Like Gaertner and Dovidio, Sniderman and Piazza seem concerned only about whites and blacks, not other ethnoracial groups.) Prime targets in this argument are various forms of "new racism" theorists who, Sniderman and Piazza believe, overstate the degree of unconscious and unacknowledged racial prejudice—especially prejudice alleged to manifest itself as a belief that blacks violate certain core American values such as individualism and a strong work ethic.[41] "New racism" theorists tend to see personal racism as implicated in opposition to policies that aid blacks.

Sniderman and Piazza are correct to resist such theories. "New racism" theories that take opposition to affirmative action as automatic evidence of racial prejudice are akin to David Wellman's definition of a racist belief as one that helps to sustain black inequality. A belief in minimal government may make it difficult to support programs necessary to reduce black-white inequality, but that does not make it a racist belief, nor adherence to it necessarily a sign of racial prejudice.

Yet Sniderman and Piazza's analysis of race-related ills on the contemporary scene suffers from two serious weaknesses. First, their conception of racism or racial prejudice is unnecessarily narrow; they appear to count only racial antipathy and not racial inferiorizing as significant forms of racism. Second, and more significant, although theirs is a work of social science rather than moral philosophy, Sniderman and Piazza very much intend their argument to have moral implications concerning legitimate forms of criticism of racial attitudes and policy stances on race-related issues. On this score, they operate with a moral vocabulary that is uncomfortably close to the all-or-nothing reasoning I criticized in chapter 1. If an individual's stance on race-related issues can not be chalked up to personal racism, they imply, it is immune to moral criticism—simply a matter of political ideology or policy about which reasonable persons may disagree.

The authors find that holding what they call "nasty" stereotypes of blacks—for example, blacks as violent—does not correlate with opposing social spending targeted to blacks, affirmative action, and governmental efforts to ensure nondiscriminatory treatment in employment.[42] They conclude that personal racism, or bigotry, does not signal opposition to black advancement at the policy level.[43] They find, however, that avowal of a range of what they regard as less vicious stereotypes—blacks need to try harder, blacks on welfare could get a job if they tried—do correlate with such opposition. By regarding such stereotypes as indicators only of "low level prejudice" they do not count this finding as a counter-example to their view that racial prejudice correlates with policy stances.[44]

These stereotypes, however, are indicators of holding inferiorizing, and in that sense racist, stereotypes. The ideas that blacks need to try harder, that blacks on welfare could get a job, and that their failure to do so is a major cause of their lot in society are extremely damaging stereotypes without foundation. Obviously *any* individual or group that exerted more effort would be likely to advance further in life. But to single out and stigmatize the entire group of blacks and fail to apply this banal truth to members of any other racial group is to do serious damage to blacks—and to evidence a deep misunderstanding of American social reality. The stereotype is a somewhat softer form of the perennial notion of blacks as lazy, a paradigm form of inferiorizing racism.

A more serious deficiency in Sniderman and Piazza's argument is the delegitimizing of a moral language for characterizing the unequal life chances of whites and blacks. Independent of how much one agrees with the authors' account of the relation between racial prejudice and ideology on race-related public policies, one must take issue with their confining moral concern to the personal side of the ledger; they essentially imply that while personal racism and prejudice are clearly moral matters, political ideology is not. (This counterposing of morality and politics is implied in the following passage: "Prejudice is at work, and there are still questions of race that have moral issues at their center. But the politics of race is complex. . . . The politics of race is driven not only by racial sentiments but also by politics."[45])

But is not a rejection of the principle of equal opportunity a moral stance? Is it not a moral matter how one comes to terms with the historical injustice perpetrated uniquely on blacks, and with the contemporary legacy of such injustice? Why should it be accounted a moral issue if someone is personally prejudiced against blacks, but not if that person supports unequal opportunity for blacks? Of course the latter issue is "political" in a way that the former is not; ensuring equal opportunity is a matter for public policy. But this does not make it any less a moral issue. Commitment to these moral/political principles (equality of opportunity, rectifying historical injustice) does not, to be sure, automatically dictate a specific stance on every issue of race-related policy—affirmative action or welfare policy, for example. But the existence of this complexity should not be allowed to imply that moral language is inappropriate in discussing such policy issues, just because one can not reduce stances on them to personal prejudice.[46]

By severing racial attitudes from policy stances, Sniderman and Piazza imply that one can be a racial egalitarian and yet oppose government action to reduce unjust racial inequities. They say explicitly that both support for and opposition to social welfare policies are consistent with "the American Creed."[47] In doing so they imply rejection of the view that racial inequities are themselves contrary to ideals of justice and equality to which our nation allegedly aspires.[48] In the course of arguing that bigotry is a minor factor in contemporary racial politics, Sniderman and Piazza imply that stances regarding the deeply troubling historical legacy of slavery, segregation, and widespread, institutionalized racial discrimination can be consigned to a realm of "politics" shielded from moral assessment.[49] By cordoning off the "political" from the "moral," they feed into a mindset that says that if something can not be characterized as "racism" or "racial prejudice," it is removed from serious moral concern.

White Privilege

In the past decade, the idea of "white privilege" or "white skin privilege" has emerged as a powerful tool of moral critique of the racial social arrangements in Western societies and the United States in particular. What is white privilege, how is it related to racism, and what is the moral foundation of criticism of it?

At one level the idea of white privilege is a morally distinctive approach to what has more frequently been thought of as racial disadvantage. As Harlan Dalton puts it, "We have long since grown accustomed to thinking of Blacks as being 'racially disadvantaged'. Rarely, however, do we refer to Whites as 'racially advantaged' even though that is an equally apt characterization of the existing inequality."[50] For example, because of housing discrimination blacks are frequently unable to move into neighborhoods they desire to and could afford to live in. We might decry this injustice or misfortune. If we are white, we are decrying an injustice or misfortune that happens to a group other than our own. The "white privilege" perspective forces our attention on the fact that we enjoy the privilege, or advantage, of being free from such discrimination. We are likely not to have thought about it this way, for privilege is something most white people simply take for granted. Indeed one of the benefits of white privilege is precisely that one does not have to think about it and face up to its possible injustice.[51]

There are two distinct forms of advantage or privilege involved here. One is simply that of being spared racial discrimination, stigmatizing, indignities, stereotyping, and other race-based wrongs. As Peggy McIntosh says, "Whether I use checks, credit cards, or cash, I can count on my skin color not to work against the appearance of financial reliability."[52] A second, however, consists in material benefits accruing to whites because of discrimination against racial minorities. When a black is denied a job because of discrimination, there is one more job available to a non-black (usually a white). When poor schooling leaves many blacks and Latinos inadequately prepared for higher education or the job market, jobs and places in colleges become more available to whites (and to others, such as some Asian groups, positioned to take advantage of these opportunities). If one includes not only contemporary forms of discrimination but the legacy of historical discrimination, the unearned material advantage becomes quite considerable.

Even if they acknowledge the disadvantages suffered by large numbers of blacks, Native Americans, and Latinos or Hispanics, most whites do not recognize these advantages. What is the relation between this white privilege and racism? Some writers have placed white privilege at the center of their definition of "racism"; for them, racism is a system of privilege, or beliefs that support such a system.[53]

We discussed David Wellman's example of the latter in chapter 1, and saw why this is misleading as a definition of personal racism. The whole point of the idea of white privilege is that it does *not* depend on the attitudes of its beneficiaries toward disadvantaged racial groups; nonracists still partake of white privilege. Even if I deplore discrimination, jobs are still available to me, I still reap the accumulated advantages of decades, even centuries, during which nonwhite people were denied opportunity, even if my own ancestors have been Americans only for several generations. What is so disturbing about white privilege is that you need not be in any way personally blameworthy for having it, but it is still unfair that you do. It is not personally racist to have white privilege.[54]

Nevertheless, one understands why some commentators do not wish to abandon a connection between individual racism and white privilege. If "racism" is the only way one can express racial wrongfulness, one will certainly want to count white privilege as a form of racism. I suggest a different approach. Let us give up the idea that the only way to talk about racial wrongfulness is by means of the concept of "racism." Let "white privilege" be permitted to carry its own moral force, just as "racial justice," "respecting racial identity," or "promoting interracial community" should do.

Yet if white privilege is to join the pantheon of race-related ills, its moral foundations require a bit more scrutiny. Peggy McIntosh notes a difference between privileges that are morally suspect—such as being able to ignore the perspectives of less powerful individuals at no personal cost—and those that are morally worthy and should be available to everyone—such as not being expected to speak for all persons in one's racial group. McIntosh also asks whether some of what look like privileges are so in fact. In part this question is related to the moral suspectness of certain privileges. Being able to glide through life without being aware of the experiences and perspectives of important social groups in one's society, and of marginalized or discriminated-against groups in particular, constitutes a form of personal ignorance or obliviousness that can be regarded as an "advantage" only within a very narrow value system.

More generally, even with regard to privileges that are genuine benefits, an individual who, having become aware of the injustice of her having an advantage, embraces it nevertheless, is arguably morally damaged by her deliberate collusion in injustice.

A different issue relates to the long-term and short-term dimensions of such alleged advantages. Although whites on the lower end of the income scale have often been willing to avail themselves of the society's offer to consider themselves superior to blacks, it can be argued that this status gain was a diversionary sop that prevented them from recognizing their class interest as workers, and their possible commonality of interests with blacks. W. E. B. Du Bois put forth a powerful version of this argument in his 1935 work, *Black Reconstruction*.[55] Even if many white workers benefited from wage discrimination against blacks, that benefit was arguably outweighed by the loss of being played off against blacks through what Du Bois called the "psychological wage" of white superiority. Even if all whites do benefit in some respect from white privilege, it is a mistake to think of "whites" (as of "blacks") as a single, unified, homogeneous grouping. On a larger social canvas, some benefit much more than others.

Whites are differentiated by forms of privilege with a structure similar to racial privilege. McIntosh mentions age, ethnicity, religion, physical ability, nationality, and sexual orientation. (Indeed, she was led to a recognition of white racial privilege through her experience on the disadvantaged side of gender privilege.) Many whites who do genuinely benefit from white privilege may be on the disadvantaged side of many of these divides. They may not be "privileged" in any overall sense, and the notion of white privilege should take care to avoid this implication.

A different pitfall in the use of the term "white privilege" lies in conflating some of these other forms of privilege with race. Louise Derman-Sparks and Carol Brunson Phillips say that only whites "who are affluent, male, adult, and generally Protestant" gain "the full economic, political, and cultural benefits of racism."[56] The privileges of wealth, maleness, adulthood, and majority religious status may in practice often be intertwined with those of whiteness, but they are distinct sources of privilege in themselves. Persons advantaged on some dimensions may be disadvantaged on others. A poor white woman is not subject to racial stigmatizing and discrimination. A wealthy black man avoids the insecurity and material depredations of poverty, and need not fear being raped as he takes an evening stroll in his neighborhood.[57] (He may risk being stopped by the police, however.) Conflating the privileges of wealth with those of race can, in addition, encourage stereotyping whites as wealthy and blacks as poor.

The discussion so far implies that the wrong involved in white privilege depends on a prior determination of injustice. Speaking of privilege becomes another way of speaking of injustice; it may be a way that elicits moral attention and concern more readily or forcefully than the invocation of "injustice" alone. (Indeed, the idea of white privilege may help to return to public attention a concept of racial injustice that has been absent from public discourse for a decade, perhaps two.) But it has no different moral status from that injustice.

If white privilege is a way of talking about injustice, we must recognize that not all racial inequality is racial injustice; hence not all forms of benefit to whites will count as "white privilege." Consider number twenty-four on McIntosh's list of white privileges, "I can be reasonably sure that if I ask to talk to 'the person in charge,' I will be facing a person of my race." (Ignore for the moment that this seems a morally suspect "privilege.") Let us imagine that in such a setting the percentage of "persons in charge" of each racial group exactly matches their percentage in the general population. Then a Latino or Hispanic asking to speak to the person in charge will be much more likely to face a white than a fellow Latino or Hispanic. But is this a (racial) injustice? It seems similar to a Jew or Muslim encountering Christmas lights in a large majority of houses in a residential area. The Jew or Muslim may be uncomfortable being reminded of her minority religious status and thus her exclusion from the dominant culture. But it does not seem an instance of injustice. Some inequities may be unfortunate, but not unjust.

Yet injustice may not be the only morally problematic dimension of "white privilege" or "unearned white advantage." Consider the above analogy of "Christian privilege." The idea of privilege may not invoke an injustice but could serve to encourage the Christian to recognize explicitly that she indeed represents the dominant group—not simply to take this for granted as if it were part of the natural order of things, but to acknowledge it as historically and socially contingent. In doing so, the idea of Christian privilege invites her to extend recognition and empathy to members of minority religions—to try to imagine what it is like for one's religion to be other than the norm.

The class inequality discussed above is another example. It may or may not be unjust for the child of the upper middle class to have greater resources than the child of the working class. But it still constitutes a kind of privilege that the former does not earn. It is a privilege that is easy to take for granted, but wrong to do so. In recognizing the privilege, the child is more readily led to recognize and empathize with the situation of those with fewer resources then she.

This understanding of "white privilege" can apply to race-based inequities or disparities that are not unjust—for example having less power, visibility, and cultural influence purely because of minority status.

"White privilege," then, is a complex idea. Some of what are so named are unworthy privileges, and some are not privileges at all, except perhaps in a very narrow sense. Among morally acceptable privileges, some are distinctly unjust, and speaking of white privilege is a way of naming that injustice that explicitly calls attention to whites' benefiting from it. Other morally acceptable but not unjust privileges are still things the privileged should not simply take for granted or fail to recognize. It is not racist to have white privilege; white privilege is a different sort of racial ill than personal racism. But it is morally wrong to be complacent about or accepting of racial privileges once one knows one possesses them; one is (often) thereby being complicit with injustice.

The range of race-related wrongs, misfortunes, and missteps is quite vast. I have considered a somewhat random sample of those often referred to as "racism." Few of these, however, are racism in the sense of antipathy or inferiorization. Recognition of personally-significant racial (or ethnic or cultural) identities; recognition of internal diversity in a racial group; appreciation of individuality (but not by denying the importance of group identities); and sensitivity to recognition issues in vulnerable groups are all important values, but violation of them is not generally racism. Gaertner and Dovidio's influential idea of "aversive racism," based on experiments that expose troubling racial attitudes, conflates racial discomfort with genuine racial antipathy, though certainly racial discomfort is itself damaging to interracial relationships and understanding. It is not in itself racist to judge a person by her race; the content of the judgment, or its purposes, alone can make it racist. Jim Sleeper conflates "racialism"—the attaching of inappropriate importance to race or racial identity—with racism; but racialism can nevertheless be quite damaging. Same-race socializing among students of color (in educational institutions) is almost never racist. It can serve some valuable race-related goals of personal and academic support; comfort, safety, and security in the not always welcoming environment of white-dominated institutions; and cultural expression. At the same time, exclusive same-race socializing can be constricting to individual development, unduly exclusionary, and harmful to interracial community; it is especially likely to be so when fueled by racialism.

We should not be required to regard something as "racist" in order to view it as worthy of moral concern. Sniderman and Piazza's *Scar of Race*, while helpfully cautionary about inflation of the term "racism" and about the danger of oversimplified thinking about relations between racial prejudice and race-related policy, yet fails to avoid this pitfall. The authors imply that because race-related policy stances are not generally fueled by personal racism and are related to political ideology, moral critique can not be applied to them. They thereby imply that racial inequities in life chances are not matters of moral concern.

"White privilege" is a recent important concept to help us talk about racial wrongfulness. It both enables and presupposes a conception of racial justice and injustice, but also invites moral concern about advantages that, while not unjust, should not be taken for granted as if they were natural or cosmically justified. Empathy for the disadvantaged is the proper moral response to such advantages. Though white privilege is a personal matter in that each white individual partakes in it, it should be kept clearly distinct from personal racism.

4

Racial Discrimination and Color Blindness

Alleging "racial discrimination" is one of the most frequently employed forms of moral criticism of behavior related to race. It is often viewed as a form of racism, both personal and institutional. What is "racial discrimination" and why is it wrong?

Linguistically, "to discriminate" originally meant merely to make distinctions. It can be used honorifically to mean "to distinguish superior from inferior quality," as in wines or associates, and to say that someone is "discriminating" is to praise her. But the verb is now generally a term of reproach, implying that the agent has used some characteristic as an unjustifiable basis for treating otherwise similarly situated persons unequally. We do not say that a college has discriminated against applicants with a D average in high school if it fails to admit them, nor do we say that a state university discriminates against nonresidents if it favors state residents. Because of the continuing presence of the older meaning, however, "discrimination" sometimes conflates the two strands of meaning to imply that *any* making of distinctions (justified or not) is morally wrong (for example, allowing only people from Indiana into a Hoosiers Club).

Even when the word is more carefully confined to unjustified distinctions used as a basis to benefit and burden categories of persons, it turns out not to name a single, unified moral wrong.[1] Forms of discrimination are morally wrong for distinct reasons, depending on the reason or mo-

tive for the differential treatment, the characteristics utilized to discriminate, and the social context.

Discrimination and Treating Persons as Individuals

One oft-cited account of the wrong of discrimination can be dispensed
with at the outset. Some say that discrimination is wrong because it fails to
treat a person as an individual, instead treating her simply as a member of
a group. This is either misleading or false. When we select applicants for a
job, an award, a place in college, and the like, we are always interested,
and rightly so, only in certain of the person's characteristics and not others. Applicants admitted to college on the basis of grades, test scores, and
recommendations are no more being treated as individuals than those admitted on the basis of those three factors plus their racial identity. In both
cases a collection of group characteristics is used to make the selection.

Racial identity differs from grades and test scores in being an involun-
tary (sometimes called "ascribed") characteristic—one is simply born into
it and, normally, can not escape it—whereas the applicant must exert
some personal effort in acquiring the other characteristics. But the difference between acquired and ascribed characteristics is a different difference from that between being treated as an individual versus a member of
a group.[2] In general, ascribed characteristics—race, gender, parentage,
ethnicity, place of origin—are no less central to most persons' sense of individual identity than are acquired characteristics.

Perhaps because of the strong cultural cachet of individualism in American culture, people often complain that they feel some part of their experience or qualifications has been overlooked or insufficiently credited
by saying they have not been treated as an individual. But this seems to me
a confusion. As we saw in chapter 3, being treated as an individual is indeed an important value. But it is seldom what is at stake in potential contexts of discrimination.

Discrimination as Unfairness: Reliance on Irrelevant Characteristics

One common understanding of the wrong of discrimination is that it involves using an irrelevant characteristic to select someone for disadvantage
or benefit—for example, to select someone for pilot training because he

has dark hair. Typically such discrimination is also seen as socially costly because it prevents the selection of appropriately qualified individuals. Discrimination on the basis of irrelevant characteristics is understood to be *morally* wrong as well, in being unfair to qualified persons not selected.

This idea of discrimination is a more conceptually and empirically complex idea than its popular use often acknowledges, for it requires distinguishing between relevant and irrelevant characteristics. That distinction in turn depends on the goals and tasks of the job or institution; qualities or characteristics are relevant or irrelevant only in relationship to such goals and tasks.[3] For example, the goals of a restaurant chain are presumably to run effective and profitable restaurants. Assume that to accomplish these goals the company currently needs a chef and a computer programmer. It would not be unfair to an experienced and first-rate computer programmer to be rejected for the chef job.

But let us consider a more complex example, especially pertinent to disputes about affirmative action. A selective university may have several goals—preparing knowledgeable and engaged citizens, with an appropriate range of communicative skills, for a democratic and culturally pluralistic society; training leaders for different communities comprising the nation; conveying a body of core knowledge to the next generation; instilling a passion for lifelong learning; preparing students for socially valuable occupations; and the like. These goals provide a basis for distinguishing between relevant and irrelevant qualities in aspirants for positions in the student body.[4] Relevant qualities in admitted students will be those that best enable the institution to realize these goals.[5]

Quite often aspirants' qualities that are popularly considered to be related to institutional goals, hence relevant to selection, are not especially likely to advance those goals. For instance, SAT scores are not strongly predictive of the likelihood of an aspirant becoming an engaged citizen, skilled in communication with those of different experiences and backgrounds, or committed to utilizing her knowledge for civic purposes. Indeed, the scores are not even particularly predictive of academic success after the first year in four-year colleges.[6] Thus the normative and empirical structure underlying judgments about discrimination can be difficult to establish with much precision,[7] even though certain characteristics will almost always fall into the category of the "irrelevant"—for example, the interviewer did not like the applicant's looks—and so will provide instances of wrongful discrimination and injustice to the applicant.[8]

To see how this structure underlying judgments of unfair discrimination works, and bears on issues of race, let us imagine that I am forming a club of high school students. The purpose of the club is to help students learn to communicate honestly and fruitfully with members of other racial groups, and to learn to work cooperatively in cross-racial groups in community-improvement activities. Suppose that the school population is somewhat evenly divided among the five principal ethnoracial groups, but a plurality are Latino and a small minority are white. One of my criteria for selection is interest, which I assess through interviews, speaking with teachers, and a written statement from the applicant. Among the white students, half seem to meet that standard unequivocally; another half are minimally qualified in that respect. On the other hand, many more of the Latinos appear to have the requisite degree of interest. To further the goals of the groups, I feel I need to have a "critical mass" from each of the groups, so I admit some of the marginally interested whites and turn down some of the clearly enthusiastic Latinos.

It might seem that I am turning down more qualified Latinos; but this interpretation would be misleading, since "would contribute to the racial makeup required to carry out the goals of the club (fostering interracial exchange, and allowing the students to work in racially mixed teams on community projects)" amounts to a qualification that an individual white student possesses to a substantially higher degree than a Latino student. So the aspirants' racial identity is clearly pertinent to the institutional goals and hence to the relevant selection criteria.

On the other hand, if I exclude an applicant because I don't like his mother, this judgment is based on an irrelevant characteristic, is unfair to the student, and constitutes wrongful discrimination.

An analogous argument was made for the relevance of racial identity in college admissions by Justice Lewis Powell in the famous 1978 Bakke case.[9] He allowed that an educational institution could plausibly argue that a racially diverse student population would serve important educational purposes, and that, under the First Amendment, educational institutions should be free to make such judgments and draft race-sensitive admissions policies (subject to certain restrictions) to advance them.[10] Under that rationale, racial identity becomes one qualification among others.

My point in citing Powell's ruling is not to argue in favor of affirmative action. Rather, I suggest that an incomplete argument *against* Powell's diversity rationale is to say that it involves "discrimination against whites," on the sole grounds that black and Latino racial identity are taken as characteristics pertinent to admission.[11] A finding of discrimination requires plausibly defending a certain normative background—a conception of the goals of the institution in question and a plausible account of how these determine qualifications in applicants for scarce positions.

Skin Tone Discrimination vs. Racial Discrimination

The injustice of selection on irrelevant characteristics is independent of the personal motive behind the selection. The selector may not like the applicant's looks; hold a grudge against him; not like his mother; or mistakenly believe the irrelevant characteristic to be relevant. Such motives may have moral implications regarding the discriminator, but the injustice to the excluded person lies simply in the intentional use of the irrelevant characteristic.

Whatever the complexities of establishing a structure that undergirds discrimination based on irrelevant characteristics, such unfairness can not be the central moral wrong involved in many forms of group discrimination, and of *racial* discrimination in particular. To see this, let us imagine an employer, Yvonne, who has a fondness for a certain skin color—say, the somewhat golden or tawny color of the actress and singer Jennifer Lopez.[12] Yvonne attempts to select only job seekers with this skin tone; she rejects those with very pale skin or very dark skin. Some members of every racial (and virtually every ethnic) group possess Yvonne's favored skin color, and Yvonne makes no racial distinction at all; her work force includes Asian Americans, blacks, Latinos, Native Americans, and whites. They just all have a skin tone like Jennifer Lopez's, or as close to that as Yvonne can get given her pool of applicants.

Granted, in the real world Yvonne is an unlikely figure, for skin-color preference is generally bound up with race. A Mexican American student ruefully relates her father's remarking to her that she was dark, but beautiful;[13] and a preference for lighter skin color permeates most Latin American cultures.[14] White preference for lighter skin color among blacks is reflected in the substantially greater earnings of light-skinned than dark-skinned African Americans.[15] Prejudice exists among African Americans on the matter of skin tone, reflecting Eurocentric standards of beauty in the dominant culture.[16] Nevertheless, Yvonne's skin color preferences are intelligible, conceivable, and instructive.[17] We can all agree that hers is not a fair employment policy, for she utilizes a characteristic that is irrelevant to the performance of the jobs for which he is hiring. She does practice "skin tone discrimination."

But Yvonne's policy is not the same as discriminating on the basis of race. Imagine that a black applicant, Terry, applies for a job in Yvonne's business and one in Amy's business, and that he is well qualified for both. Yvonne rejects Terry because his skin tone is not like Jennifer Lopez's. Amy rejects him because he is black—black in the sense that he is regarded, and regards himself, as a person who is "racially black." Amy is prejudiced against black people—in the racial, not the skin color sense (no one's skin color is, strictly speaking, black)—and does not want them working for her.

Most Americans would, I think, agree that it is worse to discriminate on the basis of race than merely on the basis of skin tone. Why is this? It is sometimes said that discrimination based on any ascribed and immutable characteristic is especially wrongful, since the subject can not do anything about it.[18] Both race and skin color are, however, immutable characteristics, so that fact cannot explain the moral difference.

Confusing Race with Skin Color: The Hopwood Decision

Before answering our question directly, let us look at how confusions between race and skin color, and consequent misunderstandings of the character of racial discrimination, vitiated the court's reasoning in the important *Hopwood* case in 1996.[19] The University of Texas law school, attempting to compensate for decades of its own and the University of Texas system's exclusion of blacks and Latinos (especially Mexican Americans), adopted a policy of admitting some blacks and Latinos with somewhat lower test scores than nonadmitted whites. The policy was also meant to reap the educational benefits of a more racially diverse student body under the *Bakke* rationale. But the Fifth Circuit Court of Appeals ruled that the university could no longer use the racial identity of its applicants in selecting admittees.

In its decision the court concluded that "the use of race, in and of itself, to choose students simply achieves a student body that looks different. Such a criterion is no more rational on its own terms than would be choices based upon the physical size or blood type of applicants."

The court appears to confuse race and skin color. Mere skin color, or skin tone, considered entirely apart from its racial significance in our society, is indeed an arbitrary feature. Like blood type or physical size, it is unrelated to any legitimate educational purpose. If we look at skin color in this way, the University of Texas's preference for more blacks and Latinos in its student body is as arbitrary as Yvonne's preference for workers who have Jennifer Lopez's skin color. An admissions policy based on skin color would be irrational and unfair, and discriminatory for that reason.

But race is not skin tone, and it is not arbitrary in relation to university admission in the way skin tone is. Race, like gender, is a deeply significant social identity arguably pertinent to legitimate goals of institutions of higher education.[20] College admissions offices do not ask applicants to describe their precise skin tone but to state their racial identity.

The court is somewhat disingenuous in this portion of its argument. Cheryl Hopwood, a white applicant who might have been admitted but for the existence of the affirmative action program, brought (with three other whites) a claim of racial not skin tone discrimination against the university.

So let us return to our earlier question. If racial discrimination is morally wrong not only because it unfairly utilizes an irrelevant characteristic to allocate benefits and burdens, what *is* the further moral wrong? Antidiscrimination law is suggestive. Laws prohibit discrimination on the basis of various characteristics, which thereby define "protected categories." Race, national origin, religion, sexual orientation, weight (obesity),[21] disability, and age are protected categories in different legal venues. Robert Post suggests that the purpose of antidiscrimination laws is to neutralize widespread forms of prejudice targeted at the possessors of such characteristics, and he cites Justice Byron White's opinion in *Cleburne v. Cleburne Living Center, Inc.* that statutory classifications of "race, alienage [immigration status], or national origin" "are so seldom relevant to the achievement of any legitimate state interest that laws grounded in such considerations are deemed to reflect prejudice and antipathy—a view that those in the burdened class are not as worthy or deserving as others."[22]

Expressing judgments of inferior worth that are widespread in the society is surely a wrong over and above the wrong of arbitrary discrimination, burdening the victims beyond the material injustice they suffer merely from being discriminated against on the basis of irrelevant characteristics. Amy's, but not Yvonne's, rejection of Terry is discrimination as prejudice. Amy's discrimination involves two forms of wrong; Yvonne's only one.

The prejudice *must* be widespread to embody the wrong I speak of. An individual may, for idiosyncratic reasons, have an animus against people from Kansas. But prejudice against Kansans does not meet that condition, whereas prejudice against women, Latinos, or lesbians does. Such widespread judgments of lesser worth or deficiency constitute *stigma*.[23] Anti-Kansan bigotry may in an individual case be no different in degree than anti-Latino bigotry, but the latter invokes a stigmatizing that the former does not, and so harms its targets more substantially.

The harm of group stigma involves targeting an entire group that has an identity as a group, and regarding which the standing of the group affects the standing of individuals, an important part of whose identity is as members of that group.[24] Groups defined by race, religion, national origin, immigrant status, and gender are groups in this sense, and are thus, when they are the target of widespread devaluing judgments, vulnerable to the harm of group stigma.

The harm of maintaining a group in a subordinate, marginalized, or inferiorized position is a material counterpart to stigma. If blacks, Native Americans, or women recognize their identity as part of a group that is unequally placed with regard to economic, political, civic, or social standing, discrimination that excludes or subordinates them perpetrates an injustice on the entire group. Such harm is not inflicted on groups that, although having a distinct conception of themselves as groups, are not subordinate (men, whites), nor on merely nominal groups, which share a common characteristic but do not conceive of themselves as a group in the sense described above (such as "people who do not have the same skin color as Jennifer Lopez").

Although subordination involves a material dimension that stigma lacks, typically it is not only material. Subordination, when recognized by the larger society as a salient inequality, tends to generate inferiorizing and stigmatizing rationales about the nature or culture of the group.[25] Nevertheless, stigma is not the same as subordination. Andrew Koppelman suggests that disabled people are subordinated but not devalued or despised; institutions discriminate against them by failing to provide adequate access and accommodation, but this is not generally intentional.[26] I am not sure that Koppelman is right about the devaluing; disabled people are generally thought incapable along a wider range of activities than they actually are, and the condition still seems to me to carry a general stigma. Still, it is possible for a group to be marginalized or subordinated without being stigmatized. Conversely it is possible for a group to be stigmatized without being subordinated. The vulnerable groups discussed in chapter 2—Jews, Japanese Americans, and especially Arabs—suffer from some degree of stigma.

A discriminatory policy need not involve a stigmatizing motive or a desire to subordinate in order to inflict the harms of either stigma or subordination. Discrimination from innocuous or reasonable motives, but directed toward already stigmatized or subordinated groups, can inflict such harms.

Statistical or "Rational" Discrimination

Statistical, or what has been referred to as "rational," discrimination illustrates, among other things, the wrong of contributing to stigma and subordination from a nonprejudicial motive. In its most pristine form, statistical discrimination involves taking racial identity as a probable sign of some other characteristic, one which it is reasonable to take into account in the context at hand. Taking it into account need not involve racial animus or prejudice, and thus some regard statistical discrimination as morally unproblematic. But this is mistaken. Let us consider an oft-cited example.

In several American cities, cabdrivers frequently pass by prospective black customers, citing fear of being robbed, or of being asked to take the customer to neighborhoods they consider unsafe.[27] Were the cabdrivers able to interview customers to find out where they were heading and to determine whether they seemed unthreatening, presumably the drivers would gain the information necessary to make a well-informed decision as to the probable safety of picking up a given customer. But since cabdrivers are not allowed to interview prospective customers, the cabdriver makes a decision based on incomplete evidence—most conspicuously, the customer's race (when this is phenotypically obvious) and attire.[28]

The cabdrivers' actions are called "rational discrimination" because it is assumed that they are not a product of racial prejudice or animus but of generalizations concerning the likelihood of the prospective customers' posing a threat. It is important to examine whether such a phenomenon is morally problematic, and whether it should count as racial discrimination. But it can not be assumed at the outset that every case of a cabdriver bypassing a black prospective customer should count as rational discrimination. For one thing, the driver's citing of "statistical" danger may mask racial animus, his real motive.

Less obviously, the nature of the cognitions the cabdriver cites as supporting his fear may be suspect. At the most basic level, he might be operating from the same racial stereotypes (associating blackness with danger) shared by many Americans, rather than from genuine knowledge of the probabilities of danger to him, even when he cites statistics that turn out to be true. (He might be aware of cases of victimized cabdrivers, without having any idea how likely that victimization is.) In his discussion of cabdrivers and racism, Dinesh D'Souza manifests (and contributes to, especially since his book was a best-seller) such stereotyping or overgeneralizing when he says, "These fears [of blacks] seem to be borne out by cabdriver muggings and killings," citing in support only a single example of murder of a cabdriver and not providing the race of the assailant.[29]

In addition to baseless stereotyping, cabdrivers might overgeneralize on the basis of their own experience or experience of other drivers. They may have been robbed by a black person, or know of someone who has, and jump to the conclusion that they have reason to fear black customers in general. Although overgeneralizing from one's own experience is hardly confined to race, it is especially fostered by the cultural salience of race, which invites such overgeneralization, stereotyping, and homogenization of racial groups. If I have once been mugged by a red-headed man, I am unlikely to believe it reasonable to fear all red-headed men in the future.

We can not assume that any individual case of presumptive rational discrimination is such; when operating in an area of powerful antiblack stereotypes, it may not be possible to disentangle facts from stereotypes in a given individual's motivation.[30] Still, it is important to investigate what a morally appropriate response would be to the sort of information alleged to warrant rational discrimination. Consider the following statistic: blacks are arrested for 62 percent of armed robberies, though they make up only 12 percent of the population.[31] How do these statistics translate into the comparative threat of a black individual about whom nothing else is known? Can we conclude that the average black is approximately five times more likely than a white to commit armed robbery? We can not, since arrest rates are affected not only by actual rates of perpetration but by stereotypes and other racial biases.[32]

It is important to recognize the difficulty of securing figures that indicate actual differentials in violent criminal activity. Nevertheless, let us suppose for the sake of argument that blacks commit robbery at three times the rate of whites. This is a significant difference, but from the perspective of danger to the cabdriver it is not the relevant statistic. What he needs to know is not whether person X is *more likely than* person Y to rob him but *how likely* person X is to rob him. A gun owner is more likely to shoot me than a non–gun owner; but this does not mean that the former is in the least likely to shoot me. Comparative statistics are relevant only to the extent that they bear on actual likelihood of harm.

So consider the statistic provided by Jody Armour (see note 30) in his discussion of rational discrimination: in 1994, 1.86 percent of black males were arrested for violent crimes. Does that statistic provide a basis for a cab driver to be fearful of a black male prospective customer? If one extrapolates (keeping in mind that violent crime has declined since 1994), it means that in a given year less than one out of fifty black males might commit a violent crime. This is not trivial (remember, however, Armour's is only an arrest statistic), but it does not license a cabdriver's general fearfulness that would lead to passing up every black male customer.

Thus it is not clear that the cabdriver case is really a case of rational discrimination, where that is understood to mean not only making a decision based on statistics rather than bias or stereotypes but making a *warranted* decision. And even if the fear were rationally warranted, this does not settle the matter of whether it is morally correct or not. There is a high cost to black people of cabbies acting on such fears. Being unable to get transportation is not a trivial matter; it can seriously hinder one's work, home life, and social life. But there is a stigmatic harm as well. Being unable to avail oneself of public accommodations is a sign of second-class citizenship. Licensing the general idea that black males are to be feared plays in to a stigmatizing of blacks as appropriately shunned in public places. Moreover, black females are bound up with males as a group, and hence they will experience a sense of public devaluing as well. New York City appears to recognize the moral and civic costs of allowing cabdrivers to shun a racially defined category of customers by making it illegal for a cab driver to refuse a fare.[33]

The form of rational discrimination surveyed here causes stigmatic and inferiorizing harm to a racially-defined population. The harm is not itself an aim of the discriminatory acts, only a by-product. But the discrimination sends the message that blacks are a group to be feared and shunned. The cabdriver may deeply regret his decision to pass up the black customer, yet by doing so he contributes to the stigma suffered by blacks. As Jody Armour points out, by riding in cars and airplanes, we take small risks every day, and "incremental race-based risks are not meaningfully different from thousands of other risks we assume every day in return for a comfortable, convenient, decent, and democratic way of life."[34]

Not all statistical discrimination is unwarranted and immoral. Suppose for example that a white man has committed several rapes in a small geographical area, and has been identified as between twenty-five and thirty-five years old and over six feet tall. Women walking in that area would be justified in avoiding any white men who seemed to fit that description, even though many innocent persons would be shunned and might well experience a sense of insult at being regarded as a potential rapist. The same would be true with regard to a black man.[35] The point is that even when the statistical basis for the contemplated racial discrimination is sound, there are moral costs to engaging in that discrimination and these must be acknowledged and weighed on the moral ledger. The costs might not always involve as strong a stigmatizing, or depriving of an important personal and civic good, as is involved in the cabdriver case. Still, they must be taken into account; the subject should also consider bearing the burden of trying to acquire the information that would allow her to make a judgment not based on the individual's race.[36]

Not only can discrimination from an innocuous motive contribute to stigma, but a group can *become* stigmatized as a result of discrimination, even where it was not before. This argument is plausibly made by those who oppose allowing insurers to engage in, or be privy to the results of, genetic screening of potential insurees. If insurers utilize such information to charge higher premiums, and especially to deny coverage, to those found to have genetic predispositions to certain medical conditions, this is likely to have the effect of creating the latter as a stigmatized group—as something like "biological undesirables."[37]

I do not mean that every group-based discriminatory policy has the effect of stigmatizing the group in question. The group must be vulnerable to being stigmatized, as persons with genetic "defects" are. But able-bodied people, or white people, are not comparably vulnerable, and policies that discriminated against them would not have the effect of stigmatizing them as groups.

I have discussed discrimination in relation to the allocation of various benefits and burdens. There are two importantly distinct classes of these. One is *reward goods*, the other *equality goods*. Rewards are goods appropriately allocated to some but not all. Prizes, jobs, and places in selective institutions are examples. Equality goods are those to which everyone is equally entitled. Failure of a group, however defined, to secure reward goods is not necessarily a form of discrimination. Failure of a group to be given its share of equality goods, however, is by itself an injustice; and an institution (or individual) charged with delivering such goods discriminates if it fails to do so. This is why Ms. Verano, the teacher in chapter 1 who fails to hear her black students' parents, can be said to be doing an injustice to her students. Without adequate input from the parents, she is unable to provide an education equal to that of her other students. The "rationally discriminating" cabdrivers also deprive blacks (or black males) of an equality good—access to transportation and a sense of civic equality.[38] By contrast, the racially discriminating employer is at fault not for depriving blacks of a good to which all are entitled, like education and transport, but for acting out her prejudice to deprive blacks of a reward good.[39]

To summarize the argument about the multiple wrongs involved in discrimination, an act or policy of discrimination can be wrong for four different reasons: (1) it unfairly excludes a qualified individual on the basis of a characteristic irrelevant to the task for which selection is being made; (2) it is done out of prejudice; (3) the prejudice is pervasive and (for that or other reasons) stigmatizing; (4) the discrimination helps to sustain the group whose members are discriminated against in a subordinate position. These four reasons carry different moral valences. Discrimination against a stigmatized or subordinate group is more harmful than that against a nonstigmatized or nonsubordinated group. Thus women but not men, gays and lesbians but not straights, obese but not thin persons, blacks and Latinos but not whites suffer this harm.[40] So moral asymmetry such as argued for in chapter 2 governs many group-based discriminations (and not only racial ones).

Race as a Uniquely Invidious Basis for Discrimination

Many people would regard racial discrimination that is stigmatic or inferiorizing as the most morally odious kind of discrimination there is. The cultural and legal salience of the idea, and ideal, of "color blindness" is an important symptom of the special status granted to race.[41] No other form of discrimination has generated a corresponding ideal of non-discrimination with anything remotely like the power of race blindness; we do not generally speak of "gender blindness," "sexual orientation blindness," or "disability blindness," although most people think it wrong to discriminate against the groups in question. The power of the ideal arises from racial discrimination having proven historically, within the United States in particular, to be a particularly socially destructive form of discrimination.[42] African Americans and Native Americans especially have been subjected to unparalleled discriminatory inferiorizing and dehumanizing ill-treatment.[43] Latinos and Hispanics and Asian Americans, as racial groups, have also been subject to destructive forms of prejudice, stigma, exclusion, and discrimination. (As we shall see in chapter 6, the very idea of "race" itself was essentially invented to justify the mistreatment of these groups by "whites.") The special status of race as a particularly invidious basis of discrimination is reflected in contemporary judicial developments. In a series of cases in the past several decades, the Supreme Court has declared that any law or policy that makes use of racial distinctions must be subject to "strict scrutiny." Strict scrutiny is the most stringent of all tests of the legitimacy of group differentiation in law or policy, and involves demonstrating that the classification is necessary to achieve a compelling state interest; that the objective could not be achieved by a race-neutral policy; and other component standards that, taken together, are difficult to meet. Justice Lewis Powell, in one of the canonical cases in this development (the *Bakke* case), stated that "the perception of racial classifications as inherently odious stems from a lengthy and tragic history [that gender-based classifications do not share]."[44] Among classifications defining protected categories, only racial classifications are subject to this level of scrutiny.

Three Meanings of "Color Blindness"

As a moral (and sometimes legal) ideal, color blindness has been under-stood in roughly three distinct ways, which I will call *race neutrality, race egalitarianism,* and *racial harmony.*[45] I will discuss the first two here, and the third at the end of the chapter. Race neutrality denotes that racial cate-gories are not to be utilized in the formulating of policies. The underlying moral idea is that since race is an odious social category, we should at-tempt as much as possible to jettison it. Race egalitarianism takes existing racial discrimination and the present effects of past discrimination as a reference point, and seeks to craft public policy that will counter the re-sultant inequalities to achieve some acceptable egalitarian norm, reflect-ing an ideal of nondiscrimination in opportunity. Whether race-neutral policies will serve that end is an empirical matter, but it is that end, not race neutrality itself, that constitutes race egalitarianism.

In recent years, in tandem with the legal developments mentioned ear-lier, public discourse, especially as it bears on race-related policy issues, has come increasingly to settle on the race neutrality understanding of "color blindness." Indeed this principle has taken on an almost absolute, foundational status in moral discourse. A policy that makes explicit refer-ence to race, or racial identities, is taken to stand condemned by that fact alone, independent of whatever the policy aims or is likely to accomplish (for example, to foster race egalitarianism).

The dispute over college admissions illustrates this extraordinary status of race neutrality as a moral principle. Complex questions about the pur-poses of educational institutions, the character of "merit" and "qualifica-tion" and the like, are swept aside in face of the view that it is simply wrong to take account of applicants' racial identity in admissions. Stricter re-liance on grades and test scores, a result of this stance, is professed while exceptions for athletes, "legacies" (offspring of alumni and alumnae), and geographical diversity are countenanced. No principled reason for allow-ing such exceptions while excluding race is given other than a circular re-liance on the absolute principle of color blindness as race neutrality.

Particularly striking evidence that "color blindness" as race neutrality has become a bedrock policy principle thought to require little support-ing argument for its use in a range of policy prescriptions is the public re-sponse to so-called "percentage plans" in college admissions. These plans guarantee places in state colleges and universities to graduating high school seniors within a certain percentile class rank in their school.[46] The plans do not make qualitative distinctions between high schools, as most selective colleges currently do; a student graduating in the top 10 percent (or whatever percent) in a poor-quality school has as much right to a space in the state system as a student with the same rank in a more demanding school.

Percentage plans are clearly intended to serve the same racial egalitarian and diversity ends as the affirmative action policies that have been jettisoned (as a result of court rulings such as *Hopwood* and popular referenda). The racial segregation of high schools in states utilizing or contemplating the percentage plans guarantees that the plans will in fact generate the desired diversity. In all high schools that are virtually 100-percent black or Hispanic (or 100-percent black *and* Hispanic) the top 10 percent of the graduates (in the Texas plan, for example) will obviously include a substantial contingent of those groups. Prior to 1996, the University of Texas at Austin had, under a regime of affirmative action, 14.5 percent Hispanic and 4.1 percent black students in its entering class. Those figures dropped the next year, in the wake of *Hopwood.* In 1999, as a result of the 10-percent plan passed in 1997, the percentages were up again, to 14 percent Hispanic and 4 percent black.[47] The plans make no explicit reference to race. They are color blind in the "race neutrality" sense. But, like affirmative action, they are race egalitarian, in seeking to reduce racial inequalities in college acceptance.

These plans appear to be widely acceptable to a public that rejects affirmative action's explicit use of racial identity in admissions.[48] There is something absurd in this differential acceptability. Both policies have the exact same race-sensitive and race-egalitarian and diversity purposes—to rectify past racial exclusions, and to ensure racial diversity in the student bodies of the states' public colleges and universities. Both policies utilize less demanding standards for students of color than for white (and perhaps Asian) students. Students of color will be admitted in preference to whites with higher standardized test scores. Under affirmative action, a Latino applicant is essentially compared with all other Latino applicants, and, taking a variety of factors into account, is held on the average to a lower standard of test scores and grades than whites and Asians. In the percentage plans, a Latino student is compared only to members of her high school class; if her grades place her in the top 10 percent, she is admitted even if her standardized test scores are lower than the affirmative action cut-off point would have been. So affirmative action actually involves a *more* stringent qualification standard for admission than does the percentage plan.[49]

In both types of plan the explicit goal is racial—race egalitarianism and greater racial diversity. Moreover, in both plans the process of selection utilizes different standards for different racial groups, and in both some

Latinos and blacks are admitted with scores inferior to those of unadmitted whites and Asians.[50]

The only difference between the two plans is that affirmative action explicitly utilizes racial identity in the selection procedure, while the percentage plan does not. This difference parallels one found in the Supreme Court case mentioned in chapter 1, in which a South Carolina voting district, enjoined from explicitly preventing blacks from registering to vote, imposed literacy requirements which it knew would have the same effect; the Supreme Court did not see a legally significant difference between these two situations, and most of us would be unlikely to see a relevant moral difference either. That so many people now do see a significant moral difference in the analogous college admission policies is testimony to the ascendancy of race neutrality as a bedrock moral principle in current popular discourse about race.

But conferring an almost absolute moral status on race neutrality does not accord with the historical and social basis for opposing racial discrimination. The historical record does not reveal odious use of *all* racial categorizing, but primarily its use to advantage whites and to subordinate blacks, Native Americans, and Latinos.

A different history might have supported race neutrality as a fundamental moral principle. Suppose, for example, that American history had been one of shifting racial power dynamics in which now one and now another group was dominant, and each made use of racial ideas to subordinate other groups. Blacks sometimes victimized Asians, sometimes whites; Asians sometimes victimized Latinos, sometimes blacks; and so on. Such a history would lend credence to a general and near absolute prohibition on all racial classifications. But that is not *our* history.

Race Egalitarianism

Our history does, however, provide the moral basis for an understanding of color blindness as racial egalitarianism (a social order in which racial identity does not affect basic life chances, and racial discrimination and its legacy are opposed). That understanding animated the Civil War amendments to the Constitution (thirteenth, fourteenth, and fifteenth), whose purpose was ending the racial caste system exemplified by slavery. They were not successful in this (see chapter 7), and the Civil Rights Act of 1964 and Voting Rights Act of 1965 had a similar purpose of integrating blacks into the mainstream of economic and political life, dismantling the forms and vestiges of the racial caste system that held sway in the southern United States and, in lesser forms, elsewhere as well. Although this legislation prohibited discrimination on the basis of race (and "color, religion, sex, and national origin") in general terms, the context and legislative history of the Acts make it clear that race egalitarianism was its ultimate aim.[51] The wording of the Civil Rights Act suggests that Congress might well have believed that race egalitarianism could be achieved by a prohibition of *all* forms of racial classification in employment (benefiting as well as burdening blacks), that is, by race neutrality. Its literal wording was in any case not implausibly read by the courts in subsequent decisions as forbidding affirmative action programs designed to correct for past racial injustice. Nevertheless, even though the courts ended up depriving employers, schools, and governments at all levels of an important means to achieve racial egalitarianism, that goal still remains a central component of the legislative intent behind both Acts.[52]

A violation of race neutrality, or "discrimination on the basis of race," if it is unconnected to current and historical prejudice, stigmatizing, and inferiorizing, does not rise to a level of moral opprobrium that warrants according race neutrality status as a fundamental moral principle. For this reason, the kind of discrimination involved in affirmative action, if there is any, is not sufficiently odious to compel its condemnation independent of a moral assessment of the goals it aims to promote and the likelihood of its success in doing so. The violation of race neutrality involved in affirmative action is plausibly outweighed by the legitimate purposes of historical correction of exclusion, of encouraging diversity, and of creating a society in which all major racial groups are fully integrated.[53]

Color Blindness as Racial Harmony

A third, distinct, meaning of "color blindness," infrequently articulated as such but occasionally implicitly supplying some of the moral luster that idea conveys, is color blindness as racial harmony.[54] This ideal builds on racial egalitarianism but goes beyond it. An important (if not primary) strand within the Civil Rights movement, racial harmony seeks a society in which different racial groups live harmoniously and interdependently with one another on a plane of equality. The groups do not lose their distinct racial identities, with the valued cultural dimensions attached to such identities (especially black identity); but race is neither a devalued nor a divisive identity. Color blindness here (as in racial egalitarianism as well) does not mean that the racial identities are literally *not seen*.[55]

A somewhat distinct and competing ideal is for no one to have racial identities at all; one can imagine this, perhaps, by envisioning so much in-termarrying that it would become impossible to sort people into racial groups, and the idea of race would eventually become a relic of the past. But I think the more modest, yet still barely imaginable ideal of harmony and equality among racial groups is a worthy ideal, which captures some of what is at times meant by "color blindness".

"Discrimination on the Basis Of"

If "discrimination" is confined to the wrongful allocation of burdens and benefits based on some group characteristics, the common expression "discrimination on the basis of race, gender, sexual orientation, and so forth" is misleading, in two ways. First, it implies that all differentiations based on race, gender, or sexual orientation are unjustified, no matter what their purpose. This is very implausible. We saw, with the two earlier examples of the discussion club and college admissions that race is some-times a bona fide qualification for a reward good. Even if we confined "discrimination on the basis of" to the wrongful use of group classifica-tions, the expression would, or could, still be misleading, since, as gener-ally understood, it morally equates discrimination against stigmatized and inferiorized groups with discrimination (otherwise of the same type) against advantaged groups. In line with the argument of chapter 2, these forms of discrimination are not morally symmetrical. For these reasons, I suggest that we jettison the expression "discrimination on the basis of," es-pecially in contexts of moral asymmetry, for the foreseeable future.

What, then, is rightly called "racial discrimination"? That expression de-rives its moral valence from systemic, prejudice-based discrimination, and, although its use (like that of "racism") has definitively extended beyond that context, I suggest that we confine it to forms of discrimination involv-ing race that *either* stem from race-based prejudiced *or* that disadvantage an inferiorized or stigmatized group; it should not be used to denote all forms of racial differentiation.[56] (Discrimination against whites that is motivated by antiwhite animus—for example, on the part of an admissions commit-tee biased against whites—would be racial discrimination.)[57]

Discrimination against whites that is motivated by a benign, if mis-guided motive, would not, however, count as "racial discrimination."[58] For example, let us imagine that K-12 education in some particular state has improved to the extent that the grades and test scores of blacks, Latinos, and Native Americans are on a par with those of whites and Asians. Yet the state universities, which have been operating with affirmative action programs, continue to give preference to blacks and Latinos in admissions, simply because they have done so in the past and no one is paying much attention. However, the goals for which such programs were formerly necessary—providing a racially diverse educational environment for the development of personal and civic educational aims, training leadership from major racial groups, correcting for historical exclusions, promoting racial egalitarianism, and the like—can now all be met without taking applicants' racial identity into account. In this context it would be wrong to do so.[59]

The admissions committee continues to favor black, Latino, and Native American applicants because they believe—incorrectly—that doing so is required to meet valid institutional objectives. They do not act from animus or prejudice toward white and Asian applicants, nor do their actions disadvantage inferiorized or stigmatized groups. Nevertheless, their acts constitute discrimination against the individuals in question; so it constitutes a form of wrongful racial differentiation, though not a wrongfulness of the level of "racial discrimination." The wrongfulness is close to that involved in "discrimination based on an irrelevant characteristic."

Nevertheless, I think a somewhat *greater* wrongfulness attaches to racial differentiations than to others. The adherents of color blindness as race neutrality are onto something that is relevant here. Race *is* an especially invidious category, both uniquely inferiorizing and uniquely divisive; when its inferiorizing dimension has been neutralized, in affirmative action contexts, its divisive dimension still remains. Although it is entirely right and necessary to take race into account in the service of morally urgent goals such as racial justice, nevertheless race should be used as sparingly as possible in achieving that and other legitimate goals. Any use of racial classification, no matter who its intended beneficiary, should be carefully scrutinized to ensure that the goals for which it has been crafted are sound, and that the means used to attain them make as limited use of racial difference as is essential to meeting the goals. This is the moral truth in "strict scrutiny" legal doctrine, which the courts have wrongly utilized as virtually an absolute prohibition on racial classification.

Evolving judicial doctrine is correct in treating race as a particularly invidious basis of discrimination, but incorrect to infer from this that taking race into account to serve goals of egalitarianism and nondiscrimination should automatically be enjoined because doing so involves intentional use of racial classification. A tacit recognition of this uniqueness of race as a classification underlies the cultural force of the ideal of color blindness, but this ideal has been misunderstood to mean race neutrality rather than race egalitarianism or racial harmony, the promotion of both of which require rejecting race neutrality. Yet, although the promotion of racial justice requires preferences for stigmatized groups, all race preference is indeed, considered purely in its own right, morally suspect.

5

"Race": What We Mean and What We Think We Mean

Racism, racial injustice, racial discrimination, racial insensitivity, and so on, all involve something going wrong because of someone's race. But what exactly does "because of someone's race" mean? What exactly *is* a person's "race"?

The Popular Account

Probably few Americans who routinely use racial language in talking about human groups have given much thought to this question. Nevertheless, I believe we are able to recognize an account—which I will call, for convenience, "the popular account"—that many would, if pressed, offer. (This is the most common account proposed by my own students in many years of putting this question to them.) The account goes something like this: Races are large groupings of persons, distinguished by physical features such as skin color, hair texture, and facial features. Some people have dark skin and woolly hair, others light skin and straight hair. These so-called racial differences are captured in what adherents of the popular account might regard as more scientifically precise form, in a UNESCO statement from 1953 describing the three "major racial groups" and attempting to summarize what was known about race at the time: "'Asians' tend to have a fold of skin (the 'epicanthic' fold) over-hanging the eye opening that the other groups don't have; 'blacks' have much darker brown skin and tightly curled hair; whites have lighter skin, narrower noses, and more bodily hair than the other two groups."[1] Races are just part of what the world consists of, like stars, trees, and animals.

In the popular account, race appears to have a greater solidity—to be more "natural"—than some other large-scale groupings to which humans belong, such as nations (in the sense of nation-states) and ethnic groups. These seem to be human creations in a way that races are not. Nigeria, for example, was created through colonization, and Mexico has had different borders at different times, depending on military and political forces. Eth-nicities are also human creations, groups that view themselves as having a common (humanly created) culture and common ancestral origins. But in the popular account, races are not created; there have always been "blacks," "whites," "Asians," and so on.[2]

This popular account views racial classification as essentially scientific—more or less in agreement with Ashley Montagu's claim in 1964: "All but a few persons take it completely for granted that scientists have estab-lished the 'facts' about 'race' and that they have long ago recognized and classified the 'races' of mankind."[3] Perhaps some would distinguish a rough-and-ready common-sense understanding of races from a more complete, and deeper, scientific one. For example, the American popular account might reflect certainty about which racial groups people of Euro-pean, sub-Saharan African, and east or southeast Asian descent belong to: white or "Caucasian", black, Asian.[4] But that account might leave it to sci-entists to say which races North Africans (Maghrebins), Turks, and South Asians belong to.

Seeing race as a scientifically validated idea suggests that racial classifi-cation is, in the popular account, evaluatively inert. To say that some people are members of the "white (Caucasian) race," while others are members of the "black race" is not in itself to imply any value judgment about either group, or about their relationship to one another. Of course some people may attach value to a racial group; that is what racism is. But they may also regard tall people as superior to short people, or men to women, without those classifications being inherently value-laden. Ameri-cans are aware, of course, that for the Nazis and for white Southerners under segregation, superiority and inferiority were built into the idea of race itself. But they now regard racist attitudes as distinct from racial clas-sification; in the popular view, merely *classifying* someone as racially "black," "Asian," or "white" carries no evaluative valence.

Our actual practices of racial classification, however, do not accord with the popular account. The racial groupings we employ do not merely correspond to differences in somatic characteristics.[5] For one thing, there are many ways of classifying people by distinctions of physical appearance—eye color, height, ear shape, weight. Yet none of these is what we mean by "race." We do not think of people over six feet tall as a different race from those under six feet, or people with blue eyes as a different race from those with brown eyes.[6] Only some bodily features are accorded a distinctly "racial" significance. So race can not simply be "classification by somatic characteristics." The physical attributes linked to race clearly imply some further significance.

Moreover, even those bodily characteristics the popular account takes to be racial do not uniformly correlate with what are commonly regarded as races. Take skin color. Many Indians, especially from the southern part of India, have much darker skins than many American blacks, as do many Australian aboriginals; yet in the United States we do not generally think of Indians or aboriginals as "blacks."[7] And the hair of many people regarded as "white" is much closer to the woolly texture of most people of pure African descent than it is to the straight hair of other whites. So again there must be something more to race than a neutral classification by physical appearance.

What we mean by "race" certainly has something to do with somatic characteristics, but it is as true to say that thinking in terms of race *shapes* the way we perceive people's bodily being as that it *reflects* it. This is amusingly but tellingly illustrated in a cartoon by Robb Armstrong.[8] Two black friends are talking about a third, Edmund (also known as "Crunchy"), and also about Edmund's cousin Edward, whom one of the friends has not yet met. The friend who has met Edward says that the minor name difference is "about the only difference between them." In the final frame, the two cousins appear. Edward is "white" but his facial features, height, and the like are virtually identical to those of Edmund; the one character says to the other, "Crunchy is a hair taller," not taking notice of the skin color difference.

We can imagine a visitor from Mars who would not see why this cartoon was funny. Edward and Edmund *do* look almost exactly alike, if one stands outside a racial way of viewing them. (It is a sign of hope that it is possible to do this, at least temporarily.) But to an American, the joke depends on blacks and whites not being experienced as looking like one another, even if they have identical physical features apart from skin color.[9] People of different races "appear" more different than they would in the absence of race-perceiving.

The phenomenon of "passing" further demonstrates this point. Historically, when a black person was of sufficiently light skin and possessed other phenotypic features that could lead white people to regard her as white, and when that person allowed white people (and other blacks not personally known to her) to regard her and treat her as if she were white, then she was said to be "passing."

If race were nothing more than features of physical appearance, the distinction between "looking" white yet "actually being" black could not be made; if someone "looked white," she would *be* white.[10] But our practices of racial classification do make this distinction; if a person's parents are regarded as unquestionably black, then the person herself is taken to be or classified as black.

The concept of "passing" suggests that, contrary to the popular account, not only skin color but ancestry determines how we classify people into races. Regardless of her physical features, we will call an individual "white" if we learn that her parents are both white. Phenotypic ambiguity reveals a more general assumption about ancestry that structures our concept of race—a child is the same race as her parents when they are of the same race. (We will discuss the case of parents of two different "races" in chapter 9.)

Reluctance to Refer to People by "Race"

People's reaction to the practice of racial designation suggests that they do not always experience race as so innocuous as the popular account implies; frequently they will tiptoe around identifying someone as "white," "black," or "Asian." In one detailed study of a racially integrated middle school created as a model for the goal of racial comity, both black and white teachers shied away from referring to students as "white" and "black," often to the detriment of their ability to discuss and understand individual students.[11] If race were merely a way of referring to people's somatic characteristics, why such reluctance?

Suggestive also about the meanings we actually attach to race (in contrast to what the popular account alleges) is a comparison between race and ethnicity—both referring to large groupings that are seen as distinct "peoples" and that provide important social identities. Americans, especially whites, are much less skittish about referring to people's ethnicity than their race.[12] Moreover, ethnicity can provide a cross-ethnic bond for which there is no racial analogy. An Irish American can think "We're both ethnic" as a way of attempting to forge a connection with an Italian American, and perhaps with a Korean American or Caribbean American as well. But race virtually never functions as a source of commonality in that way. No one thinks, "We're all racial" or "We all have a race" as a way of connecting across racial boundaries. Race seems divisive in a way that ethnicity does not.[13]

The reluctance to use racial terminology may stem in part from a misunderstanding of color blindness (see chapter 4)—a feeling that it is somehow wrong, or even racist, to notice people's race. But I want to suggest that the reluctance is a window onto the limitations of the popular account of race as a morally and evaluatively neutral system of scientific classification of natural biological groups.[14] Race is not just a way of classifying people, or of talking about people; it is not just a "discourse." It is a way of thinking about, experiencing, perceiving, and relating to people.[15] I suggest that it is a morally problematic way of doing so, and that our reluctance to go in for racial labeling may well reflect an often unarticulated awareness of its moral liabilities.

The Moral Dangers of Racial Thinking

The full argument for the deleterious meanings of "race" as it is actually employed in contemporary American popular consciousness will have to await the historical account of the development of "race" provided in the next chapter. But I hope the reader will recognize, upon reflection, that thinking of persons in racial terms does indeed generally carry morally problematic implications, and not only when that thinking is racist.[16]

Moral Distance

First, racial thinking implies a moral distance among those of different races—an intensified consciousness of a "we" of one race counterposed to a "they" of another.[17] This distance is bound up with the idea of deep, inherent, and ineradicable differences among races. The scientific conception of race (see chapters 7 and 8) as a fundamental division of the human species—race as "subspecies" or "basic human type"—provides a metaphor for this idea of deep-rooted division, difference, and "otherness."

This sense of differentness or otherness is independent of any specific characteristics that might be attributed to different racial groups. Race thinking encourages us to invent differences and to focus on them rather than on similarities. Thus it inhibits empathy and connectedness. One vaguely feels that the racial other's experiences are entirely opaque; or at least one is discouraged from attempting to understand them. Thus the idea of race is inherently divisive. It tends to mask from our consciousness deeply significant commonalities shared by all human beings—the capacity to suffer and to experience loss, to care about one's place in the world, to be capable of human attachment, to possess human dignity. It hinders a lived sense of the moral unity of humankind.[18]

Race also discourages individuals from experiencing more particular commonalities with individuals of other races—commonalities of interest, taste, sources of enjoyment, background, religion, shared institutional membership, aspirations, and the like.[19]

Although all racial language and consciousness carries an implication of fundamental and immutable difference, certain racial designations carry it more than others. "Black" and "white" are the most polarized, as the color language suggests. Asian (or, in its more archaic but more explicitly racialized forms, "Mongoloid" or "yellow") and Native Americans ("red") are somewhere in between.

False Commonality

A second, unfortunate aspect of race thinking is an imposition of false commonality on all those classified as members of the same race. Just as such thinking inhibits persons of different races from seeing commonalities, so it encourages people of a given race to expect commonalities with members of their own race when none may exist, and to overlook or minimize differences that do exist. A black student of mine, Mohamara, related an experience in a high school class in which there was only one other black student. Mohamara would always sit next to this student, assuming that she and this other girl would have a lot in common. It took Mohamara a long while to recognize that they did not. Racial thinking had led her to false assumptions of commonality.

This racial homogenizing leads us to overlook or accord insufficient weight to differences—for example, of family background, class position, profession, religion, gender, personal interests, region—within a racial group. Related to this, it invites stereotyping and overgeneralizing about other racial groups. Failure to see the internal diversity in racial groups other than one's own is both a cause and product of racial stereotyping.

One sees racial others as "the same" in an overall sense, and not only with respect to stereotypical characteristics. To some extent, the tendency to overgeneralize is a product of group identity itself. Lawyers stereotype doctors and accountants. But because of its history (discussed in chapter 6) and its special divisiveness, race thinking tends to be both more prone to such stereotyping and overgeneralization[20] and to invite more noxious stereotypes (as stupid, lazy, violent, alien, morally deficient, uncivilized) than other groupings.

Inescapable Racial Fate

Because race implies the possession of immutable characteristics, it suggests an inescapable "racial fate." If, by virtue of their race, blacks are lazy, or whites racist, or Asians passive, their laziness, racism, or passivity is part of their very nature. On this way of thinking, it is then impossible for members of the group to avoid the characteristics in question. Of course, as with many generalizations, exceptions may be allowed; some whites might not be racist, or Asians passive. But, in a fully racial mindset, exceptions will be seen as quite uncommon; avoidance of alleged racial characteristics will be achievable only with unusual effort. Race, then, invokes a sense of being trapped in or stuck with the characteristics attributed to one's group.

In this respect, attributing general characteristics to groups in a racial manner differs from doing so in a nonracial manner. It is quite possible to attribute characteristics, even to a racial group, without implying that those characteristics are inherent in the group's character. One might believe that African Americans tend to vote Democratic without thinking that this is the racial fate of African Americans; indeed, one might well be a Republican who, while noting this generalization, hopes it will become less true in the future. Not all generalizings, even about racial groups, buy into implications of immutability.

At the same time, if the groups being generalized about are racial ones, even careful generalizings made with the intention of avoiding implications of inherent and inescapable characteristics will stand in tension with the tendency of all invocations of race to imply that attributed characteristics *are* inherent and immutable.

Dominance and Hierarchy

A fourth morally deleterious consequence of race is that racial categories tend to evoke associations of superiority and inferiority of value. The claiming of a "white" identity, for example, tends to imply the acknowledgment of the appropriateness of, or the attempt to stake a claim to, the privileges and higher status historically associated with "whiteness," even though those claiming it may not be conscious of this implication.

All other racial color terms, and especially "black" generally connote inferiority, deficiency, marginality, or some lesser human or civic status.

These associations are powerfully reinforced by racial stratification in
society. That blacks and Latinos are disproportionately concentrated in
the lower socioeconomic rungs of society reinforces the already-present
idea that their situation is due to something amiss within the groups
themselves (be it their "genes" or their "culture" [see chapter 7]). But
merely thinking in racial terms carries such associations anyway. The popular account is wrong to imply that racial designation is entirely separate
from the placing of value on those so designated.[21]

Lack of Reflective Endorsement

In marked contrast to the classic nineteenth-century period of racial
thought that we will discuss in the following chapter, it is characteristic of
contemporary racial thinking that many, perhaps most, people who engage in it would not reflectively endorse the elements implied in its usage.
If one asks persons who appear to be making the racial assumption that
blacks and whites differ in their fundamental natures whether they in fact
believe this, many would deny it. They might say, "Of course not. The differences are the products of culture and environment" or "People—including blacks and whites—are much more alike than different." Similarly, if someone seemed to imply a belief that all Asians are smart or
diligent students, and one pressed her on this implication, she might well
deny it. "Of course not all Asians are smart. Many Asians are stupid, just
like in any other group. You can't generalize about an entire group like
that." Or if someone appeared to imply that blacks had an inherent tendency toward criminality and was asked to consider that view reflectively,
she would be likely to deny it. Nevertheless, people continue to engage in
racial thinking and language that does carry these deleterious implications.

The lack of reflective endorsement is probably clearest with respect to
the implication of racial hierarchy. Few people would reflectively endorse
the idea that some races are inherently superior to others, or are inherently more deserving of superior socioeconomic position. This is no
longer a respectable position to avow in mainstream culture. Yet many
people do believe it. (Racial differences with regard to this belief will be
discussed below. Nor do I mean to deny that many people would be perfectly willing to avow belief in these deleterious implications of racial

thinking, at least in settings in which they are not concerned about disapproval for doing so.)

Why are many, or most, Americans reluctant to endorse racial thinking? It reflects, I believe, a combination of scientific, sociopolitical, and ethical assaults waged in the latter half of the twentieth century against the idea of race, or at least its most harmful dimensions. We will discuss these in more detail in chapters 6, 7, and 8. But we should be equally struck by the other side of this development—the continuing vitality of the idea of race in the face of these assaults. Racial thinking has manifested substantial staying power in American life. And it has done so in part precisely by remaining outside the domain of reflectively endorsed ideas.

The "popular view" helps keep this structure in place. It supplies a benign or innocuous image, or official story, of what is customarily meant by race—namely, an evaluatively neutral classification of groups by somatic, and perhaps ancestral, characteristics. Thus contemporary Americans are enabled to believe that they have put a much greater distance than they in fact have between themselves and the classic racial ideology of the nineteenth century.

Blacks' Use of Racial Categories

Blacks seem distinctly less reluctant than whites to use racial designations, for perhaps two quite different reasons. First, for American blacks, the term "black" tends to carry ethnocultural associations along with racial ones. That is, it is not a purely racial designation. Thus it carries some of the positive associations that ethnic designations—Irish American, Polish American, Korean American—have come to possess in the United States since the late twentieth century. When Jesse Jackson promoted "African American" as a designation for American blacks whose roots could be traced to slavery as a way to garner ethnocultural recognition, more blacks continued to prefer the designation "black," at least in part because that term already carried ethnocultural significance.[22]

A second possible reason for the lack of reluctance of blacks to self-designate as "black," and to feel comfortable using racial designations for other groups, is that blacks are much more able than nonblacks to do so without an implication of their own inferiority. In her study of black views of whites and of racial difference in the nineteenth and early twentieth century, Mia Bay documents that many blacks, both educated and uneducated, challenged white claims to inherent moral superiority. They generally accepted the idea that blacks and whites possessed distinct characteristics, but they defended the equal humanity (and sometimes the moral superiority) of blacks. What blacks did not generally do, Bay argues (with few exceptions, Frederick Douglass being one), was challenge the very idea of race itself; they did not, for example, argue that blacks and whites were the same except for their somatic characteristics, though many did regard alleged racial traits of mind and temperament as a product of environment.[23] I will follow Anthony Appiah's suggestion that we use the term "racialism" to describe the view that races are biologically real divisions of the human species that imply no hierarchy of value.[24] Racialism is race without inferiorization, and this is the view held by many blacks in the nineteenth century.

Although challenges to racialism (not only to racial hierarchy) have made their way into popular thought, I believe the situation Bay describes still generally holds true for African Americans. Popular movements challenging white superiority, such as the Civil Rights movement and its forebears, and those promoting black pride, such as the Black Power movement of the 1960s, have made it easier to resist the implication of inferiority carried by the dominant culture's use of racial language.[25]

But aside from hierarchy of value these movements have generally not done battle with the other elements of the idea of race—immutable characteristics, false commonality, and exaggerated difference between races. (Indeed, some black pride movements, such as Marcus Garvey's nationalist back-to-Africa movement in the 1920s, and the Nation of Islam, embraced race no less fully, although with a different racial hierarchy, than did white supremacists.) For this reason, these features remain central to the contemporary conception of race among blacks (as well as whites), even while the connection between racial thought and the implication of white superiority has been somewhat weakened.[26] The racialist and the hierarchical strands coexist within the popular meanings of race. But the egalitarian use of race can not drive out the inegalitarian one, especially if the society remains racially stratified, because the historical associations of hierarchy are too central to what race means. It can, however, provide new strands of meaning that compete with the older ones.

Many people think that when they categorize people racially, and think of others in terms of race, they are simply classifying people by skin color, nose shape, and other somatic characteristics. But our actual shared practices of racial classification show that race is not a mere reflection of somatic differences. And a widespread diffidence about referring to people's race suggests that racial meaning is evaluatively charged rather than inert.

I suggest that a central strand in the concept of race in actual practice carries four morally unfortunate connotations. It exaggerates the differences among persons of different racial groups and thus encourages moral distancing and discourages a lived sense of common humanity. It exaggerates the commonality among those of the same race. It implies that alleged racial characteristics are permanent and inescapable. And it suggests, though less definitively, a hierarchy of worth among different racial groups. Blacks' greater willingness to think in terms of race in part reflects (I suggest) an ability to think racially without an implication of their own inferior worth.

6

"Race": A Brief History, with Moral Implications

"**R**ace" is not a primordial category of human diversity. Racial prejudice is not an inevitable noxious response to phenotypic or cultural diversity. We have come to see the world in the racial way we do now, with its deleterious moral consequences, because we inherit a conception of race that developed from the sixteenth century until its zenith in the late nineteenth century. Tracing that history will reveal why we now see human diversity in terms of a false sense of immutable intraracial similarity and interracial difference and hierarchy. A historical perspective, which allows us to pinpoint the entry of distinct aspects of racial thinking and to see how our notion of race changed over time, can dislodge the sense of naturalness and inescapability of our present racial way of viewing people. History shows, moreover, how the U.S. conception of race is virtually unique among conceptions of cultural and somatic diversity.

Finally, the history of race will enable us to do justice both to the falsity of our idea of race and yet to the reality that being treated as a distinct race has profoundly shaped the social and historical experience of the groups we call "blacks," "whites," "Asians," "Native Americans," and "Latinos" or "Hispanics."

Skin Color Difference without Race: The Ancient Greeks

Human beings have seldom been "color blind" in the sense often touted today as ideal—not actually noticing differences in skin color.[1] In the ancient Greco-Roman world, Africans were identified primarily by skin color, nose shape and hair texture. (The Greek word for an African, "Aethiops," literally means "burnt-faced person.") The Greeks were quite interested in the dark skin color of Ethiopians, which they attributed to climatic conditions; but they did not homogenize all darker-skinned persons into a single social grouping. They were clearly aware of distinct shades of dark skin.

The Greeks were respectful of dark-skinned Africans, whom they encountered in war, as both allies and adversaries, and in commerce. Nubia, an African civilization south of Egypt inhabited by persons of "Negroid" features, was respected as a military power. Dark-skinned Africans were identified generally as "human beings with the capacity for freedom and justice, piety and wisdom."[2]

The Greeks sometimes (but not uniformly) identified light skin as more beautiful than dark, but this was an aesthetic preference, not a judgment of deeper human deficiency or inferiority. Moreover, culturally and aesthetically both the Greeks and the Romans, who were often quite ethnocentric, were no more so toward Aethiopees than toward northern Europeans, with their blond hair and blue eyes. Skin color was just that; it was not seen as linked to characteristics such as honesty, intelligence, or courage in battle—a striking difference from the racialized way that we now view skin color.[3] Sexual relations between Aethiopees and Greeks were generally accepted. The Greeks did note distinct cultural characteristics accompanying bodily characteristics, but saw no intrinsic connection between them. An Aethiops brought up in Greek society—for example, the offspring of a war captive, or even the captive himself—although ineligible for citizenship, would be able to take part in much of the economic, social, and cultural life of the polis.

The absence of any conception of races, hence of racial prejudice, hardly renders ancient Greece an ideal society, though its early practice of a form of democracy in some city-states was a vital contribution to the Western democratic tradition. Greeks did, after all, practice slavery. Slaves were generally conquered peoples, but were not identified with any particular somatically defined or cultural group, even though they were often of a different ethnicity than the Greeks. Indeed, most slaves were of light complexion.

The Greeks seldom attempted to produce a general justification for slavery. An exception was Aristotle, who said that some individuals were "slaves by nature." He admitted that one could not discern this nature by outward appearance, though he felt it an unfortunate deficiency on the part of nature not to have provided such external markers.[4] In any case, even for Aristotle what made someone a slave had nothing to do with race, color, or ethnicity.[5]

The value of considering the Greeks' nonracial understanding of human somatic and cultural diversity is to illustrate that "race" is not a primordial category of human beings, as our current understanding tends to suggest. While we can not simply will away a concept that so deeply structures our own consciousness and social reality, outlooks such as the ancient Greeks' can spur a search for alternatives suitable to our own time and place.

Origins and Development of the Concept of "Race"

The modern U.S. idea of race had its origins in sixteenth- through eighteenth-century Europe. The word surfaced in all European Romance languages at approximately the same time. "Race" was originally a folk, or popular, mode of categorizing animal, plant, and human groups; it did not carry the aura of scientific legitimacy attached to our current concept of race.[6] As the term came to be applied more and more exclusively to human groups, it referred to a "people," or population group, of common lineage or "stock," and a supposedly common origin or history. Such groups as Anglo-Saxons, Normans, Basques, and Teutons were referred to as "races." Originally the term "race" did not carry an implication that racial groups were biologically distinct from one another, nor did it carry the implication that they possessed distinct sets of personality, temperamental, characterological, mental, or aesthetic characteristics. Neither did it imply a distinct hierarchical relation among the groups.[7]

Ideas of superiority and inferiority of entire peoples were largely a product of the encounter of Europeans with Africans and the indigenous peoples of the Americas, through conquest, colonization, and, later, the Atlantic slave trade. Contact with these groups *prior* to a full commitment to colonization and expansion by no means resulted in primarily negative images of them. Columbus, for example, landing on the island of Hispaniola, spoke of the native Arawak as "a loving people without covetousness."[8] In 1584, Sir Walter Raleigh led an expedition to Roanoke Island (to establish a colony for England) and described the inhabitants thus: "We found the people most gentle, loving, and faithful, void of all guile and treason, and such as lived after the manner of the golden rule."[9]

Africans and people of mixed African and European descent had been part of Spanish and Portuguese society for several centuries prior to these nations' colonial expeditions to the New World. The English, in contrast, had less exposure to dark-skinned persons, but in their few encounters with Africans through trade or adventure, impressions were far from uniformly negative. Africans were certainly not seen as less than human. Sir Francis Drake, who pirated Spanish ships in the Caribbean, made alliances with cimarrons, groups of slaves who had escaped from the Spanish and established their own communities. "The alliance seems to have been untroubled by racial prejudice," according to historian Edmund Morgan.[10] Although emphasizing that the negative connotations of "blackness" in the English language and religious worldview of the time contributed to a negative view of Africans, the historian Winthrop Jordan nevertheless notes that the English were aware of the relative sophistication of political organization of West African societies.[11]

Basil Davidson, a historian of Africa, summarizes European attitudes toward Africans in the period of initial encounter:

> In short, and again with the exceptions that so vast a subject must allow, the Europeans of the sixteenth century believed that they had found forms of civilization which were often comparable with their own, however differently and variously dressed and mannered. A later age would prefer to forget this, and would roundly state that Africa knew nothing but a savage and indeed hopeless barbarism.[12]

It was only when the European powers turned definitively to conquest, subjugation, displacement of native peoples, and slavery that they began to develop rationalizations in which the latter were viewed as inferior and subhuman. Cultural and religious differences aided in the quest for such rationalization. Both Native Americans and Africans were viewed as "heathens" (that is, non-Christians), and in that regard inferior to Europeans. Heathenism is nonracial, referring to peoples' religious practices and beliefs, and the modes of life based on them, and it carries no necessary implication that the peoples are inferior in other ways, or that the inferiority of heathen ways of life is part of the heathen's very nature.

Eventually both Native Americans and Africans came also to be viewed as "savages," a step further on the way toward racialization. "Savagery" implies a more pervasive deficiency than does heathenism, yet it was still regarded as remediable through a process of cultural change, which the Europeans thought of as "civilizing." The image of Native Americans and Africans as savages became much more pervasive as a result of conquest and enslavement.

So Europeans were not primordially racist in their view or treatment of

Africans and Native Americans. The seventeenth-century English colonists referred to themselves primarily as Christians or Englishmen when contrasting themselves with these other two groups; the racialized language of "white," "black," and "red" was not yet widely used.[13] In a very real sense, Europeans were not yet "white," nor Africans "black."[14]

Certainly many Europeans showed few qualms in subjugating African and Native American peoples in the name of expansion, power, acquisitiveness or general economic gain, and their fellows at home readily accepted the benefits of such subjugation. This greed helped to produce, or to greatly intensify the salience of, negative views of Africans and Native Americans. Such greed-based willingness to subjugate may seem little better than being racist, yet distinguishing greed and racism is essential for both historical and moral understanding. Greed is obviously a motivation found in most human groups, not only Europeans (although some cultures and social circumstances may provide it with greater outlet and legitimation). Many civilizations have engaged in conquest in which subject people were treated appallingly. Myriad factors—level of technological development, development of armed forces, nature of resistance, forms of religion—having little to do with the intrinsic motives of the conquerors determined the form of damage done to subject populations. A willingness, in the name of conquest, to overlook the humanity of peoples seen as strangers or "other" can be found within most societies or cultures. Now that racism has been invented, however, it is fair to say that no groups have nearly matched Europeans in carrying out large-scale race-based forms of oppression.

There were marked differences among the European colonizing powers in their treatment of Africans and indigenous American peoples, and in the social systems of race emerging therefrom. The English (and northern Europeans more generally) were much less tolerant of cultural and somatic differences than the Spanish and Portuguese, a difference due in part to the Iberians' much greater exposure to such differences. But perhaps a more historically significant factor in the differing systems of slavery and conceptions of race was the difference in the purposes and patterns of colonization. The Spanish and Portuguese initially saw their colonies as a source of wealth rather than settlement, and the colonizers were therefore mostly males. They intermarried and mated with indigenous women and later (to a lesser extent) with African slave women. The English, by contrast, always intended to settle in the New World, and so came over in families. Thus there were greater numbers of "mixed" persons (mulattos and mestizos) in the Spanish than the English colonies; the comparative absence of such mixed persons was one important factor that enabled the English colonies to enforce, by law and custom, a rigid sense of racial difference and separation, which never emerged in Iberian America. The English developed customs and eventually laws that forbade interracial marriage and mating (though a good deal of it took place anyway).[15] For these and other reasons, Latin American countries and Brazil never developed the notion of races as discrete groups marked by somatic differences taken to correspond to humanly significant characteristics of mind and character.[16]

Only with a full commitment to conquest did the Spanish, Portuguese, and English colonists come to view Africans and Native Americans as savages and heathens, providing a seeming rationale that rendered the cultures and interests of these groups unworthy of the colonists' respect. Even then, however, these groups were not seen in a fully racial manner; they were not yet regarded as inherently and immutably inferior.

Slavery and Race

Forms of slavery have been practiced since Greek times in virtually every part of the world. Some Muslim nations and groups owned slaves and engaged in extensive overland slave trading. Many African peoples (Muslim and non-Muslim) practiced slavery.[17] Prior to the eighteenth century, slavery was not generally thought to require justification in terms of qualities possessed by or absent in those enslaved. As in ancient Greece, slaves were often captives of war, or debtors, both considered sufficient rationale for their enslavement, though perhaps only against a background in which the institution of slavery itself was seen as acceptable. Bernard Williams, in his insightful discussion of the justification of slavery in ancient Greece, argues that the Greeks were quite aware that it was a terrible misfortune to be a slave, and saw that there was a certain arbitrariness about who fell into this unfortunate state. Yet they could not conceive of a form of social existence that "preserved what was worthwhile to them" without slavery.[18] So though they saw slavery as a misfortune for the slave, they did not see it as an *injustice* perpetrated on the slave. Seeing no alternative to slavery, the ancient Greeks did not develop a broadly shared popular justification for it, although as we saw earlier, Aristotle did claim that some people were "slaves by nature."[19]

Some Africans first brought to the English colonies in the early 1600s were, like many English and Irish, indentured servants. After completing their term of service some gained their freedom, acquired property, and were able to vote in some colonies.[20] In the early form of slavery in the colonies, slaves were restricted and regarded as property, but they were not fully deprived of all human status, as they would come to be later with the advent of racialized, hereditary chattel slavery. In the seventeenth century, Africans were by no means seen as the racial group "blacks," nor (integral to that racialization) were they viewed as virtually subhuman, as, with the rise of the plantation system, they would later come to be.[21]

As mentioned earlier, the English sense of superiority to many other groups was initially expressed in the counterposition of "Christian" and "heathen," used to justify driving Indians from their lands, as well as attempting to enslave them. Gradually religion gave way to race in the conception of superiority. A seventeenth-century slave owner in Barbados bluntly articulated the disadvantages of a religion-based view of the differences between slaves and masters; responding to a slave who asked to become a Christian, the master replied, "We could not make a Christian a Slave . . . [nor] a Slave a Christian . . . , [for] being once a Christian, he [i.e., a slave master] could no more account him a Slave, and so lose the hold they had on them as Slaves, by making them Christians."[22]

This slave owner had not yet adopted a racial way of viewing his slaves. But he implicitly saw the advantage of a justification of slavery that does not allow slaves to opt into a category (for example, by converting to Christianity) that protected them from the rationale given for slavery. Race provided such a justification.

One might think that Christians and Muslims could see that slavery was inconsistent with their shared teaching that humans are all equally creatures of God. But both Christianity and Islam contained scriptural and other justifications that seemed consistent with slavery, or with regarding some humans as lower than others.[23] (Significantly, neither Christians nor Muslims would enslave their own coreligionists.) More important, however, the economic attractions of the slave trade, which made harvesting of tobacco, sugar, cotton, and rice so lucrative, gave slave-owning societies a compelling reason to reconcile themselves to behavior inconsistent with their religion. Racist ideologies arose to accomplish this rationalizing function.[24]

The selection of Africans to be the sole slave population of the United States was dictated almost entirely by the economic aim of finding a stable, captive, productive, reliable labor force rather than by prejudice against Africans, hostility toward persons of darker skin, or a belief that Africans were a people in whose unique nature it was to be slaves. In the seventeenth century, three groups other than Africans—pauperized English persons, Irish, and Native Americans—were at various times used as slave or slave-like labor in the English colonies, in the Caribbean as well as

North America. But none of these groups proved viable in the long run, especially given the increased demand for slave labor beginning in the late seventeenth century.[25] Impoverished Englishmen were too small a group, could readily blend in with the general population if they escaped their masters, and diminished in number as economic conditions in England improved in that period. The Irish too were better able to elude captivity and blend in with the nonslave population; in addition (in contrast to Africans), they were not accustomed to agricultural work or the climate of the southern colonies. Native Americans too could escape into their tribal groups, and they resisted customary labor discipline. Moreover, their ranks were decimated by European diseases. In addition, they knew the terrain better than the colonists and were often able to evade their would-be captors.

None of these drawbacks applied to Africans. They were readily identifiable and could not, therefore, easily escape. They were not familiar with the territory. They were of many different linguistic and cultural groups, and slave owners purposely mixed them together to inhibit communication that might enable escape or rebellion.[26] Most important, the Atlantic slave trade, already put in place by the Portuguese and Spanish, promised an endless supply of bound labor for the economic needs of the colonial economies.

A striking event in the degrading of the status of Africans, and more generally in the construction of "race" in the English colonies, was Bacon's Rebellion of 1676 in Virginia. Originally directed against Native American tribes whose land was coveted, the rebellion eventually brought together disgruntled former indentured servants unable to find land, African slaves, and white and black indentured servants chafing under bonded labor—all to fight the oppressive power of the planter elite. The willingness of Europeans and Africans in similar economic and social circumstances to make common cause reveals that the divisions we have come to think of as "racial" did not yet exist. But the threat to planter social control led the planters to seek in such divisions a means to securing their hegemony. "In quick order [planters in the Virginia colony] elaborated a slave code that singled out people of African descent as slaves and made their status hereditary."[27]

So slavery was not originally a "racial" institution in the United States. Somatic characteristics played a role only in relation to relative ease of escape (and perhaps a form of mild prejudice), not as a badge of inherent inferiority. Africans were not yet seen as a grouping of people created by God or nature as an inferior breed of human destined to no better life than to be the property of others. Such a racial rationalization was not fully and unequivocally employed in the dominant culture until the nineteenth century. Until that time, then, dark-skinned persons of African descent were not fully regarded as (and inferiorized as) "blacks" in the true racial sense of that word familiar to us today.

The absence of racial thinking in the early Colonial period should not, however, be equated with an egalitarian world outlook. Landowners and ruling elites saw the world in hierarchical terms. They regarded those who worked the land for them, or provided personal service, as lower than themselves. The difference between slave and servant was a matter of degree. This inferiorizing was based on class rather than race, although it could take an ethnic or proto-racial form when the laboring class was primarily a specific ethnic or national group, such as Native Americans, Irish, or Africans. Even when ethnicized, this viewpoint lacked the imputation, present in "race," of inherent and inescapable inferiority grounded in a group's biological nature.

Because race and slavery later came to be so intimately linked in American history and consciousness, blacks have been burdened by a deep association between blackness and slavery. For this reason it is important to keep clearly in mind that the historic *foundation* and function of slavery was economic rather than racial, though eventually whites, whether slave owners or not, did become psychically invested in white supremacy and a racial outlook that ranged far beyond their attachment to slavery itself.[28]

Slavery and Racial Ideology

What pressed slave owners and others toward a distinctly racial rationalization of slavery was the increasing salience of ideals of Christianity and the Enlightenment, especially the moral equality of all human beings as creatures of God or as possessors of secularly grounded natural rights. In the U.S. the constant invocations of the injustice of tyranny leveled against English rule in the pre-Revolutionary period rendered slavery a troubling contradiction, which slaves themselves recognized. In 1777, for example, a group of slaves petitioned the Massachusetts legislature for freedom, with the following statement as part of their argument: "Every principle from which America has acted in the course of their unhappy difficulties with Great Britain pleads stronger than a thousand arguments in favor of your petitioners."[29] The slave trade to the United States was abolished in 1808 (a compromise forged at the Constitutional Congress in 1789), and slavery itself abolished in the various northern states, where it was of marginal economic significance, by the early 19th century.

But the moral and philosophic contradiction between slavery and freedom and equality did not translate into a widespread public challenge to slavery in the northern or southern states for several decades after the Revolution.[30] Indeed, the slave system became stronger than ever, with smuggling and natural reproduction increasing the number of slaves even after the trade itself was abolished. The invention of the cotton gin in 1793 made cotton production and the plantation system of slave labor especially profitable, and gave the South an even stronger stake in slavery. As George Frederickson notes,

> Although gradual emancipation had been instituted in the North, slavery in the South had survived the Revolutionary era and the rest of the natural-rights philosophy without an elaborated racial defense—without, indeed, much of an intellectual defense of any kind; for the institution had never actually been seriously threatened.[31]

Northern industry had many ties to southern slavery. Moreover, even the increasing numbers of white Northerners, and Southerners such as Thomas Jefferson, who were uncomfortable about slavery on both moral and practical grounds did not believe that freed slaves could be integrated into the national polity.[32] In the early 19th century, though the seeds of racial thought had taken root in the widespread view of slaves as an inferior people, a full-fledged racial ideology that came to grips with the Revolutionary-era natural rights challenge had barely been articulated. That development had to await the public visibility, beginning in the 1830s, of the Abolitionist movement in the United States (with assistance from its earlier manifestation in England).[33] So it was the combination of the official egalitarian beliefs that made up an important component in American political culture, combined with the South's (and to some extent the North's) economic and social stake in slavery, that set the stage for the full articulation of a racial ideology.

If all human beings had an equal right to freedom, those of African descent had to be construed as not human for slavery to be justified. To justify permanent and hereditary slavery, as practiced in the slave states, the supposedly subhuman qualities had to be seen as permanent and heritable. The rights in property that played such a strong part in the English natural rights tradition could take precedence over any claim that blacks could stake as human creatures. And these ideas were legitimized and solidified by the contributions of 19th century natural science (see below). Only with the moral advance of the idea of human equality as a norm to be expressed in social and political institutions would slaveholding require a denial of the slave's humanity.

While the goal of racist ideology was to shore up the moral foundations of slavery, its logic required it to encompass all black persons, including free blacks in the North (and a lesser number in the South). The presence of free blacks had always been a source of anxiety to slave owners, for it reminded slaves that people of African ancestry were not predestined to their lot. As racial ideology solidified, free blacks' situation became increasingly anomalous, and they were more and more restricted in their civil rights.[34] Thus the ideology of racial inequality penetrated all sectors of the society. Among whites, only a small group of Abolitionists were full racial egalitarians; most white Abolitionists condemned slavery for a variety of moral reasons but did not regard blacks as full human equals.

The developing logic of "race" attained its most striking public legitimation in the Supreme Court's ruling in the 1857 *Dred Scott v. Sandford* case. The case concerned the status of fugitive slaves only, but the Court's decision, written by Chief Justice Roger Taney, proclaimed of *all* blacks that they had "no rights which the white man was bound to respect."

The same processes that re-created persons of African ancestry as "blacks" created "whites" out of persons of European ancestry; as Africans and their ancestors were regarded as possessing immutable characteristics signifying their inferiority, so Europeans came to possess a guarantee of intrinsic superiority. The idea of "whiteness" was never a neutral characterization of skin color, nor an innocuous way of referring to persons of European origin. It was a racialized way of conferring the moral right to hold power over and regard themselves as superior to other groups of persons.

The role of slavery in generating racist ideology reminds us that race is not an inevitable system for classifying human biological diversity. Its U.S. form is virtually unique in the world and is intimately connected with its particular form of slavery. Yet if we link slavery and racism too closely we might be led into the moral error discussed earlier of thinking that slavery stands as an appropriate metaphor for racism more generally. As a result we would either overstate the horrors of lesser but still very objectionable forms of racism (such as job discrimination or racial harassment) by analogizing them too closely to slavery; or be led to the opposite error of seeing as insignificant many such forms of racism because they are not sufficiently akin to slavery. We must, then, keep firmly in mind that slavery has existed without racism, and racism has existed without slavery.

Eighteenth-Century Classifications of Human Diversity: Linnaeus and Buffon

Slavery alone demanded the racializing only of Europeans ("whites") and Africans ("blacks"), though the earlier subjugation and displacement of Native Americans also embodied an inferiorizing, hence proto-racial strand. Developments in eighteenth-century natural science provided a way of thinking about human groups that dovetailed with elements of the evolving slavery-inspired folk view in the United States, while providing it with much greater scope and the authority increasingly attached to scientific thought. The Swedish naturalist Linnaeus (1707–78), considered the founder of scientific taxonomy, played a key role in this development, establishing a paradigm in the mid-1700's that remained influential in physical anthropology until the 1960's.[35]

Linnaeus attempted to understand human diversity by drawing on zoological classification. He was the first scientist to clearly situate human beings as a species within an encompassing system of nature that included animal and plant species. He saw the naturalist's task as a search for basic and unchangeable biological divisions among humankind, analogous to differences within classificatory groups of animals such as rodents and carnivores. Although he affirmed the religiously-grounded and widely accepted principle of the unity of the human species, Linnaeus thought that human diversity could be adequately captured in a system of a small number of such groups, seen as radically distinct from one another in something like the way species differed, and created as such by God. In particular, he postulated four such groups—Asiaticus, Europaeus, Africanus, and Americanus—the latter three of which matched the evolving racialized groups in the English colonists' outlook in North America.

Linnaeus did not regard this classification as a mere mental convenience for bringing provisional order to the complexity of human difference. He regarded the four groups as real entities within nature—"natural kinds." Although he recognized the theoretical possibility of interbreeding, Linnaeus nevertheless conveyed the impression of species-like differences among these four "variations." Biologist and anthropologist Jonathan Marks usefully designates Linnaeus's scheme as "Platonic," as it ignored actual diversity within each category of human in favor of seeking out the ideal form to which all this variety could be assimilated.[36]

The implications for racial thought are obvious. Linnaeus's classificatory schema implies permanent, natural, and fundamental differences of character among, and commonalities within, races. Naturalists and physical anthropologists do not ordinarily take themselves to be engaged in an explicitly moral enterprise, but classifying humans, in contrast to classify-

ing plants and animals, into distinct "types of beings" has moral consequences. It implies that some persons "belong together" (in not only a
classificatory but a social and moral sense) and that some groups share
very little with other groups, thus suggesting that moral and social distance among them is appropriate.

Linnaeus's typological descriptions also combined physical with behavioral and temperamental characteristics. He described "Homo Sapiens
Asiaticus" (East Asians) as "sallow, melancholy, stiff; hair black dark
eyes . . . covered with loose garments; ruled by opinions." "Europaeus"
was "white, serious, strong. Hair blond, flowing. Eyes blue. Active, very
smart, inventive. Covered by tight clothing. Ruled by laws."[37] His fourfold
scheme was deeply value-laden, with the European group ("ruled by
laws") accorded the most favorable characterization, and the African
group ("ruled by caprice") the least, with the other two somewhere in between. Linnaeus thereby contributed to the hierarchical dimension of
"race," though he himself avoided an explicit value ranking.[38]

It was not merely fortuitous, of course, that Linnaeus's groupings cor-
responded so closely to the dominating and subordinated proto-racial
groups involved in the European encounter with Africans and indigenous
peoples of the New World. He drew his descriptions of these groups from
the writings of travelers, explorers, plantations owners, traders, and mis-
sionaries, and he shared the Eurocentric prejudices and outlook of his
times. Linnaeus's "scientific" approach supplied a refined and solidified
framing of proto-racial thought for this Eurocentrism.

That Linnaeus's approach was not an inevitable mode of comprehending human diversity is evidenced by his intellectual rival of the same period, Louis Leclerc, Comte de Buffon (1707–88). Buffon also sought to
understand and bring order to human variety. In contrast to Linnaeus,
however, Buffon was not interested in searching for permanent types of
human being but rather in explaining human variety given a basic assumption of the unity of the human species. Without claiming compre-
hensiveness, Buffon eschewed a small number of race-like groupings in
favor of an account of peoples of the world in their manifold cultural variety—Eskimos, Lapps, Tartars, Chinese, Japanese, Persians, Arabian,
Egyptians, Filipinos, Swedes, Russians, Congolese, Hottentots, Madagas-
carans, Caribbeans, and the like. Of the variations of humanity, Buffon
said, "Those marks which distinguish men who inhabit different regions
of the earth are not original, but purely superficial."[39]

Linnaeus's proto-racial approach prevailed, however, among natural
scientists of the 18th and 19th centuries. Its racial legacy comprised: (1)
describing human biological and cultural variety in terms of a small num-

ber of allegedly somatically and characterologically similar human groups; (2) implying vast and immutable differences between such groups; (3) confusing cultural and innate factors in human difference; (4) providing the underpinnings of a hierarchy of human worth; and (5) undermining a sense of the moral unity of humankind (while officially adhering to a doctrine of common ancestry).[40]

The emphasis on common humanity was nominally retained in Linnaeus and others, such as Johann Blumenbach, the inventor of the term "Caucasian" to refer to people of European ancestry, who believed that God created all humans as a single species. But even this compromised sense of human unity was abandoned by a 19th century development known as "polygenism," the view that different races arose separate from one another in different regions of the globe as essentially distinct species. The Swiss naturalist Louis Agassiz, of the Linnaean school of taxonomy, was converted to the polygenist cause upon coming to the United States in the 1840s and encountering black people for the first time. Agassiz was an influential voice in the United States, and polygenism came to be known as "the American school" on matters of race and origin. Agassiz' views were appropriated and widely disseminated by southern defenders of slavery,[41] and they also influenced respectable thought in the academy and in the North more generally.[42]

Polygenism was opposed by "monogenists," who affirmed the unity of the human species. In sharing the widely-held views of black inferiority, white superiority, and permanence of the groups coming to be thought of as "races," however, monogenists were hardly racial egalitarians. But polygenism contributed most strongly to the American idea of species-like, fundamental differences between "races." Laws against miscegenation both reflected and reinforced the idea of racial differences as akin to species-like differences.

Darwinism and Racial Thought

By the mid-nineteenth century the popular idea of "race," developed to rationalize enslavement of imported Africans and displacement of native peoples, had acquired scientific character and respectability, embedded as it was in a more general scheme for comprehending all human and other natural variety. Science, politics, and morals were indissolubly bound in this racial thinking.

Darwin's theory of evolution undermined the idea of permanent and unchangeable species and subspecies that undergirded nineteenth-century racial thought. Darwin's 1859 work—whose full title is *The Origin of Species by Means of Natural Selection or the Preservation of Favored Races in the Struggle for Life*[43]—held that life forms evolved and changed rather than becoming permanent and immutable in their differences. Differences between dogs and wolves, for instance, were not God-given but rather classificatory conveniences with somewhat arbitrary boundaries.[44] In a later work that concerned the human species, Darwin (countering polygenism) emphasized the unity and common biological origin of all human beings.

> As it is improbable that the numerous and unimportant points of resemblance between the several races of man in bodily structure and mental facilities (I do not here refer to similar customs) should all have been independently acquired, they must have been inherited from progenitors who had these same characters.[45]

But on the other hand, elements in Darwin's thought bolstered, or were at least consistent with, key aspects of the reigning conception of race. By greatly extending the historical timescale in which populations developed, the theory of natural selection allowed that, despite remote common ancestry, populations differing in biologically significant characteristics could emerge, through natural selection among random variations and adaptation to different circumstances. Common evolutionary ancestry was compatible with evolved biological difference. In addition, Darwin accepted the idea that different human groups had attained quite distinct levels of "civilization"; employed the vocabulary of "savagery" to describe these differences; used the term "race" to refer to groups thus characterized;[46] and had in mind the same groups commonly referred to as "races."[47] He rejected only the idea that the differences were species-like.

Herbert Spencer, a British philosopher and sociologist whose work was very influential in the United States, developed what came to be called "social Darwinism."[48] Although Spencer used biological analogies for society in a manner largely foreign to Darwin's own thought, social Darwinism picked up on the racist strands in Darwin to develop a philosophy that explicitly provided support for the preservation of racial hierarchies as they had developed in the United States, rationalizing them as a product of natural processes of social evolution that separated groups into the more and less "fit." In Spencer's work the groups in question were defined explicitly by race, using the now-standard classifications, as well as by economic class. Though not racial thought in its purest 19th century form—since it avoided the explicit claim that each racial group's characteristics were fully determined by its biological endowment—Social Darwinism came very close to it. In this way, partly within and partly against the spirit of Darwin himself, Darwinism came to serve a reinvigoration of racist thought in the last decades of the 19th century.

Race and Naturalized Citizenship

Certain factors besides slavery and science contributed to the general racialization of the American polity. Race, and the privileging of "whiteness" in particular, were built into the foundation of citizenship in the new republic from its origins. The first act of Congress in 1790 limited naturalized citizenship to "free white persons." As A. Leon Higginbotham has pointed out, that restriction was a natural outgrowth of the pre-union colonists' understanding of citizenship, which (as explicitly expressed in congressional debates) was inextricably bound up with the suppression of slave insurrections and the overcoming of Native American resistance to encroachments on their land.[49]

This racial restriction was first used outside the "white/black/red" framework with the immigration of Chinese to the West in 1849, and especially after their importation to work on the transcontinental railroad. In a series of federal policies beginning in 1880, the Chinese were excluded from immigration, with justification appealing frankly to racial notions of their inherent unfitness for self-government and unassimilability to American life.[50]

Naturalization was extended to blacks in 1870, but East Asians and Filipinos were not included until 1952, when the Congress, embarrassed that Germany was the only nation other than the United States that placed racial restrictions on citizenship, struck all racial language from naturalization laws.[51]

The most consistent cultural image in the racialization of East Asians was their "alienness"—the idea that they were perpetual outsiders, never really able to be fully assimilated to the American body politic. The most egregious manifestation of this racialization was the internment of Japanese Americans during World War II, upheld as constitutional by the Supreme Court in *Korematsu v. U.S.* (1944). Nothing comparable befell American descendants of Germans and Italians.

In the nineteenth century a broadening pantheon of racial targets felt the bite of American domestic and overseas endeavors. Racial rationalizations permeated the Mexican-American War of 1846–48. At the century's end, racial themes were an integral part of the debates about incursions against Hawaii and against the Spanish in Cuba and the Philippines, and the inhabitants of those territories were viewed in racial terms. Native Americans were denied citizenship until 1924, although the reasons for this delay were only partly racial.

Post-Slavery Racial Thought

After Emancipation, racial thinking about blacks expanded beyond its specific function in rationalizing slavery. One might speculate that had Reconstruction been successful in its original promise of bringing freed slaves into full civic and political equality, and enabling a degree of economic self-sufficiency, the material foundations of race thinking might have been severely weakened.

Emancipation and Reconstruction did improve the lot and standing of African Americans in substantial ways, and gave them a modicum of political power. The thirteenth, fourteenth, and fifteenth Amendments, the Civil Rights Acts of 1866 (collectively intended to nullify the *Dred Scott* decision), and of 1870, 1871, and 1875 were meant to guarantee suffrage and political participation to blacks, to guarantee certain civic rights (making and enforcing contracts, suing, buying and selling property), and to forbid various forms of discrimination. But support for these measures by the so-called Radical Republicans who controlled Congress during much of the Reconstruction period did not entail a full commitment to racial equality. Belief in the inferiority of blacks remained widespread,[52] and these modest attempts to confer political power and civil rights on the black population were met with powerful resistance. By 1877 federal support of Reconstruction had ended, and "white supremacy" was the rallying cry for political campaigns to return the former elite to power and to disenfranchise new black voters. A series of Supreme Court decisions quickly eroded the legal underpinnings of Reconstruction progress.[53]

Eventually, by the mid-1890s, the southern elite was able to reimpose a form of state-sanctioned white supremacy in the "Jim Crow" form of segregation. Not until the 1950s was this structure subject to serious legal damage, and the legal props to segregation were not fully dismantled until the 1960s. Nor were blacks outside the South generally regarded as full equals before the law until the 1960s. Anti black forms of racial thought thus rationalized legally-enforced and socially and politically sanctioned subordination for at least one hundred years after the demise of slavery. The racializing of blacks (and, correlatively, of whites) has lingered as both cause and effect of the continuing economic, political, educational, and social inequality suffered by blacks.

No respectable scientist challenged the idea of race and its corollary, white supremacy, until the early decades of the 20th century. (And few did so even then.) Emblematic were the views of Daniel Brinton, president of the American Association for the Advancement of Science and the individual credited with "changing anthropology from a romantic pastime to an academic discipline."[54] Brinton rightly took himself to be reflecting both popular and scientific opinion when he stated, in his 1890 book *Races and Peoples*: "We are accustomed familiarly to speak of 'higher' and 'lower' races, and we are justified in this even from merely physical considerations. These indeed bear intimate relations to mental capacity . . . Measured by these criteria, the European or white race stands at the head of the list, the African or negro at its foot."[55] We still very much live with the legacy of this "classic" conception of race as if it were a natural and unavoidable way to comprehend human diversity.

European Variants of Racial Thought

Prior to the twentieth century, European and American racial thought, especially in their popular versions, developed in relative independence from one another, and in distinct historical circumstances. One distinctive element in European racial and proto-racial thought bears a brief mention here. Immanuel Kant (1724–1804), J. G. von Herder (1744–1803), and G. W. F. Hegel (1770–1831) developed a form of proto-racial thought involving "the spirit of a people" (*Volksgeist*), a set of characteristics alleged to inhere in a people's nature viewed both spiritually and quasi-biologically.[56] The European tradition linked inherent characteristics more closely to nations or peoples than did the American version, and became a forerunner of European racialized nationalism. The contrasts are most striking in Nazism, a culmination of a major form of European racial thought. Groups the Nazis thought of as distinct races—Jews, Slavs, Aryans, Teutons, French, Italians, Celts—were what Americans would more likely call ethnic or national groups (sometimes fictitious ones). This strand of racial thought gave somewhat less prominence to phenotypic difference than did its American counterpart; the groups involved were rather identified by ancestry, language, and nationality, although the tendency to ascribe phenotypic differences was still present.

American thought always contained elements of the intellectual strand I am noting in the European tradition, and the European always contained phenotypically based and biologistic forms.[57] With the substantial movement in the latter half of the twentieth century of phenotypically distinct populations to European countries—either as former colonials, immigrants, or guest workers—the way Europeans have come to conceive of race has moved closer to the American model.[58]

The Elements of Classic Racial Ideology

Here, then, are the elements of the "classic," nineteenth-century conception of race in the United States:[59]

1. Human beings fall into a small number of ancestral groupings called "races," linked historically to certain geographical regions of the globe. These are natural, discrete, fixed subdivisions of humanity. These races are radically distinct in character from one another. Every human being is a member of one and only one race.
2. Races differ from one another in significant qualities of mind, character, personality, and temperament. Blacks are lazy; whites are industrious; yellows are cunning; and the like.
3. Every member of a given race possesses the characteristics distinctive to that race—what is sometimes called the race's "essence."[60] Sometimes race thinking allows for aberrant or untypical members not to possess the characteristics constituting the racial essence.
4. The race's essence of mind, character, and personality is grounded in biology.
5. The racial essence is passed from one generation to the next.[61]
6. Races are generally also distinct in certain aspects of physical appearance. These somatic or phenotypic features are, therefore, indicators of the group's racial essence, its inner reality. For example, light skin and straight hair indicates initiative and inventiveness; dark skin and woolly hair indicates musicality and laziness.
7. Racial differences are fixed, innate, and unchangeable, because they are grounded in biology.[62]
8. Races can be ranked in terms of superiority and inferiority generally, or at least with regard to particular significant characteristics. This ranking should be and generally is reflected in the relations of power and status in society and civilizations.

9. The social order appropriately reflects, through its legal, institutional, and customary norms, the distinctness in nature between races by separating them as much as possible in occupational, social, personal, and public space. Segregation is "natural" and mixing is "unnatural," especially in regard to sexual and marital relations. When individuals of different races do interact, their interactions are to reflect the hierarchical order, the inferior group members showing deference to the superior.

Classic late nineteenth-century race involved both a vertical and a horizontal dimension. Horizontally, races were radically distinct from one another, and social distance and separation were meant to reflect this. Vertically, races were superior and inferior to one another, and the hierarchical social order was to reflect this as well.

This conception is the culmination of several centuries' development of the idea of race, a product of the interaction of economic, political, historical, social, and scientific factors. Yet it is not really coherent. No groups large enough to be "races" on this conception could possibly have the internal commonality, nor the comprehensive difference from other races, demanded by this view. Nor can somatic features plausibly be linked to the wide range of significant human characteristics involved in the view. Entire racial groups can not be inherently "inferior" to entire other ones in any intelligible sense, though of course they can be treated as if they were. That classic race is a false idea will be demonstrated in detail in the next chapter. But historian Barbara Fields is surely right when she says that many white people knew, or had a basis for knowing, from their own experience of blacks that this racial worldview was not correct; yet they believed it anyway, or at least pretended to, since it generally rationalized their privilege.[63]

Twentieth-Century Developments

Especially within the sciences, the twentieth century witnessed several revolutions in thought that bore on the validity of the idea of "race." By the century's end, little of classic racial thought still commanded the assent of the preponderance of scientists in any relevant discipline (genetics, psychology, anthropology, biology, and others). Yet popular thought, by and large, more responsive to continuing racial inequalities and the deep and extensive roots of racial thought in American social and political history than to developments in science, retained the core of classic race. In the next chapter I will delineate the differences between contemporary popular racial thinking and classic race. But first let us look briefly at some twentieth-century forms of scientific thought that themselves retained a strong continuity with classic race.

The rediscovery in 1900s of Mendel's experiments on heredity in fruit flies promised to fill a significant lacuna in the classic theory of race by showing how racial characteristics were transmitted through successive generations. The idea of a single gene for intelligence (and for distinct temperamental features such as adventurousness) was embraced by racists and eugenicists who thought the influence of heredity could thereby be separated entirely from environment.[64] Through the staggering advances in genetics as the century progressed, there remained and remains to this day a distinctly geneticist strand of racial thought—the idea that races differ significantly in genetic makeup and that the sources of important human characteristics (especially intelligence) are largely genetic.[65]

A related development of twentieth-century racial science was the IQ test, regarded by its American developers and proponents as measuring "intelligence," which they took to be a single trait and assumed to be hereditary.[66] The psychometricians utilized a concept of averages—the average possession of a given trait in a given population—that, considered by itself, seems very different from racial thinking. Average differences between groups still allows for substantial group overlap in possession of the characteristic in question (intelligence, industry, secretiveness), especially if the alleged difference is small; but racial thought inclines toward absolute differences between groups.

As used by racialists, however, the idea of averages as a summary of the attributes of individuals has turned into an assertion about the characteristics of groups as a whole, in a manner that preserves the nineteenth-century implication of whole-group differences. Moreover, as Smedley points out, racial thought has tended to latch onto virtually *any* differences between racially defined groups and magnify and distort them into a judgment of whole-group difference, in the nineteenth-century mold.[67] Attaching the assumption of genetic underpinning to the assertion of group difference preserves the basic structure of classic race.

The geneticist, eugenicist, and psychometric turns in racial thought coincided with a racialized or semi-racialized understanding of the southern and eastern European immigrants who flowed in unprecedented numbers to American shores beginning in the 1880s. These groups had been permitted to immigrate and naturalize as "white" from the point of view of the 1790 naturalization law, but what constituted "whiteness" had never been clearly defined. The influx of new immigrants, coinciding with the deeper penetration of racial ways of thinking in the late nineteenth-century, precipitated a kind of crisis of "whiteness," which is explored in Matthew Jacobson's *Whiteness of a Different Color: European Immigrants and the Alchemy of Race.* Poles, Jews, Slavs, Greeks, Italians, and the many other immigrating groups came to be viewed as something like distinct races with distinctive inherent characteristics linked (although less decisively than in the case of "blacks," "reds," and "yellows,") to distinctive physiognomies.[68] They were seen as inferior to Anglo-Saxons and northern Europeans ("Nordics") more generally.[69] In 1917 psychometricians weighed in with a mass psychological testing of army recruits that allegedly found these groups to be inferior in intelligence to Nordics. The culmination of this particular racial development was the 1924 Immigration Restriction Act, which drastically curtailed the immigration of southern and eastern Europeans.[70]

The rise of Nazi-tainted eugenicist ideas, and the curtailing of immigration (until restrictions were lifted in 1965), enabled southern and eastern Europeans to assimilate, and thereby removed from public concern the issue of their questionable "fitness" (what Jacobson calls their "probationary whiteness"). Then the revelation after the World War II of the Nazi horrors led to a widespread rejection of racial thought, and scientists from many disciplines began to develop critiques of classic race theory, including its hereditarian, geneticist, and inegalitarian components. The appellation "racism" was coined to express the moral revulsion at ideologies of racial supremacy, and even milder forms of nonsupremacist racialist thought were tainted by association with them.

Geneticist strands of racial thought held on within science, but as a decidedly marginal voice.[71] That *The Bell Curve* (the most recent manifestation of this tradition, published in 1994) became a popular best-seller is testimony more to the continuing vitality of popular racial thinking—and to the continuing controversy and sensitivity concerning allegations of racial inferiority of African Americans—than to scientific influence.[72] By and large twentieth-century science has distanced itself from classic race theory. Popular thought, by contrast, has, as I suggested in chapter 5, retained important elements of racial thinking, though these are frequently unacknowledged. To the precise differences between classic and contemporary racial thought we now turn.

7

Do Races Exist?

In chapter 5 I suggested that the contemporary American conception of race contains certain morally troubling features independent of its use in specifically racist contexts: exaggerated difference and moral distance between those of different races, which discourages an experienced sense of common humanity; an overdrawn and falsely grounded sense of commonality among members of the same race;[1] a notion of being trapped in one's racial fate; encouragement of stereotyping racial others rather than seeing them as individuals; and an implication that, because of their racial membership, some persons have greater worth or ability than others.

In chapter 6 I traced the history of how these features came to be present in classic nineteenth-century racial thought. We can assume neither that contemporary ideas of race are simply carryovers from that period, nor that racial thinking has entirely jettisoned its nineteenth-century forms.[2] What remains, then, is to pin down precisely which elements have been preserved and which abandoned or qualified. Once we have done so, we can address the vital question whether there actually *are* races, and, if so, whether the groups we currently call "races" are actually races.

Contemporary popular racial thinking follows classic racial thought in most respects. It divides the human species into several large ancestral groupings linked historically to certain geographical regions, marked by alleged somatic commonality, and constituting natural, discrete, fixed, and fundamental subdivisions of humankind that can be ranked as superior and inferior in important respects. There seem, however, three major differences between contemporary and classic notions of race. First, racial beliefs are today seldom explicitly avowed. In the nineteenth century almost all white people were explicit believers in race; in contemporary terminology, they were avowed racists. I have argued that blacks were avowed racialists as well.

A second difference is a general softening of the content of racial beliefs. Characteristics currently attributed to the nonwhite races are less noxious and inferiorizing than their nineteenth-century counterparts. Then blacks were regarded as uncivilized and virtually subhuman—"humanoid but not fully human" in Charles Mills's apt phrase.[3] They were seen as like both beasts and children—in neither case capable of directing their own lives, and requiring whites to do this for them. These figurations did not vanish with slavery but continued, revitalized, in the Jim Crow era, and not only in the South. Blacks are still viewed as inferior in certain respects—as violent, lacking in motivation, intellectually deficient—but, except in the far extremes of racism, seldom in such degrading and vicious ways as in classic racial ideology.

In the nineteenth century, Asians (primarily Chinese) were thought of as unfit for self-government, devious, potentially treacherous. The latter two stereotypes have not disappeared, but contemporary racial thought, though still carrying implications of irrevocable alienness, is much less vicious and insulting in its portrayal. Many racial stereotypes of Asian Americans—as high achievers, having strong families, being good in math and science—are at least partially flattering, even if they come with all the moral harms of stereotyping in general,[4] and often with negative counterparts as well ("geeky," lacking independence, not good at humanities subjects).

The same softening applies to the belief in racial hierarchy. In the nineteenth century, for almost all white people, the distance in worth and ability between whites and all other racial groups was quite vast, with blacks generally the least capable, least human, least worthy. Though contemporary racial thinking still carries implications of unequal value and capacity, the degree of inequality has greatly diminished, thanks to challenges by science and by the Civil Rights and Black Power movements, and by the movements for equality of other ethnic and racial groups (Latinos, Native Americans) that were inspired by the latter.[5]

Inherentism

A third important difference between contemporary and classic racial thought concerns the claim of "inherency"—that certain traits of mind, character, and temperament are inescapably part of a racial group's "nature" and hence define its racial fate.[6] The mindset of racial inherency is that blacks just *are* intellectually inferior, Asians studious, whites racist, Mexicans lazy, and so on. Classic racial thought located that inherent nature in the groups' biological endowment, and so may he called "biological inherentism." Twentieth-century science has waged a multidisciplinary attack on biological inherentism, and contemporary racial thinking has followed mainstream science in largely abandoning it.[7] Contemporary racial thought has not, however, abandoned inherentism itself—only its definitively biologistic forms.[8]

Inherentism can take a qualified or unqualified form. In its unqualified form the characteristic attributed to the group is viewed as present in every member of the group. Qualified inherentism, by contrast, involves attributing a characteristic to a group but allowing that some members do not possess the characteristic; the latter are seen as exceptions, as not typical of the group. For instance, Laverne might think that white people are basically racist but that a few manage to escape this characteristic. The implication that racism is somehow rooted in white people's nature is what makes her thinking inherentist. Qualified inherentism is similar to one form of what in chapter 1 was called "selective racism." There the young black male was thought of as "really black" and the black grandmother was thought of as somehow less black. Here the nonracist white person is thought of as "less white" or "less exemplifying of whiteness," though still acknowledged, in a purely classificatory sense, to be white.

Qualified inherentism must be distinguished from a different intellectual stance with which it might be confused, but which is not inherentist at all. That stance is that *on the average* a given group possesses a certain characteristic, but those who do not possess the characteristic are no less representative or typical of the group than those who do. For example, Tony says "Asian Americans are, on the average, better at math than other groups" but he in no way implies that Asian Americans who are not good at math are less fully Asian American, or less representative of the overall character of Asian Americans. Tony may well not have adequate evidence for making this generalization; he may, indeed, be drawing on stereotypes of Asian Americans that others hold in an inherentist fashion. Nevertheless, his stance is not itself inherentist; it postulates no natural or necessary link between being Asian Americans and being good at math.

To understand contemporary inherentism, we must first consider the difference between race and culture. Generally, to attribute characteristics to a group's culture is a way of saying that the characteristics are *not* inherent, for cultures are human creations and potentially changeable. Mexican American culture may place a strong emphasis, value, and reliance on families, but over time this emphasis could diminish.

Changeable cultural characteristics may be attributed even to a racial group.[9] Consider the views of William E. Cross Jr., a theorist of black adolescent identity development.[10] Cross plausibly argues that many young blacks develop an "alienated oppositional identity," a cultural orientation detrimental to their acquiring the skills to negotiate a successful relationship with the white-dominated world. This cultural orientation is rooted in norms and expectations that, Cross argues, are an understandable outgrowth of a history of racism, of a racially segregated existence, of a community in which the young people's parents and other adults are often unemployed and in which little hope for their own future appears on their horizon. The alienated oppositional identity is not a mere bad habit. It pervades the norms and modes of life of the black youngsters who possess it, which is why it is appropriate to call it "cultural."

Cross regards this identity as changeable (if not easily). He argues that, in the long run, job programs in urban neighborhoods can help to reverse the hopelessness brought about by parental unemployment that he sees as a source of the oppositional identity, and that, in the short-run, school-based programs recognizing the problem can help change this cultural feature. Cross's view is clearly not inherentist; he recognizes social and structural features that produce the culture, and looks to the possibility of changing it.

Cultural Inherentism

The retreat from biological inherentism in contemporary racial thought has led some persons to a view one might call "cultural inherentism." The culturally inherentist mindset is, roughly, "These people (Jews, whites, Asians) just are that way (stingy, racist, studious); it's part of their culture." Cultural inherentism is more socially and intellectually acceptable than biological inherentism, which is tainted by association with classic racial thought.[11]

To be sure, cultural inherentism is not intellectually coherent, since cultural characteristics are not inherent; and it is unlikely to survive sustained reflection by someone who manifests an unacknowledged belief in it. Nevertheless, in popular thought, some racial inherentism survives in a culturalist form.

We must therefore distinguish between cultural inherentism and cultural noninherentism. Only the former is characteristic of racial thinking; the latter, even when one regards the group to which it is applied as a racial group, as Cross does, is not a racial way of thinking about that group's alleged characteristics.

Some observers, noting the contemporary waning of biologistic racism have suggested that "race" has now come to *mean* "culture," which sometimes includes religion, language, or ethnicity.[12] Though the word "race" is indeed sometimes used in these ways, the usage undermines any attempt to decide whether a particular usage of the word has drifted so far from its agreed-upon earlier meanings that it has come to constitute a new or different concept. Although there can be no pretense of locating a single true meaning of "race," I would suggest that inherentist understandings of culture preserve the idea central to the moral and social significance that the notion of "race" has always possessed, and that is of characteristics that are fixed and unchangeable because they are part of a group's nature.[13] Noninherentist notions of culture, which attribute explicitly changeable characteristics, are entirely different.[14]

One suspects, as with the conceptual inflation of "racism" discussed earlier, that some of the impetus to expand the scope of reference of "race" is a desire to garner for religious, ethnic, cultural, and national groups the sort of moral and political attention generally associated with racially inferiorized or demonized groups.[15] An individual can, however, give up her religion and change her nationality (neither easy to do, of course), but she can not change her race. (She can "pass," but that is a different matter.) Ethnic groups can change their cultural characteristics, as French-Canadians, for example, became much less religious in the 1960s and after.[16] Linguistic groups are defined by first language, but are not typically thought of as possessing other distinctive characteristics. Race differs from all these other group-defining characteristics in being an inescapable identity and in implying a range of other inherent characteristics. Of course ethnic, linguistic, religious, and national groups can be the target of discrimination, vilification, inferiorization, and demonization. But this just shows that such depredations are not confined to racial groups, not that those groups *are* racial.

As we saw in chapter 6, a distinct strand in nineteenth-century European racial thought attributed inherent characteristics to something like the spirit of a people or race. We can call this "metaphysical inherentism," as it posits an entity which can be understood in a more or less religious way as the source of the allegedly inherent characteristics. This metaphysical source is distinct from a genetic or a cultural one.[17] Some current inherentism has something like this metaphysical form.

Uncommitted Inherentism

Biological, cultural, and metaphysical inherentism all postulate a distinct basis for attributing characteristics to a group. At the same time, there can be an "uncommitted" inherentism that takes the form of neither genetic, metaphysical, nor cultural inherentism. Here the subject attributes characteristics to a racial group, and gives every evidence of regarding these characteristics as inherent in the group. Miguel thinks, "That's just the way these people are"—lazy, stingy, prone to drunkenness, good at dancing, exploitative, and the like. But Miguel has never thought through the implications of his views, and holds no definite opinion as to whether the group is "that way" because of culture, biology, or spirit. I suggest that much inherentist thinking takes this uncommitted form.[18] People have soaked up inherentist ways of thinking about racial groups and may not be entirely aware of having done so. More generally, many persons maintain elements of racial thought without reflectively endorsing them. Not entirely aware of their inherentism, they experience no requirement to justify the belief that the racial group in question possesses the characteristics they attribute to it.

Thus uncommitted inherentism is psychologically unstable. If someone presses Miguel to say why he thinks the group is stingy or lazy, he would naturally seek to provide some sort of account—in culture, genetics, or metaphysics. Alternatively, however, he might find all these explanations implausible, and thus be led to question whether he has any basis for his inherentism at all.[19]

But an uncommitted inherentist might stick to his guns while either rejecting or remaining agnostic about geneticist, cultural, or metaphysical explanations. Miguel might say, "I don't know what makes them lazy. Maybe it's their genes; maybe it's their culture; maybe it's some metaphysical spirit. Maybe it's none of these. I have no idea. What I know is, they *are* lazy."

If Miguel is further pressed, not so much for a rational basis for his belief but simply for an account of how he arrived at it, he might cite his own experience. Of course it is illegitimate to infer from a small sample in one's experience to an entire group; and, in any case, people's interpretation of their own experience—for example, what they perceive as laziness in others—is itself quite often suspect, driven by the very stereotypic generalizations it purports to provide evidence for.[20] Nevertheless, just as familiarly, people do engage in such unwarranted generalizing all the time.

So uncommitted inherentism tends to fall either into genetic, cultural, or metaphysical inherentism, or into an abandonment of inherentism entirely; but it can also persist in the face of self-reflection. An individual might even explicitly and sincerely disavow inherentist thinking, but slip back into it when her mental guard is down.[21]

The Nonexistence of Races: Somatic Variation and Genetic Commonality

Having examined what contemporary belief in races consists in, let us turn to the question whether the groups we call "races"—whites, blacks, Asians and Native Americans—are such. In one sense, the question seems absurd; these are precisely the groups we in the United States *mean* when we speak of races. But racial thinking requires that each group possess a set of distinct characteristics; if they do not possess these characteristics, they are not races.

One argument frequently given against the popular understanding of race is that populations have moved around so much that no race is "pure."[22] Africans and Europeans, for example, have so intermingled with one another that neither group is any longer a pure race. But this argument assumes that a group that is "pure" *would* count as a race—for example, that a group of pure (sub-Saharan) African descent would be a race. This concedes too much to race thinking. Races, in the common view, are not merely groups that share certain somatic characteristics and geographical ancestry that distinguish them from other groups; they are also assumed to differ in mental, emotional, and characterological traits expressed in the idea of a "fundamental division of humankind." Unless the visible characteristics correspond to inherent psychological commonalities within the alleged race, and mark differences among alleged races, the groups defined by those visible characteristics are not races.[23]

Nevertheless, this point about racial mixture does tell against one component of the racial outlook—that the groups we call races can be sharply distinguished in their somatic characteristics. In fact, neither blacks, whites, Native Americans, nor Asians are sufficiently uniform in physical appearance to be fully distinguishable from the other groups; their differences are a matter of degree, not of kind. This lack of clear somatic boundaries around groups classified as different races is, indeed largely a product of the mixing of geographically defined races.

This is particularly obvious with regard to blacks. American and Caribbean blacks, especially the former, have a wide range of skin colors, hair textures, and size and shape of facial features. Many are of lighter skin than others classified as "white," "Asian", and "Native American" and are otherwise physically similar to whites and Native Americans. The reason for this variation is, of course, the peculiar system of classification used in the United States to define "black"—the so-called one-drop rule, according to which an individual with any degree of sub-Saharan African ancestry is counted as black, even if she has a predominance of European ancestry.[24] In the context of the one-drop rule, racial coupling between those of European and African ancestry during the period of slavery (consisting primarily, but not only, in slave masters' sexual relations with their female slaves), helped to create, in subsequent generations, a population of blacks with substantial variation in somatic characteristics. Blacks and Native Americans have also interbred for several centuries, with offspring generally counted as "black."

Because of this wide variation, many blacks have been able to pass as whites, availing themselves of opportunities denied blacks and avoiding the stigma of black racial identity. If passing is possible—if a black can look white enough to be taken as white by whites—then blacks can not be uniformly physically distinct from whites. Hence, according to the common understanding of race, the group designated as "black" in the United States lacks one requirement for being a genuine race.[25] And yet for most Americans the one group most clearly and consistently thought of (by others as well as themselves) as a race are blacks.[26]

Race, as we have frequently noted, is much more than classification by somatic characteristics. How would we determine if racial groups also differ in deeper characteristics inherent in their nature? One obvious place to look would be genetics. Are the groups we call "races" genetically distinct?

Genetic diversity *within* any racial group is far greater than genetic difference *between* races (that is, between the statistical averages of different races).[27] Although there is not yet agreement on the precise percentile estimate of genetic commonality and difference, several respected studies agree that approximately 84–85 percent of *all genetic variation in the entire human species* can be found among a random sample of two people from the same tribal or ethnic group in the same geographical region. This extraordinary fact runs entirely counter to the idea that members of different races are fundamentally different from one another and fundamentally similar to those of the same race.

Of the approximately 15-percent genetic variation not found between "neighbors," slightly less than half—in other words, 6–7 percent of the total average genetic variation among individuals—is distinctly racial in character.[28] To put this another way, genetic differences between two random individuals of different races are only marginally greater than those between two individuals from the same racial group. Moreover, and particularly relevant to the idea of blacks as a race, there is more genetic diversity in sub-Saharan Africa than in the rest of the world combined.[29]

The amount of genetic material that two random individuals share is, according to one estimate, 99.8 percent of their total genetic material; of two random individuals of different races, the shared amount decreases by only .02 percent.[30] So genetically human beings are vastly more alike than different. The groups we call "races" are, as far as all available evidence suggests, only marginally more genetically different from each other than any other random divisions of the human population; they are not races.

This does not mean that there are no statistically significant differences in genetic makeup between racial groups as conventionally understood. (Obviously, genes that control for somatic characteristics conventionally defining races differ significantly among racial groups, although, again, only by a matter of degree.) In addition, molecular polymorphisms are genetic characteristics that are present (or not) in a binary manner; a given individual either possesses the characteristic—for example, a particular blood group, immune type, or enzyme—or does not. Molecular polymorphisms, in contrast to characteristics such as eye color, height, or metabolic rate, are not a matter of degree. Such a blood group allele known as "Duffy Fy^a" is found in 6 percent of blacks, 42 percent of whites and 90 percent of Asians.[31] This degree of racial group difference is significant. If there were a broad range of such genetic differences, they might bear on our ordinary understanding of race; as just mentioned, however, available evidence is that such genetic difference as is found in the Duffy blood group is not broad.

This difference in the presence of a blood group allele, by itself, lends no support to the idea of race for another reason as well: so far as we know, differences in such polymorphisms have no bearing on the mental and behavioral traits that inform our idea of "race." Indeed, *purely* genetic differences—differences described at the level of genes and alleles with no link drawn to traits of character, mind, and temperament—are only tangentially related to popular understandings of "race." Consider the following thought experiment. Imagine two geographically distinct populations numbering in the millions—one located in central Asia and one in Latin America. Research reveals that the two populations are genetically

virtually identical. They contain the same proportion of genetic differences of all significant types. But because they have developed distinct cultures, the two groups are behaviorally and psychologically very different.
One is very cooperative and nonviolent. The other is aggressive and war-
like, constantly threatening its neighbors. Are these two groups of the
same race? If race were simply a question of genetics, the answer would be
obvious, but at the level of the popular notion of race, it is not obvious,
since they are so different in behavior.

Now suppose we imagine a small genetic difference between the two
groups—with respect to genes that determine somatic characteristics traditionally associated with race (skin color, hair texture, and so forth).
Popular thought would now be much more likely to declare these distinct
races, since they differ both somatically and behaviorally. But the judgment would not be based on the marginal *genetic* difference, which is too
minimal to be of significance.

It is not possible to rule out *a priori* the possibility that some respect in
which conventional racial groups do differ genetically will turn out to
bear strongly on some important mental or behavioral characteristic; but
the burden of proof is with the proponents of this view, and there is little
in our current understandings of genetics to support such a view. Regarding this possibility, moreover, the racial group difference in allelic frequency in the Duffy blood group can be positively misleading; it is ex-
ceedingly unlikely that any psychologically or behaviorally interesting
trait is explained by the presence of such an allele. No one has come remotely close to demonstrating a causal link between psychological traits
and the sort of genetic material that has been found in significantly different proportions in different "racial" groups. This is true even of scientists who postulate a genetic underpinning to some humanly important
trait, as Herrnstein and Murray do with regard to "intelligence" in *The Bell
Curve*. They infer a genetic substratum, but have not in any way located or
even attempted to locate it.[32] If there is to be a link between genes and behavior, it will certainly not be in the form of a distinct behavioral or temperamental trait—moodiness, compassion, hyperactivity, laziness—being
the direct expression of a distinct gene or allele.

Let us step back a moment and reflect on the bearing of genetics on
the popular conception of race. It is relevant not because race is itself a
genetic concept. Genetic differences unconnected to psychological traits
have little relevance to the commonsense idea of race. It is relevant because racial thought is inherentist and the only plausible account of how
psychological characteristics could be inherent is that they are genetically
based. This is not to say that racial thinking distinctly affirms the genetic

basis of allegedly inherent traits. Nineteenth century American pre-genetics racial thought did affirm a biological basis for traits but, as we have seen, contemporary racial thought is more frequently of a cultural, metaphysical, or uncommited—that is, nongenetic—inherentist form. If the deep, inherent differences racialism claims do exist, however, they can do so only if there is a genetic basis for them. This is why the evidence that the substantial genetic diversity that does exist in the human species as a whole is mostly present within any geographically located population group, but not between racial groups, is so striking.

The Racial Significance of Sickle-Cell Anemia

Statistically interesting differences in some genetically based characteristics among racial groups are not inconsistent with the overwhelming genetic similarity within the human species. A frequently cited difference concerns sickle-cell anemia (a breakdown, expressed in a sickle-shaped formation, in red blood cells). American blacks are much more prone to this disease than are whites of northern European extraction. The reason for this difference is apparently that in the processes of natural selection Africans and other residents of tropical climates have developed a gene that provides immunity to malaria (a tropical disease), but this gene causes sickle-cell anemia.[33]

Seeing this and other statistical correlations as "racial" in character, however, tends to impose a false commonality that distorts the significance of the correlations. In the sickle-cell case, the source of correlation is not racial but geographical (proximity to the equator). Persons of tropical African descent share this genetic tendency with Arabs of the Arabian peninsula and southern Indians, who would generally be regarded, in our familiar racial schema, as of different races. But the Xhosa tribe of Southern Africa is a nontropical group and does not carry the sickle-cell antimalarial gene.[34] It is not blacks per se but people with ancestors from tropical climates whose grouping is evolutionarily related to a propensity to sickle-cell anemia; and even in this group, by no means all carry the gene. Of course such statistical correlations should be utilized in relevant medical or other practical contexts; American doctors should be more alert to certain symptoms in their African American than in northern European–American patients. But doctors are misled if they see race as the causal factor in such conditions.

In the sickle-cell case the causal and evolutionary factors are known. Frequently, though, researchers are presented with a statistically interesting racial generalization in which the causal links are not known. For example, African Americans are almost twice as likely as whites to suffer from hypertension, or high blood pressure. Here the causes are likely to be a mixture of social (such as poorer health care and greater stress because of societal racism) and perhaps genetic ones. But if one is primed to think in racial terms, one may too quickly ignore the possible social causes, assuming the primacy of an underlying biological one.[35]

Focusing on genetic differences and similarities may mislead us about the character of human behavioral differences and their relation to the groupings we now call "races." Notwithstanding the staggering advances in genetic understanding in the past century, represented by the final mapping of the chemical structure of the human genome in the year 2000, we actually know precious little about the relation between genetic features and the wide range of psychological and behavioral characteristics associated with races—intelligence (in its various modes), artistic propensity, industriousness, apathy, violence, secretiveness, compassion, sociability, trustworthiness, athletic ability, and so on.

Popular writing regarding genetics often falls into the error that has been called "geneticization."[36] Consider the following from a *New York Times* article about recent advances in human genomics: "By contrast with the tiny number of genes that make some people dark-skinned and doe-eyed, and others as pale as napkins, scientists say that traits like intelligence, artistic talent, and social skills are likely to be shaped by thousands, if not tens of thousands, of the 80,000 or so genes in the human genome, all working in complex combinatorial combination."[37] Though overall the article is making the valuable antirace point that all the genes for such important characteristics as intelligence are extremely unlikely to be transmitted in way that would allow for differentiation among races, the passage could easily be read to imply that characteristics such as intelligence and social skills are strongly genetically determined (even if in a complex way).[38] But no such correlation has ever been demonstrated. It seems highly likely that human social skills for example, are strongly affected by culture and learning. The current fascination with genetics should not lead us to believe that the contribution of genetic structure to qualities of mind and psyche vastly outstrips that of culture, learning, habituation, and other processes of human social and cultural life.

Science and Race

Natural and social scientists in the twentieth century have disagreed about the scientific value of the concept of "race." This disagreement cannot be settled by showing (as I have attempted to do) that the groups popularly called races do not possess the features required by the popular concept of race. For particular sciences may have reason to utilize "race" as a theoretical term that does not carry the associations that it carries in popular thought.

But if geneticists or anthropologists do craft a viable meaning for "race," this will not necessarily tell us anything about whether races, in the ordinary understanding, exist. For example, population geneticists, drawing on an increasingly sophisticated understanding of the structure of DNA and of the processes of genetic transmission, have developed a notion of a "breeding population"—a relatively reproductively isolated human group that differs significantly from others in the frequency of certain genes—and some have proposed calling such a group a "race."[39] The choice of terminology has a historical basis within the biological sciences; "races" have been considered biologically significant subdivisions of the human species. And the definition accords with the assumption in evolutionary theory that breeding populations represent "the primary unit of analysis for evolutionary change."[40]

Nevertheless, this definition contains an arbitrariness regarding racial classification that could sow confusion when brought into relation with popular understandings of race. First, genetic characteristics are frequently not "concordant"; that is, they do not vary together. So populations that differ with respect to one characteristic may well not differ with respect to another. For example, scholars of an earlier generation grouped African and New Guinean pygmies together on the basis of body shape, skin color, hair form, and nose shape; but later scholarship has indicated significant differences between the two groups in the hereditary components of their blood.[41] Hence selecting distinct genetically significant characteristics as bases for classifying races will result in a hodgepodge of different classification schemes. For instance, if an antimalarial gene is the criterion, Swedes and Xhosas will be one race and Italians, Greeks, Saudi Arabians, and most sub-Saharan Africans another. Possession of the enzyme lactase (enabling digestion of lactose) would place Northern Europeans, North Indians, and west African Fulani in one race, with Japanese, Native Americans, and most other sub-Saharan Africans in another.[42] There are many such possible classifications, depending on the genetic trait in question, and the resultant groupings almost never correspond with one another. Moreover, few such classifications are likely to generate groups that correspond to racial groups as traditionally understood.

Within scientific discourse this multiplicity of "racial" classification schemes may not be a problem; for particular purposes, each may contribute to scientific understanding. But such an understanding of race, a contextual one allowing for multiple racial categorizations, is far different from the popular one, in which races are understood as fundamental human subdivisions. Using the same term for these two very different beasts could lead to misunderstanding when the lay public "overhears" conversations among population geneticists.

A deeper problem for the idea of a race as a breeding population is the character and degree of reproductive isolation required for a group to count as a race. Audrey Smedley asks if we are to regard the inhabitants of a small town in Colorado in which a high percentage intermarry as a distinct race from those in a similar town in Vermont, because these are very reproductively isolated from one another.[43] Are small, geographically localized ethnic minority groups that set up strong cultural barriers to interbreeding with the wider society—such as the Amish—to be counted as races?[44]

Finally, this definition of "race" may involve unwarranted assumptions, such as that each reproductively isolated group will in fact possess distinctive frequencies of genes and their allelic variants in relation to significant traits.[45] Such an assumption seems implausible if the reproductive isolation is understood literally, as in Smedley's above example. Such groups are unlikely to be genetically distinct from one another in any interesting way.

If this assumption is jettisoned and the definition of "race" is confined only to those reproductively isolated groups that do in fact possess distinctive gene pools for significant traits, many geographically isolated groups will not be races at all. And the ones that satisfy this condition will still be subject to the contextual multiplicity—the degree of arbitrariness involved in selecting genetic characteristics to count as "significant" for classificatory purposes—that renders this definition far distant from that of race in the ordinary sense.

Scientists in a given field, then, may define "race" in a manner that can be defended by criteria of theory construction in that field, but one must then look closely to see whether that definition is so distant from popular understandings as to provide nothing in the way of support for the idea that races as we ordinarily understand them exist.[46]

Science is an integral part of society, and scientific findings and concepts can make their way into popular discourse. For this reason, scientific attempts to confine a particular concept such as "race" to a usage internal to a given scientific community may be unsuccessful. The concept may be taken up in popular discourse in a manner that preserves its traditional popular associations—even if the associations are explicitly rejected in the scientific definition. The deeply rooted character of racial thinking in U.S. culture renders it likely that any scientific usage of "race" in the near future will be taken, at least to some significant extent, to support current popular understandings. Even if population geneticists say that races exist *only* in the sense of a genetically significant, reproductively isolated group, popular thought may appropriate that as affirming that "races exist" in the popular understanding of that idea. Moreover, scientists are not themselves immune from influence by popular thought. It is reasonable to worry that, despite attempts to provide a theoretical meaning for a concept entirely distinct from the popular one, scientists may not be able to shake those associations. They may therefore be led unwittingly to incorporate false popular understandings into their own discourse.

Not all scientists wish to remain aloof from popular concerns and discourse, in defining theoretical terms in a manner wholly distinct from popular usage. Some of them do want to weigh in, hoping that scientific understandings can clarify confusions or misunderstandings in popular thought. To do so requires an engagement with popular vocabularies and understandings. Elazar Barkan has shown that after World War I (and especially after the ascension of Hitler to power in 1933), a group of (primarily) anthropologists in the United States and biologists in Britain had a not insignificant impact in discrediting racial ideologies among the general public in their respective nations.[47]

Nevertheless, scientific discourse proferred in popular venues has sometimes served to confuse the political core of race, and has thereby masked its full range of moral implications in popular discourse. Audrey Smedley points out that in his attempt to undermine the nineteenth-century connection between biology and personality and cultural characteristics, the German American anthropologist Franz Boas seemed to regard the concept of race that he was attacking as a purely scientific idea. He reasoned, therefore, that decisive arguments against race's scientific forms would deal a fatal blow to popular appropriation of the concept and the prejudices founded on it.[48]

What Boas missed, Smedley says, is the folk origins of the concept of race—the way it emerged as a rationalization of domination, exploitation, and slavery. This same error afflicts physiologist and geneticist Jared Diamond's account of race. Diamond argues that traditional racial classifications, and indeed any classifications grounded in phenotype, are biologically of little or no value. Yet he explains the existence of the popular phenotype-based forms of racial classification as lying in "the body's signals for differentiating attractive from unattractive sex partners, and for differentiating friend from foe."[49] Whether this account is plausible as an evolutionary explanation of the familiar differentiation of human populations along the lines of the phenotypic differences (skin color, hair texture, and the like), it certainly does *not* explain why popular thought attributes racial significance to these characteristics. It does not explain race, because race did not arise in human consciousness as a product of sexual selection, but as a way that European colonizers came to see Native Americans and Africans in the process of inferiorizing and dehumanizing them. Like Boas, Diamond sees race as fundamentally generated through processes internal to the development of scientific ideas, rather than as a political and moral idea given legitimacy through science.

Popular ideas of race, confused as they certainly are, remain in place not primarily because of scientific misunderstandings but through the weight of a racialized history and the current legacy of racial depredations. Science has a limited, though far from trivial, role to play in undermining some of the intellectual props of popular racial ideas. But seriously weakening popular attachment to race requires doing battle with the *political* foundations of race thinking; to that end the achievement of a more just and less racially divided society is the crucial task.

8

Racialized Groups and Social Constructions

D oes the nonexistence of races mean, then, that "blacks," "whites," "Asians," and "Native Americans" refer simply to collections of individuals who have nothing in common other than that a racial label has wrongly been applied to them? No, it does not.

For several centuries Americans believed that the groups we now call "whites," "blacks," "Asians," and "Native Americans" were races, and as a result of this belief the groups have been treated so. American society structured into its institutions and norms of group interaction the idea that whites were a superior and more worthy "race"—through slavery, segregation, naturalization laws, immigration policies, and discrimination in education, housing, and labor. By purveying the idea that all "nonwhites" were inferior or deficient in some regard, that this was most especially true of "blacks," and that people of different races were to be separated from one another, educational and scientific authority as well as popular thought rationalized institutional racial hierarchy and separation.

This process is what I mean by "racialization," which is the treating of groups as if there were inherent and immutable differences between them; *as if* certain somatic characteristics marked the presence of significant characteristics of mind, emotion, and character; and *as if* some were of greater worth than others.[1]

Over time, certain groups once seen as races have come to be seen as something else, for instance as ethnic groups. This is what happened to southern and eastern European immigrant groups (though they were never seen as paradigmatic races). And some groups are seen and treated as races in the present in part because they were so seen and treated in the past. Whether a group is racialized is a matter of its treatment by the larger society. Whether the group takes on a self-identity as a race is a different matter. The contrast between "whites" and "blacks" is instructive in this regard. Through law, custom, and popular understanding and behavior, people of African descent were turned into the racial group "black." They were consigned to a subordinate place in society, denied various rights, discriminated against, and subjected to norms meant to keep them separate from whites, all on the basis that they were members of "the black race." Blacks by and large accepted racialism with regard to themselves and whites; they accepted the idea that both groups were races, though often rejecting the implication of their own inferiority.

Whiteness was similarly built into the structure of American society. Until this century, it was a prerequisite for naturalization. More generally, in seeing the "nonwhite" races as inferior, people of European descent became the superior racial counterpart. (Of course it was largely powerful whites who did the creating, though powerless whites often bought into that creation.) Whiteness, however, was generally less explicitly defined than were the other racial identities. Ian Haney-Lopez points to one aspect of this inexplicitness in his discussion of the large number of naturalization cases brought before sundry courts of the nation, which determined whether Syrians, Indians, Armenians, Chinese, and Japanese persons were sufficiently white to count under the 1790 Naturalization Act and subsequent laws and constitutional amendments.[2] The courts treated whiteness as if it were a natural, biological category, yet were entirely inconsistent in its definition and application.

Although for much of American history subsequent to the development of the idea of "race" whites were not reluctant to avow their whiteness and its alleged superiority, as the dominant group they did not have to think about their whiteness or what it consisted in. They constituted the norm, the "we" against whom the various inferiorized "they"s were defined. Thus whiteness was always a kind of inexplicit identity to those who possessed it, as the color term used to represent it suggests, while at the same time it constituted an indispensable source of value.[3]

This inexplicitness, as we saw in chapter 3, deepened in the post–Civil Rights era, for three reasons. First, "color blindness" was understood to imply that it was inappropriate and possibly even racist to take note of people's racial identity. In addition, many whites came to think that the antidiscrimination legislation and rulings of the Civil Rights era had created a level playing field in which race no longer really mattered. So calling attention to whiteness was not only frowned upon; it was unnecessary, passé. Finally, the rise of white ethnic consciousness in the 1970s and its validation in the multicultural era of the 1980s and beyond provided whites with an alternative identity that appeared to replace whiteness (though actually presupposing it).[4]

Yet whiteness continues to structure life chances and opportunities in every domain of social existence. It remains a deeply meaningful social identity, even if whites do not explicitly acknowledge or even recognize it as such. Of course, few whites would actually disavow their whiteness, even their mere classificatory whiteness. That is, they know what to check off on the Census when presented with an array of "racial choices," even if they might want to add that "it doesn't mean anything." Thus "whites" remain very much a racialized group.

Because of their social and historical treatment, members of racialized groups share certain experiences (for example, discrimination, stigmatization, exclusion, and privilege).[5] Often they adopt a group identity based on the experience of racialization, and such self-claiming may further contribute to their racialization. American blacks have forged a distinct group identity in the face of being treated as a race. In partial contrast, Asian Americans have not generally embraced a racialized identity, although they are often seen as a racial group by others.

Panethnicity and Racialization

Racialization is best understood against the background of "panethnicity," the word for a grouping of disparate ethnocultural groups under a common umbrella identity.[6] "Hispanic/Latino," "Native American," and "Asian American" name panethnic groups (these designations can also be understood racially). The precise boundaries of the group are often not fixed. "Hispanic/Latino" includes U.S. Americans with ancestry from Latin America (sometimes Brazil is included, and sometimes Spain; both are matters of contention). "Native American" is also a panethnic group, an identity for the quite diverse tribal groups of North America. "Asian American" is taken to refer either to U.S. Americans whose ancestry lies in the nations of east and southeast Asia or (more recently) to that group plus South Asian Americans.

The impetus to forming panethnic groups in the United States is multifaceted.[7] Joining with others gives a racialized or ethnocultural group visibility, political influence, and power that it could not have on its own;

Asian Americans, for example, have a political and social presence that Vietnamese Americans alone cannot have. The subgroups composing a given panethnic group are often quite culturally distinct from one another, and, especially in the nation of origin, might even be hostile to one another (Japanese and Koreans, for example). But generally there is greater cultural commonality among the ethnocultural groups within a panethnic group than between those and ethnocultural groups comprising another panethnicity. Culturally, Chinese Americans share more with Laotian Americans than with Colombian Americans.

One of the strongest reasons for forming panethnicities is discriminatory treatment or stigmatizing as a member of the racial group corresponding to the panethnicity. A watershed in contemporary Asian American panethnic formation, for example, was the murder in 1982 of Vincent Chin, a Chinese American mistaken for a Japanese American (or, possibly, for a generic "Asian" on whom the murderer took out his anti-Japanese resentments).[8] Discriminatory treatment toward Asian ethnocultural groups is frequently directed toward them not as Laotians or Chinese but as "Asians."

Though panethnicity is not itself a cultural or ethnic identity, it is sometimes treated, especially by outgroup members, as if it were. That is, non-Asians often regard "Asian American" as a group with a single ethnoculture and identity. (This is not the same, though, as treating it as a racial group.) "Asian Americans" are a relatively recent panethnic formation, and those who are so called are concerned that their internal diversity be recognized. One of the ironies of Asian American political efficacy, for example, was its gaining recognition in the Census for the many distinct Asian ethnicities, while retaining the recognition that all these groups deserved protection against discrimination (a major purpose of Census categories since 1970). In the 1990 Census, respondents were asked to self-designate from a list of "Asian or Pacific Islander" ethnic categories—Chinese, Laotian, and so on—which were collectively called a "race" on the census form. (In 2000 the list of ethnic choices was retained, and, though the overall grouping was not explicitly called a race, the question to be answered was "What is this person's race?", with "white", "black, African American, or Negro," "American Indian or Alaska Native," and "some other race" as alternatives for non-Asians.)[9] It was only through the submerging of their particularity in an overall panethnicity that the ethnic particularities gained recognition on the Census.

Though panethnicity is not a cultural identity (or only a weak one at best), and though it is generally created for strategic reasons, it can nevertheless be personally important as a communal or collective identity. Many Asian Americans' identity as such may be no less significant to them than their Chinese American or Indian American identity. For very assimilated Asian Americans whose ethnic identity may be weak, it may be even more important. Or the two different types of identities might both be important, but in different contexts. On the other hand, panethnicity can also seem like an artificial, contrived identity; Eric Liu, for example, expresses this idea in the title of his book *The Accidental Asian*.[10]

"European American" is coming to be a panethnic identity for whites of European ancestry, though the political purposes of such an identity do not parallel those of the other groups mentioned; for example, there is no history of stigma and victimization to provide a common identity, nor minority status that provides a reason for common cause. "European American" is both benign—giving an ethnic-like identity to those whose backgrounds are too mixed to claim a specific ethnicity—and problematic in that it implies that all ethnicities of Americans are on the same social level (or, to put it another way, that white ethnicities do not partake of white privilege).[11]

The boundaries of panethnic groups generally correspond to those of racialized groups—European Americans ("whites"), Asian Americans ("yellows"), Native Americans ("reds"). This is not surprising, since racial mistreatment is one important reason for panethnic formation. But since it is not the only reason, the boundaries are not precisely coincident. The recent official inclusion of South Asians in the "Asian" or "Asian/Pacific Islander" Census category suggests two distinct possibilities—a racialized group (or panethnic group with a racial impetus) that *omits* South Asians; and a panethnic group that *includes* South Asians. South Asians lobbied the Census Bureau for inclusion as "Asians" partly on the grounds that they were discriminated against as Indians, historically and in the present,[12] but they are not generally regarded as the same racial group as East and Southeast Asians.

As personal identities, panethnicity and race are distinct. Panethnicity involves an awareness of component ethnic identities even where these are not important to the individual in question; race does not. Panethnicity invokes culture; race invokes stigma, discrimination, and hierarchy. Nevertheless, in practice these different elements are often mixed up together, as David Hollinger's felicitous phrase "ethnoracial groups" expresses.[13]

Latinos as an Incompletely Racialized Group

Panethnicity allows us to recognize a vital difference between race and racialization. Race is an "all or nothing" matter: groups and individuals are either of a particular race or not (though there may be disagreement as to which race some individuals should be assigned to, as Haney-Lopez's discussion of the naturalization cases shows).[14] Here I am interested in the group rather than the individual dimension of this categorization. Every group that is a race is equally a race. In contrast say, to being respected by others, being cohesive, or being politically engaged, being a race is not a matter of degree.

Racialization, however, *is* a matter of degree—determined by a particular society and a particular history. Racialization concerns the way a group is experienced, viewed, and treated in a society at a given time in its history, and it includes the character of the identity the group has appropriated for itself.

The difference between race and racialization is well exemplified by the group in the United States called "Latinos" or "Hispanics" (both terms are used, for the first time, on the 2000 Census[15]), a group I have sometimes intentionally omitted in listings of racial groups. "Latino/Hispanic," as I shall call it in this chapter, is unquestionably a panethnic group. But is it a race? In light of my argument that there are no races, I would answer that question "no." Are they a race in the popular sense of "race," in which "blacks" and "whites" are paradigm races? To this I would respond that a "yes" or "no" answer can not be provided. Are Latino/Hispanics, then, a racialized group? I would say "partially."

On the federal Census only this ethnoracial group is granted a distinct status other than race (implying that it is an "ethnicity"). The Census thus allows individuals to select a Latino/Hispanic (that is, ethnic-like) identity *and* a white, black, or Asian racial identity.[16] In this official sense, then, Latinos are not a race.

In addition, the two largest Latino ethnic groups in the United States, Mexican Americans and Puerto Ricans, explicitly think of themselves as "mixed race." (The general idea of such mixedness is captured in the Spanish word *mestizaje*.[17]) Such self-designation is especially made by Mexican Americans, as Mexican identity is viewed as an amalgam of Spanish and indigenous peoples.[18] (There were relatively few African slaves in Mexico, and this phenotypic strand has largely been physically "absorbed" into the general population, so is not generally recognized as a distinctive element in the mix.[19]) With various degrees of explicitness, most Latin American nations view themselves as similarly mixed, with different mixtures predominating in different nations. Although *mestizaje* implies a plurality of races making up the mix, some Latin Americans refer to the resultant mix as itself a race. Thus Mexicans and Chicanos (Mexican Americans) sometimes refer to themselves as "La Raza," the race. (Brazilians, though Portuguese-speaking, hence not Hispanic, and thus at best problematically "Latino," are comparable to Latin Americans in important respects, and sometimes think of themselves as a distinct, Brazilian, race.[20]) If Latinos are a plurality of national races, and if those are themselves mixtures of paradigmatic races (blacks, whites, indigenous peoples) and are viewed that way by Latinos themselves, they cannot all be one race.

Moreover, because of this historical *mestizaje*, persons of Latin American ancestry in the United States have a wide range of somatic characteristics, which span the conventional phenotypes of paradigmatic races—blacks, Native Americans, and whites. So from the perspectives of official categorization, of self-identification, especially in the nation of origin (or commonwealth in the case of Puerto Rico), and of physical appearance in the U.S. context, Latinos do not represent a race.

Nevertheless, Latino/Hispanics are by no means unequivocally regarded, either by others or themselves, as *not* a race, in the popular meaning. Several factors tilt toward a racial way of viewing this group. First, despite the wide range of phenotypes, many Latinos' skin color is a shade of brown or bronze distinct from the large majority of both whites and blacks. With the powerful propensity in U.S. culture toward racialization and seeing somatic differences in a race-like manner, it is easy for Latino/Hispanics to be viewed as "browns" in a racial color spectrum.

Furthermore, when the Latin American, in contrast to the more broadly Hispanic version of the identity is emphasized, colonization becomes salient. The original occupants of Latin American lands were colonized by Spanish conquerors, and, with the subsequent importation of African slaves, Latinos today often experience themselves as a formerly colonized and thus inferiorized people. This legacy contributes to a more racialized self-understanding in the nation of origin that carries over to the immigrant generation and to some extent beyond.

In addition, in part because the two largest Latino/Hispanic groups, Mexican Americans and Puerto Ricans, were incorporated through war and conquest (and, in the case of Puerto Rico, remain in a dependent territorial relationship), Latinos' experience in the United States also has an inferiorized, and in this respect racialized, dimension. On various standard measures of socioeconomic status, Latino/Hispanics are much closer to blacks and Native Americans than to whites.[21] Moreover, these groups, by and large, occupy a lower position on the social scale, a further racializing factor.

Also, in light of antidiscrimination legislation and affirmative action, there are benefits to the various Latino national subgroups in forming an overarching identity that can be seen as a disadvantaged racial, or at least race-like, minority. Despite its official nonrace status on the Census, the Latino/Hispanic category is there because the group is discriminated against in a manner analogous to the groups labeled "races" on the Census; so it is essentially treated, by those who make use of Census data, as a racial or race-like minority.

If we try to put these diverse and contrary tendencies together into an answer to the question whether Latinos/Hispanics are a race in the popular understanding of that concept, it is impossible to give a definitive answer. But one can say that Latino/Hispanics are a panethnic group that is viewed (both by ingroup and outgroup) as *partially* racialized.

So one group can be more racialized than another group; and the degree of racialization depends not only on historical factors but local ones. In parts of the country with heavy concentrations of Mexican Americans, like California, that group may be seen more racially than other Latinos, and also seen as something like equally racially with blacks. At the same time, some groups in the United States (whites and blacks) have fully undergone the process of racialization.

Racialized identity is context-bound and a matter of degree in another sense as well. Races are not confined to nations. There are blacks in Africa, the U.S., the Caribbean, the United Kingdom, and elsewhere. On the standard binary understanding of racial classification, all these persons are *equally* "black." But in the United States, groups inside its borders are those most distinctly regarded as races. This is most strongly true of blacks. In practice, most white U.S. Americans regard African Americans as more paradigmatically black than Afro-Caribbeans and even Africans. When they think of race, and of who is a racial group, African Americans provide the standard. It is to this group that white Americans most commonly attribute racial characteristics—"otherness," homogeneity, certain mental and temperamental characteristics, and so on. White Americans, and perhaps other nonblacks as well, especially those whose ancestors have been in this country for several generations, are much less likely to have as clearly defined a sense of Africans as possessing certain definite racial characteristics as they are of African Americans. In this sense, one might say that the boundaries around racialized groups do not precisely correspond to those around races. Again, this is in no way to deny that if asked what racial group a (sub-Saharan, nonwhite [e.g., South African or Zimbabwean]) belongs to, few white Americans will hesitate to say "black." These groups are equally classificatorily "black." But the form and extent of racialization—seeing a group as a race—is not coextensive with mere practices of racial classification. The former but not the latter comes with the social meanings described in chapters 5–7.

Alternatives to Racial Identity

This contextualization of racialization applies, to some degree, to immigrant, ethnic, and panethnic groups, as well as to groups in other countries. From a purely conceptual or classificatory point of view, panethnic groups can well also be, or overlap strongly with, racial groups. Both Asian Americans and European Americans are simultaneously panethnic groups and racial groups. Similarly, ethnic groups are parts of larger racial groups—Jamaican Americans are black, Irish Americans are white, and Korean Americans are Asian. Immigrant groups also "have race". A Nigerian immigrant is black. A Vietnamese immigrant is Asian (again, the racial, not the panethnic category). A Polish immigrant is white.

At the level of classification, then, there is no inconsistency between fully having an ethnicity, a panethnicity, an immigrant status, and a race. But in respect to the degree to which a group is in everyday life viewed by others racially, with all the baggage this normally implies, a panethnic, ethnic, or immigrant identity may at least partly crowd out a racialized identity.

Mary Waters's work on Caribbean immigrants in New York City is suggestive concerning the relations among immigrant, ethnic, and racial identities. Waters studied whites' perceptions of African American and Caribbean workers at two work sites. She found that "the whites who worked at American Food and the white teachers we interviewed tended to see the immigrants as sharing an immigrant identity with them—because many of these whites are the descendants of European immigrants." Of the immigrants themselves, she says that "the act of immigration tends to erase the slave narrative and replace it with an immigrant narrative."[22] That is, the immigrant narrative is, in part, an alternative to a racial narrative, deemphasizing victimization and the sense of inferiorization bound up with race. In its providing whites a sense that they have something in common with the Caribbeans, it dampens the strong sense of otherness that is integral to racial perception. In these ways, an immigrant identity can weaken, at least to some extent, a racialized sense of the group in question.

Countering this deracializing element is the powerful salience of "black" phenotypic characteristics, which exert a racializing force that can homogenize immigrant blacks and native blacks in the view of the white majority. This racializing factor is even more powerful toward those in the next generation who have lost the most obvious markers of immigrant identity (a Caribbean accent, for example). Waters found that the second generation much more strongly identified with African Americans—seeing themselves and being seen more exclusively as "black."[23]

What is true of immigrant identity is also true, though to a lesser extent, of ethnic identity. That is, the idea of ethnicity carries a weaker sense of both otherness and inherency than does race. Jesse Jackson's campaign to encourage American blacks to adopt "African American" as their preferred identity label is interesting in this regard. Jackson wanted to emphasize that American blacks (in the sense of those whose ancestry lay in the slave era) had a distinctive culture as well as a race. But he did not mean for this recognition to mask the fact that American blacks were a racial group. He could take for granted that, as the most explicitly racialized of American groups, blacks or African Americans would themselves never be confused as to the race-related disadvantages and stigma with which they were encumbered. The ethnicization carried by "African American" has produced some confusion, however, among nonblacks, whites in particular. For them, the ethnicized identity does in fact mask racial disadvantage.[24] It encourages whites to think of blacks as just another ethnic group.

The degree of a group's racialization vis-à-vis its ethnicization is not easy to determine. We can say with certainty that it is not revealed solely in the degree of the dominant culture's use of racial as against ethnocultural vocabulary in referring to the group. We saw that people are often reluctant to talk about someone's race, and that ethnic categories are generally less charged and more acceptable; but someone using the language of ethnicity may still be thinking about the group in question in a fully racialized way. Thus, although the label "African American" invites nonblacks to supplant a racial with an ethnic way of viewing American blacks, it very seldom has this actual effect. The actual withering away of a racial way of viewing African Americans is obviously nowhere on the horizon.[25]

Is "Race" a Social Construction?

Recent academic writing frequently refers to race as a "social construct" or "social construction."[26] This language can illuminate the meaning of "race," but only if it clearly and explicitly distinguishes between races, which do not exist, and racialized groups, which do. The statement "race is a social construction" does not draw that distinction, and can lead to obfuscation rather than illumination.

Several distinct meanings have been attached to the term "social construction."[27] One is that the thing in question has been wrongly thought to be a product of "natural" (biological or physical) processes when it is in fact a product of social ones. Masculinity and femininity are frequently cited examples. Femininity in a given society involves not merely the possession of certain bodily organs and a particular chromosomal structure ("nature") but socially prescribed ways of behaving. This notion of social construction is sometimes but not necessarily conjoined with the view that only biological or physical entities or processes are "real" while social ones are not.

In the classic nineteenth-century sense races were purported to be natural rather than socially constructed; for they were understood as biological entities, in the same sense that the human species is. A racialized group, however, is socially constructed rather than natural, a group created by social and historical forces and treated as if it were a race.

A second meaning of "social construction" is that the thing in question is defined by social convention, and so is marked by an element of arbitrariness. Conventions of games, such as strikes, passed balls, and field positions in baseball, are examples. What makes something a strike is in a sense arbitrary. Baseball could have developed, or been "constructed", in such a way that four strikes instead of three counted as an out. In this sense strikes are indeed social constructs. But within the actual rules of baseball, it is not arbitrary that a particular pitched ball is a strike rather than a ball. Strikes are perfectly real; one simply has to understand the sort of convention-bound reality they possess.

An example of social construction more relevant to race is that of nations,[28] which are historically contingent human creations that need not have existed or developed the particular character they have. The difference between baseball and nations is that everyone recognizes the conventional dimension of the former but not always the latter. Nations are sometimes talked or thought about as if they were natural human forms, primordial communities, created by God, destined to serve an historical mission, and the like. Rather, nations are, in Benedict Anderson's striking phrase, "imagined communities."[29] Because people can forget this, and especially because a "natural" view of nations provides fertile soil for virulent and destructive forms of nationalism, the idea of social construction can serve to remind us of the historically contingent character of nations. In this sense, a social-construction perspective is sometimes spoken of as "denaturalizing" that which is constructed.

Races are often spoken of as social constructions in this sense. But while there *are*, in fact, nations, there are *not* races. The groups we call "races" do not possess the features popular understanding attributes to races. In this sense "whites," "blacks," "Asians," and "Native Americans" are not races; they are racialized groups. By contrast, Nigeria, Mexico, and Thailand *are* nations.

Unlike races, racialized groups are real, and like nations they can provide a foundation for an appropriate and important social identity, for loyalty, for a sense of community and shared fate (though not a shared destiny[30]), for sentiments of shame and pride. But as social creations they may wrongly be viewed as if they were natural, and they may encourage misplaced attachments, overblown and excessive loyalties, and disproportion in how one regards one's racialized identity in relation to other significant identities. Such distortions of racialized identities are likely to stem from wrongly thinking that one is not merely a member of a racialized group but of an actual race. But they are also possible in someone who is fully aware that her racial identity is socially and historically created and contingent.

Imagine, for example, an Asian American who recognizes and accepts a racialized (not merely panethnic) identity as "Asian"—seeing the source of that identity in the resentments, discrimination, and stereotyping to which her group is subject, not in characteristics inherent in her racial group. She may exaggerate the importance of this racialized identity in relation to her other identities—professor, Korean American, parent, resident of Peoria, woman, lover of tennis. She may, for example, become blind to the fact that groups other than her own also suffer from discrimination and stereotyping. She may fail to recognize that despite differences she has much in common with other women professors.

Misunderstandings of Social Construction

The idea of social construction has been subject to misunderstandings (often with some basis in the writings of its proponents) that bear clearing up if we are to make the best use of it in understanding "race." For one thing, "social construction" has sometimes been taken to imply that we could do away with what is socially constructed (genders, nations, racialized groups) if we so chose. Certainly, to recognize something as a human creation implies that it need not exist, at least in the form that it does, and thereby provides a basis for hope that we could live without various forms of injustice, oppression, and constraint attached to such creations. But to think we can simply jettison those creations is to fall prey to a kind of social voluntarism regarding social structures and identities. Racialized thinking is deeply embedded in our social existence; its constructedness notwithstanding, we may not be able to change these social forms without far-ranging and currently barely imaginable changes in familiar structures, such as an end to racial inequality and race-based social segregation.

A related misunderstanding of the import of social construction is that it is simply a form of labeling or categorizing: to be black is simply to be labeled or identified according to the rules that govern the practice of racial categorization. But this is like saying that to be a judge is simply to be a person whom society labels "judge." To be a judge is a good deal more; it involves being accorded authority to engage in certain behavior within certain institutional structures. Similarly, to *be* a racialized black person is not simply to be called "black." For racialization imposes certain ways of viewing the person who is called or self-identified as "black"—as having something fundamental and natural in common with other black people; as radically other than persons of different races; and as possessing certain humanly significant characteristics inherent in her racial nature.[31]

If there are no races, it might seem natural to express this truth by saying that to be black is just to be called "black" by one's society, or to call oneself "black". But, consider the following incident: In 1977 two aspiring firefighters who were brothers identified themselves as "black" on a civil service exam. Under an affirmative action plan that admitted black aspirants with lower scores than whites to firefighter vacancies, the Malone brothers joined the force. They served for ten years. Then the fire commissioner noticed that they had been classified as black. They were promptly fired, but appealed, in a case that appeared before the Supreme Judicial Court of Massachusetts.[32]

All available evidence brought before the court led it to conclude that the Malones were white.[33] Despite their claiming of the category "black," they seemed quite clearly to be white. They were members of the racialized group "white," despite claiming to be black, just as I am an American even if I go to the United Kingdom, affect a British accent, and attempt to pass myself off as British.[34]

In the sense of a racialized group, the Malone brothers were white, not black; they were not merely identified or categorized as white. Still, racialized groups are social constructs, just as nations are; they are not natural, biological entities.

The social construction of race sometimes takes the form, "Biological races are not real, but social races are," or "Race is socially but not biologically real." If the social reality attributed to "race" involved decisively discarding the moral and conceptual trappings that attend popular understandings of it—as the idea of "racialized groups" is meant to do—I would not object to these expressions. Frequently, however, this social interpretation of race reimports all the associations of radical differentness among groups and commonality among all members of a group, excepting only the idea that characteristics of the group are grounded in their biology.[35] At this point in our history, I think *any* conferring of reality on "race" is likely to carry these false and invidious associations. The term "racialized groups" is preferable as a way of acknowledging that some groups have been *created* by being treated as if they were races, while also acknowledging that "race" in its popular meaning is entirely false.

Scalar Uses of Race

In the film *Boys on the Side*, a black character, Jane, calls a white character, Robin, "the whitest gal on the face of the earth."[36] The qualified inherentist regards some members of a racial group as "more black" or "more white," and the selective racist does as well. Yet some people are baffled or outraged at such "scalar" uses of racial concepts.[37] "Either he's black or he isn't. You can't be 'more black'." What sense can we make of this interpretation of scalar race?

Scalar concepts admit of degrees, binary ones do not; "pregnant" is a binary concept, and "tall" is scalar. But race admits of both versions. Classification is a binary use of "race." To which racial group does a person belong—black, white, Native American, Latino, Asian? In this classificatory sense, a person can not be "more black." She can, perhaps, be *more obviously* black. That is, it might be less or more easy to discern whether she is black. But *whether* she is black is not a matter of degree.

"Racialization" can be a matter of degree, but only at the level of the group, not of the individual. Whether an individual is a member of a given racialized group remains a binary matter. What is a scalar conception of race that applies at the individual level?

Two pertinent features of racialized groups are that they involve membership in a collectivity, and that cultural characteristics may become associated with that collectivity, and with the group identity. Thus, when Robin first meets Jane in the film, she tells Jane that she has done some singing—songs by the Carpenters. This revelation, together with the way Robin talks and dresses, prompts Jane's scalar racial remark. (Jane wouldn't have made the remark, probably, if Robin had said she sang Bonnie Raitt or Janis Joplin songs.[38]) Thus one meaning of a scalar concept of race is cultural.

There are several other scalar uses of race. (1) A person can make her racial identity less or more central to her overall identity. A "less black" person relates less of what she does and experiences to her black identity. (Or a person embraces her racial group identity, as contrasted with wishing she were something else.[39]) (2) A person can be less or more personally and socially involved with these in her racial group. A "more Asian" person hangs out primarily with other Asians or Asian American. (3) A person can be less or more devoted to the welfare of her group. A "more black" person can be what has been called a "race man" or "race woman"—someone devoted to the advancement of black people. (4) A person can adhere less or more to, and express, political values taken as appropriate to a racial group. Being a black nationalist or separatist is a way of being "more black." (Obviously there can be a good deal of disagreement over what should constitute the political values of a given racial group.)

Although empirically many of these tendencies occur together, they are distinct and can operate independently. A Latino individual may live in a very white-centered professional and social world yet make his Latino identity central to his self-conception and engage in activities aimed at bettering the lot of Latinos. A black person can be socially "more black" but politically "less black." And so on.

In general, racial scalarity has a different moral valence for whites than for persons of color. It is impossible for a white person to be devoted to the welfare of whites, or to be "politically white", without being very close to a white supremacist. Cultural or social whiteness are somewhat less suspect. Devotion to the welfare of one's inferiorized racial group, by contrast, is largely a good.

In general, the terrain marked out by scalar uses of race is quite emotionally and morally charged. For people of color, the idea of "racial degrees" raises issues of group loyalty, of deserting one's group for a taste of power and acceptance in the dominant group, of assimilation. As long as there are dominant groups, subordinate groups, inferiorized groups, and not-fully-accepted groups, it is hard to envision the terrain of scalar race disappearing. That is, it is hard to imagine not only scalar judgments being made (especially by members of the racial group themselves), but value being attached to those judgments.

Some observers worry about such judgments sowing dissension within race-based communities, and also about their constricting the autonomy of those held to standards of scalar blackness and the like. Stephen Carter, for example, strongly identifies with his black identity, and with a black community.[40] He is "more black" along most of the dimensions I have mentioned. Yet he strongly resists the legitimacy of scalar race as a way of thinking about black people. Acknowledging that "less black" is inevitably taken as a moral criticism, Carter is leery of allowing anyone to set the standards as to what should count for more and less black.[41] People should be free, Carter suggests, to make of their racial identity what they will, and others, he feels, do not have the standing to criticize those choices.

Carter's is indeed a humane position, respecting autonomy and rightly distrustful of the abuses to which the policing of racial identities can lead. But until racial identities are equally valued in the larger society—until they become something like what white ethnicities have become—that position will run up against some unpleasant realities. For example, as long as "black" is a generally stigmatized identity it will be difficult for blacks to avoid thinking ill of those who appear to avoid loyalty to other blacks, to black welfare, to black identity. Solidarity among the victimized exerts a strong and appropriate moral pull. Carter's position is a morally coherent one, though perhaps psychologically difficult to sustain.

Analogous arguments can be made for Native Americans who particularly scorn "assimilation,"[42] for Latinos and Hispanics, and for Asian Americans. Ideally an individual should be fully free to be "weakly X" along every dimension of scalar race without being scorned for doing so. But current racial arrangements are not yet hospitable to that stance, which requires full equality.

Blacks, whites, Asians, and Native Americans have been treated as if they were races. This makes them racialized groups, but not races; for there are no races. This is not merely a shift in terminology. Racialization does not, but race does, imply inherent characteristics, a virtually unbridgeable moral, experiental, and cognitive gulf among racial groups, and a hierarchy of worth. Racialization is a matter of degree; Latino/Hispanics are partially racialized, blacks fully so.

Merely *classifying* persons into racial groups does not necessarily carry all the deleterious assumptions of racial *thinking*. From a classificatory point of view of view, then, having an ethnicity or being an immigrant (Jamaican, for example) is fully consistent with having a racial designation (black). In terms of day-to-day racial thinking, however, viewing someone ethnically or as an immigrant can crowd out viewing him or her racially.

Races are not socially constructed; they simply do not exist. Racialized groups, however, are socially constructed, by the historical process of racialization. There did not have to be racialized groups, just as there did not have to be nations; but there are, they are fully "real," and there is a good deal of agreement as to how we determine someone's racialized group. Nevertheless, we sometimes speak of people as being "more black," "less Latino," "more white," and so on. This scalar way of talking about race derives from the identities, communities, and cultures that are attached to racial groups, and is potentially morally problematic yet seems inevitable as long as racial inequality exists.

9

Should We Try to Give Up Race?

If there are no races and if racial thinking has morally destructive consequences, should we not attempt to "give up race"? First, should we stop using racial words ("race," "black," "white," "Caucasian," "Asian," and so on), and should governmental units such as schools, agencies, and the Census Bureau stop asking people their racial identity? Second, should we actually stop *thinking of* and *experiencing* people in racial terms? These are two quite distinct matters; it is hardly evident that giving up official racial categorizing would have the effect of substantially reducing racial thinking, given how pervasive it is and how significant racial categories are to the social experiences and standing of different racial groups. It is plausible to suppose that racial thinking would continue largely unabated, simply driven underground by a norm discouraging its expression.[1]

Moral Benefits and Costs

Leaving aside for the moment how this daunting goal might be achieved, giving up racial thinking would involve important moral advances over our current situation. Without a racial frame, it would be much easier to see the internal diversity of racialized groups, and easier to see their members as individuals. We can get some idea of what this would be like by considering how we generally think about our own racial group. We recognize all kinds of subgroup differences, and we are not prevented from seeing members of our own group as individuals. Admittedly, we might be blinded to others' individuality by other group differences, such as economic or cultural ones. Getting rid of race is not the same as getting rid of all "group think." Race, however, tends to be a stronger force than other groupings for suppressing internal diversity and individuality.

In addition to giving up the suspicion that whites are inherently superior to blacks, Latinos, and Native Americans, doing away with race would allow us to see common interests and experiences currently masked by race. Persons of different racial groups would more readily experience commonalities as workers, persons without adequate health care, parents who want good public schools for their children, and so on.[2] And jettisoning race would rid us of one of the strongest barriers to experiencing a sense of common humanity with those now thought of as "other."

Yet jettisoning race in the two ways I've mentioned (racial language and racial thinking) would have important moral costs as well. Many would be misled into thinking that if there are no races, there can be no racism, no groups to be its target. But to be a target of racism requires only that a group is racialized, not that it is actually a race.

More fundamentally, race is part of our history and our current social arrangements. Groups defined by race are continuing targets of discrimination, inferiorizing, and stigmatizing. These groups, especially blacks, Native Americans, and some Latino/Hispanic groups, also live with accumulated deficits from even more horrendous injustices in the past. Whites possess a range of unearned advantages in virtually every major domain of social existence—education, jobs, health care, and political power; and often they harbor subtle assumptions that they are "all right" while other groups are defective in some way. If we give up race entirely, we abandon the ability to name these racial wrongs. We see this happening to some extent already. Whites have abandoned an earlier explicit consciousness of themselves as a racial group that needed to defend its privileges against threatening or inferior "others." White privilege has become largely unacknowledged; and with the exception of widely deplored racist violence by extremist groups, race-based wrongs are frequently unseen and denied by whites. Color blindness has assumed the status of an almost absolute principle that further motivates whites to be blind to continuing racial discrimination and injustice.

Jettisoning racial language and thinking would render us no longer able even to talk or think about racism, racial injustice, racial insensitivity, institutional racism, racial ignorance, and racial nonrecognition, and to make appropriate claims on the conscience of Americans.

How do we move ahead, then, in abandoning the false and destructive idea of race while retaining our ability to name and deplore racism and other racial wrongs? Distinguishing races from racialized groups is a necessary step to progress here, allowing us to do justice to both aims. In this chapter I will look at several aspects of the problem I have posed: the meaning of racial categories on the Census; Orlando Patterson's attempt to substitute ethnicity for race in order to do justice to the unreality of race; the defense of black racial identity, which attempts to preserve the ability to name racism and other racial wrongs and to retain a personally meaningful social identity; and the increasingly prevalent claiming of a mixed race identity, which has the potential to destabilize racial consciousness in general. Appreciating the difference between race and racialization, and at the same time attempting to do justice to the unreality of race and the reality of racism, may point us toward new ways of thinking and new forms of institutional practice.

How the Census Construes "Race"

Recognizing racial wrongs does not require acceding to the reality of race, but only to racialization.[3] Melissa Nobles's historical account of the use of racial categories on the decennial census illustrates this point clearly.[4] In contrast to many other nations, the United States has always "counted by race" on the Census; all the Censuses from 1790 until 1960 assumed the existence of races as real, biological divisions of the human species, though the specific understanding of what the term "race" meant changed significantly over that long stretch of history. Through 1930, science was fully implicated in the understanding of race assumed by the Census Bureau. Indeed, Nobles shows that the "mulatto" category from 1850 through 1920 (and "quadroon" and "octoroon," added in 1890) was initially placed on the Census explicitly to help racist scientists test their theories of racial purity, which implied that such categories of person were racially and reproductively defective and would die out with time.[5] The presence of this category should in no way be viewed as some sort of recognition of "mixed-race" persons, in the current sense of that term.[6]

From 1930 through 1960, political and scientific developments left racial categories without their previously presumed intellectual foundation. Yet neither was the idea of race as biologically real explicitly abandoned. The most dramatic change in the purposes of, and the implied understanding of, racial categories came with the 1980 Census. With minority groups' and civil rights groups' input, and with a much greater sensitivity to racial designations as they were understood by individual citizens, the Census Bureau began to see the major purpose of such categories as the monitoring of discrimination to ensure compliance with civil rights and other antidiscrimination laws and, more generally, as providing relevant data for federal programs targeted to disadvantaged minority communities.[7]

These purposes no longer require a belief in races, either in the classic sense described in chapter 7 or in the more attenuated contemporary form of race thinking. For a group to be racially discriminated against, it does not have to be a race in any sense at all; it need only be a racialized group—a group generally treated and regarded as a race—or, even more minimally, a group that the individual discriminator regards as a race. But Nobles says that those who created the official Census categories of the current era "viewed races as natural human groupings, each with its own original geographic home."[8] And in its continuing use of the general category "race" in an unexplained and unelaborated manner as the general rubric under which "white," "black," and "American Indian or Alaskan Native" are listed, the Census fails to distance itself from false racialist understandings.[9] Were the federal government to encourage a broad understanding that the purposes for which the Census is now explicitly used do not require a commitment to the existence of races in any form, but only to racialized groups,[10] the legitimate discrimination-monitoring function of Census racial categories could be severed from any implication of racialism.[11]

Substituting Ethnicity for Race

Orlando Patterson regards race as a false and pernicious idea, and argues that no meaningful distinction exists between ethnicity and what we think of as race. Patterson therefore proposes that we abandon all talk of race and substitute ethnicity where we formerly referred to racial groups.[12] We believe that racial differences rest on phenotypic differences while ethnicity is concerned with culture, Patterson says, but this distinction does not hold up. Jews, for example, were regarded as a racial group not only by Nazis but Europeans in general, yet in America they are now seen as an ethnic group. The distinction is arbitrary. Moreover, in England and

America both Jews and the Irish have been regarded as not white. Do we call prejudice against Jews racial or ethnic prejudice?

Moreover, Patterson asserts, "however similar people may look to out-siders, those who believe that there are differences tend to have very little difficulty identifying the believed-in different group and to see gross phys-ical differences that outsiders find it hard to identify."[13] So belief in phe-notypic differences can not be used to differentiate race from ethnicity. At the same time, Patterson suggests, retaining racial language allows and encourages us to draw invidious distinctions between people.

Patterson's historical perspective does not, however, support his pro-posal. It is true that many southern and eastern Europeans groups were not regarded unequivocally as "white" in the early part of this century (see chapter 6); nor were the Irish so regarded in the nineteenth century. Now, however, in the United States at least, these groups are seen as eth-nic groups, defined by ancestry and culture; they are no longer racial-ized—seen as having distinct inherent natures and saliently marked by phenotype.

This argument presupposes that we can and do draw a distinction be-tween race and ethnicity. A group *once* seen as racial (Poles and Jews, for example) can *come to be* seen as ethnic rather than racial. Blacks, Asians, and, to some extent, Latinos are still seen as racial, though they are seen as ethnic also. We could stop using words like "black," "white" and "Asian," and instead say "African American," "Caribbean American," "Pol-ish American," "Korean American," and "Vietnamese American." But if we are to understand what the former groups' historical experience has been, and what their status in the nation is today, we must take account of their having been seen and treated as racial groups. Patterson asks, "Why is it not enough to be simply Jewish-American, Anglo-American, Irish-American, or, if one chooses, just plain American?"[14] It may be "enough" for members of those groups, who may not wish to embrace the designa-tion "white." But it is not enough if we want to understand their social and historical experience as groups racialized as "white."[15]

If we make clear that when we use "white," "black," and so on, we mean only racialized groups, we will further Patterson's laudable goal of under-mining the legitimacy of race. To accomplish this while not rendering the social and historical experience of blacks, whites, and other groups invisi-ble requires that we hold on to the distinction between an ethnic group and a racialized group. Doing so does not play into racist or racialist thinking. Patterson is right that representing a group as a race does imply unchangeable biologically based difference, which in turn invites hostility or inferiorization; seeing a group ethnically generally does not. But we can not deracialize a racialized group simply by refusing to use racial language, or substituting ethnic language, when discussing it.

Racial and Racialized Identity

Many blacks feel a strong sense of racial solidarity or kinship with other blacks; black identity and the black community provide them a vital horizon of meaning. Of course they recognize other important sources of identity. But not only is race almost always present in the mix of identity features; it is often accorded a special and overriding place. William Cross articulates this primacy: "Many blacks . . . gain personal fulfillment and happiness from being Christians, lawyers, doctors, gamblers, police officers, gays, or believers in obscure cults. Such people cannot be said to have a black identity because their sense of personal well-being is anchored in something other than their blackness."[16]

Thus for many American blacks, questioning black identity and community would be taken as an attack on an important source of self-understanding and meaningfulness in their lives. Race is the one commonality that provides support, pride, and solidarity in the face of an often hostile, stigmatizing world.

Can there be racial identity without "race?" Isn't the honoring and preserving of black identity a reason not to jettison race? I do not think so. If there are no races, then any racial solidarity presuming them is without foundation. Based on a falsehood, it lends itself to the moral distortions described throughout this book. It encourages blacks to think they are more like each other, and more different from other groups, than they actually are. It encourages failure to recognize commonalities with individuals of other groups. It encourages stereotyping, even of one's own group. It encourages an unwarranted privileging of racial identity. On what basis does Cross say that in order to have an identity as "black" one must derive one's sense of well-being primarily from one's blackness? Why can't one be healthily, unashamedly, and responsibly "black" while making one's job, or work on behalf of refugees, or interracial family, for example, the center of meaning in one's life?

As suggested in chapter 8, a black consciousness can be based not on race but on racialized identity. This is no mere semantic trickery. Racialized identities are much less subject to the moral pitfalls just mentioned. Race assumes an inherent bond with every member of one's racial group. The bond supplied by racialization is of shared social and historical experience. But the experience of racialization is not the same across racial groups. Not all blacks are treated the same, even if all are affected by being black. Not every black person is equally stigmatized, nor equally discriminated against. Gender, class, region, and other factors make for significant differences in racialized experience. Equally significant, there is no experience unique to one group; other racial groups experience racial discrimination and stigma as well. While there are differences of degree between groups, they are not necessarily greater than differences of degree within a given group.

Moreover, nonracial groups (women, the obese, the disabled, gays and lesbians) can be discriminated against or stigmatized also. Of course only blacks have undergone slavery, and that is a unique feature of their racialized experience. The significance of slave descent for the current situation of blacks, five or six generations later, is, however, much less clear. Each group has some elements of distinctive racialization—the experience of Native Americans is also unique among American ethnoracial groups—but its overall experience contains elements shared, at least to some degree, with other ethnoracial groups, and other types of groups as well.

Shared experience does not, to be sure, fix the appropriate limit of a racialized bond. Someone of a given racialized group can choose, and feel, a solidarity with fellow members whose experience is very different from his own. That solidarity can be put to political use, to rally other members of the racialized group to join in struggle against racial discrimination and injustice. Such a political and moral choice is, however, quite different from believing that mere racial membership itself insures an inherent tie to other members. Political solidarity does not require a belief in the reality of race, even though in fact some blacks do appear to regard criticism of race as an attack on the basis of racial solidarity. Not only is racialization sufficient for such solidarity, however, but its recognition supplies a more accurate understanding of the character of the racialized social order, encourages a stronger recognition of commonalities of experience and of political and moral commitments across "racial" lines, and, arguably, would in the long run be more politically effective in mitigating racism and racial injustice than would a belief in the reality of race.

The difference between race and racialization as a basis for identity is nicely illustrated in a 1996 *New York Times* article, "New Sense of Race Rises among Asian-Americans."[17] The article describes the reaction of diverse Asian American groups to discrimination against them as Asians, rather than as members of particular Asian ethnic groups. The discrimination causes the ethnic groups to identify more with one another than they had previously. This race-based unifying has served to overcome, at least partly, historical tensions among some of the Asian American groups, especially Korean and Japanese.

In the article Peter Bersamin, a Filipino American psychologist, describes the experience of seeking a cottage rental in a complex with a "vacancy" sign, then having the owner close his doors to him. "That was my first experience with racial discrimination and the beginning of my awareness as being somebody other than white," he says.[18] The article's author goes on to comment, "The psychologist has come to feel less part of a national or ethnic group and more part of a racial one."[19]

Two quite different things might be going on for Mr. Bersamin (and the other Asian Americans discussed in the article). He might think that this experience of racial discrimination revealed something that had always been true, but that he had been unaware of—that he was a member of a particular nonwhite race, the Asian race. This would be similar to what W. E. B. Du Bois movingly describes in *Souls of Black Folk* when as a young boy in a mostly white school, a white female classmate rebuffs an innocent social overture. Du Bois realizes at that moment that he is black, of a different race than the other children and therefore "shut out from their world."[20]

But perhaps Bersamin means rather that he recognizes a commonality of racialized experience and social positioning with other Asian Americans that he had not recognized before—that they are all potential targets of race prejudice. Since there are no races, Mr. Bersamin can not have realized that he was a member of the Asian race.[21] Racialization is all he need have recognized in order to appreciate the significance of the incident to his commonality with other Asian Americans. In that sense, Asian Americans similarly situated lose nothing if they fully eschew the idea that they constitute an actual racial group.

African American racial identity in the face of antiblack racism generally functions in quite a different manner. Black identity is generally experienced by African Americans as an identity they already possess, in distinctly racial form. Blacks do not generally regard what binds them together in a common plight to be *only* that they are all subject to stigmatization and discrimination.

Culture and Racialized Identities

Culture is an additional integral part of black identity, and, as Anthony Appiah says, there are many African American cultures—youth cultures, urban cultures, rural cultures, cultures related to distinctive African American religious practice, and so on.[22] As we saw in chapter 5, the designation "black" has for a long time carried not only a racial but an ethnocultural meaning, and African American cultures are infused with racialized significance. Black Christianity, for instance, distinctively responded, in part through supporting and fashioning forms of resistance, to the experience of slavery and racial oppression. This is true as well of several distinctive black American musical forms—spirituals, gospel, blues, rap.

Asian American identity contrasts strikingly with African American. Indeed, Eric Liu says that "what's missing from Asian American culture is culture."[23] Liu says that there are distinctive Asian ethnicity-based cultural forms and practices—sushi, karaoke bars, taking one's shoes off in a Chinese home—but that these are not pan-Asian cultural forms, nor are they related to the ways that Asians have historically been racialized. The use of "Oriental," "Mongoloid," and "Asiatic" as racial terms for all Asians in the heyday of classic racial thought never had the effect of creating a widespread pan-Asian racial consciousness among the small numbers of Asian Americans prior to the large upsurge in Asian immigration in the past three decades.

For blacks, though, abandoning race might feel like giving up black culture as a distinctive expression of black identity. But I think this is not so. Black cultural forms arose partly in response to the experience of racialization, not from a racial essence inherent in all black people. Abandoning race would, perhaps, affect the way some black Americans think about their relation to their cultures. It might, for example, weaken a sense of *exclusive possession* of them. Having arisen from the distinctive experiences of racialized groups, cultural forms can be appropriated and developed by those of other racialized groups. Whites, Latinos, and Asians can learn to sing gospel, and perform and develop jazz and hip-hop. This is all to the good. Cultural forms are different ways of expressing the human spirit and should be seen as contributions to the inheritance of humanity, not the possession of a single group. All can be enriched by the expressive variety of cultural groups, as well as by the hybrid directions that outgroup members can develop.

At the same time, to say that cultural products can not be the exclusive possession of their original creators is not to deny that appropriations of those products by a group other than their original creators can be justly criticized on both moral and aesthetic grounds. African Americans sometimes assert such proprietary interest because of a history of exploitation and nonrecognition. An especially egregious example is the white music producers, promoters, and singers who have appropriated black music, rendered it acceptable to a mass white teen audience, and reaped the profits, leaving the black originators uncompensated and unrecognized.[24] It is wrong not to acknowledge the provenance and pay homage to the creators of any form of cultural endeavor, and wrong to use one's greater wealth and cultural power to exploit it. But the solution is not to racialize culture and turn it into the exclusive possession of the group that originated it.

Asserting too tight a link between race and culture by protecting a group's cultural borders from "racial interlopers" also has an unnecessarily constricting impact on members of that group themselves. For it discourages them from attempting to cross boundaries in the other direction and become proficient partakers and developers of the music, art, and lifestyles of other cultural groups. An African-American should be able to love Irish music unashamedly and without any sense either that he does not belong, or that he has somehow abandoned his racial blackness by doing so. Shifting one's self-understanding from a racial to a racialized one is of course no guarantee against inappropriate cultural possessiveness or exclusiveness, but by abandoning racialism's sense of inherent connection between culture and racial identity, one rejects a principal source of narrow racial ways of thinking.

Recognizing the ethnocultural dimension of a racialized black American identity would go a long way toward preserving what is valuable in maintaining black identity.

At this point in American history, Asian Americans and Latinos and Hispanics have a very weak sense of being distinct racial groups. Many do appreciate that they have been racialized, but do not confuse this with being an actual race. For many, a panethnic consciousness has emerged as a personally important identity. But, again, panethnicity is not the same as race. For large numbers in both groups, their ethnic identity, as Korean American, Cambodian American, Mexican American, or Dominican American, is much more important than a panethnic or racialized, much less racial, consciousness. Native Americans have been deeply racialized in American history, and no doubt possess some degree of racial consciousness as well as intensifying pan-Indian consciousness, especially in the years since the founding of the American Indian Movement in the late 1960s. Nevertheless, specific tribal identities and loyalties constitute a buffer to the form of racial consciousness developed by African Americans.

Many whites would also find the jettisoning of race for racialization difficult, though they might *think* they would be relieved by it. The specialness and superiority of whiteness is deeply embedded in American politics and culture. The idea that whiteness is not real, that it is in a sense not anything, that it was constructed to rationalize undeserved status, might be emotionally difficult to accept. Ultimately, however, the enhanced ability to live in equality with those of other racial groups would be a moral gain for whites; and this would be facilitated by recognizing their own racialization.

Multiracial Identities

The unashamed and even proud claiming of biracial, mixed-race, or multiracial identity is a genuinely new phenomenon. Although "mulattos" were recognized in former eras, including on the federal Census, that designation belongs to a period when such persons were generally regarded as defectives, even biologically.[25] Biracial and multiracial persons by their very existence pose a challenge to racial thinking; but the extent to which that challenge will translate into the actual destabilizing of racial thinking depends in part on how this group of persons position themselves in relation to existing racial groups, communities, and categories.

Interracial couples and biracial children are a small but growing portion of the population. The latter represented 3.4 percent of births in 1989, but their rate of growth since the early 1970s is 260 percent compared to 15 percent for monoracial persons.[26] Two percent of Americans identified themselves as having more than one "race" on the 2000 Census.[27] From 1970 to 1996 the number of black-white married couples has more than quintupled, to 337,000.[28] Several national organizations have formed to represent the interests and increase the visibility of multiracial people. Their visibility was greatly enhanced by their attempt to persuade the Census Bureau to seriously consider (although it ultimately rejected) including a "multiracial" category, in addition to the standard racial choices, on the 2000 Census.

What is the significance of these developments for the future of racial consciousness in the U.S.? Let us focus on the "biracial" designation first. Generally, this category comprises offspring of persons who are members of two distinct racial classifications—"Asian" and "black," "black" and "white," and so forth. On one level the biracial marriage and the biracial child constitute a triumph over racialism and racism. By loving one another, the partners have prevailed over the sense of radical difference created by racial thinking; the biracial child single-handedly refutes the idea that group difference is a species-like division. (A biracial adoptive family, in which both parents are of a different racial group than the child, poses a similar, though slightly weaker, challenge to race.) Biracials blur the boundaries between racial groups, thereby challenging the idea that every individual can be slotted into one and only one race.

Nevertheless, in some respects these challenges to racialism are limited. Biraciality still implies that each parent does indeed "have a race." The biracial child may not want to confine herself to a single racial identity, because doing so constitutes a denial of one of her parents' racial identity (often expressed, somewhat misleadingly, except in the case of blacks, as a "heritage"). Such a biracial child has two races, not one; but she still "has race," and her parents each have one, in the traditional sense.

The idea of mixed-race or multiracial is less beholden to standard racial classification. It is not tied to the racial identity of a particular parent or even a distinct familial ancestor but only to the individual's having biological ancestry of more than one racial group.[29] In this sense most African Americans are multiracial, including those whose ancestors for several generations back identified themselves as "black." Generally, multiracial (as distinct from biracial) identity is not claimed as a way of honoring a particular ancestor. For Latinos and Hispanics, mixed-race identity is a component of ethnoracial or national identity (see chapter 7.) Multiraciality does not presuppose, hence legitimize, any specific ancestor's racial identity.

Nevertheless, multiraciality does require some conception of traditional races as the contributing elements to the mix. Of course a person with a mixed-race identity could view them as racialized groups, and so could the biracial individual. But saying that "I fall into a category distinct from traditional races by being a combination of those races" is much less challenging to the idea of race than saying, "As a person whose biological ancestry includes a mixture of what have been called 'races,' I reject the idea of race entirely. My identity lies entirely outside your racial classification system."

Some biracial or multiracial persons desire acceptance in each of the traditionally defined racial groups to which they claim a connection.[30] They want to be able to be part of, say, the black community, and also the white community.[31] Actually securing such acceptance would challenge racial thinking, especially with regard to black-white mixes. Whites would have to accept as one of their own someone who is seen as "black" and such acceptance would be especially threatening to their idea of race because white racial identity has always required a purity, reflected in the one-drop rule, that denies whiteness to anyone with any fraction of non-whiteness, especially blackness. By contrast, blacks have always accepted mixed-race persons as part of the black community; someone who wishes to sustain an allegiance to a white community as well as a black one, however, poses more of a challenge to standard conceptions of black communal identity. People's claiming of multiple race-based communities would destabilize racial thinking no matter what groups are involved. At the same time, with the exception of whites mentioned above, multiracial persons seeking acceptance in multiple communities do not explicitly challenge the idea of race or the self-understanding of race-based communities. Indeed, they accept the traditional racial communities as they now exist, asking only that they not be confined to one of them.

On the other hand, some multiracial persons seek an identity *distinct* from traditional racial groups, in a new community of "multiracials."[32] Such an identity is less directly parasitic on standard racial classifications than the form involving attachment to traditional racial groups.

The attempt by organizations representing elements of the multiracial community to gain recognition on the 2000 Census reveals how the form of public recognition sought by multiracial and biracial people affects the challenge to traditional racial classifications and racial thinking.[33] These organizations have sought a distinct category of "multiracial," to appear alongside "white," "black," and the others. But despite its being separate from the array of categories currently understood as racial, "multiracial" would seem to derive its meaning and legitimacy from its position in the already existing racial pantheon; it would seem like a quasi-racial category of its own.[34] The proposal ultimately adopted in 2000 for the first time by the Census Bureau—to allow "check all that apply" as an option—avoids this ironic quasi-validation of the racial classification system. It does, however, render multiracial persons less visible as a group than does the multiracial organizations' proposal.[35] In addition (like the "multiracial" category), in a certain way "check all that apply" accepts standard racial categories in their own right, challenging only the idea that all persons must be slotted into one and only one of them. But, again, this formal acceptance is perfectly consistent with viewing such categories as naming racialized rather than racial groups.

If multiracial persons were to use their identity as a direct challenge to the idea of race, they would be likely to have a more destabilizing impact on racial thinking than would their mere presence. Cynthia Nakashima notes that one impetus within the multiracial movement is "to dismantle dominant racial ideology and group boundaries and to create connections across communities into a community of humanity."[36] But the multiracial community is very diverse, not only in its racial composition but in individual desires for distinct forms of recognition and acknowledgment. Though it is, in one sense, well placed to lodge assaults on the idea of race, it is not particularly right or fair to expect it to do so.

Whatever impact multiracial persons and the multiracial movement have on destabilizing the idea of race, we should not confuse that benefit with the potential impact on racial injustice. Because race as an ideology arose as a rationale for oppression, undermining race has been confused with undermining racial inequality. Even without this direct confusion, the public interest in racial matters could simply shift from racism and racial injustice to multiracial people, their identities, communities, families, and the like.[37] The latter topics are safer for whites; they don't challenge white privilege.

A desire to keep the racial justice purposes of classification clearly in view underlay the Census Bureau's decision not to include a "multiracial" category on the 2000 Census. Although we have seen that the Bureau is not entirely clear where it stands on the question of whether races exist, its major purpose in collecting race-based data is to monitor racial discrimination and target programs to racially disadvantaged communities. This purpose requires knowing an individual's public racial identity—that is, her racialized identity.[38] It is mostly on the basis of how she is seen in society, not how she sees herself, that she is discriminated against, stigmatized, or inherits a history of racial advantage or disadvantage. This racialized identity can be at odds with an individual's own identity preference, and the Bureau chose to privilege the needs of racial justice over those of individual identity expression and recognition.

In rejecting the "multiracial" category, the Census Bureau (and civil rights groups that pressed for this position) reasoned that if the category were offered as an alternative to "black", many blacks, a significant percentage of whom have European racial ancestry might prefer it.[39] They might do so because they feel the "multiracial" designation better expresses their personal sense of identity, or because they feel that "black" is a more stigmatized identity in the United States than "multiracial."[40] But such persons would often face the same discrimination as those who identified themselves as "black" and for the same reason—they would still be seen as black. The purposes of collecting racial data, and the cause of racial justice, would be adversely affected.

Achieving Racial Equality and Harmony and Abandoning Race

Although racial justice is an urgent goal, ridding ourselves of false and divisive racial thinking—abandoning race—is a worthy aim in its own right. At first glance these two aims seem at odds, since we require racial categories in order to keep in view the way that racialization has affected life chances. Yet doing so would seem to reinforce rather than weaken a consciousness of race.

In the larger scheme of things, however, the achievement of racial justice itself weakens racial consciousness. Racial consciousness thrives on social, economic, political, educational, and civic inequality, and on the social, residential, and occupational segregation that is both a cause and a consequence of that inequality. The tendency to think that those lower on the social and economic scale are in *some* way inherently inferior is very difficult to resist, even if the weight of science undermines any foundation for such belief. And social separation feeds the idea that "those people" are fundamentally different from oneself. Social intercourse among racial groups on a basis of equality and in a spirit of comity would do more to undermine a lived sense of those groups as races than would the increasing presence of multiracial people or scientific arguments about the unreality of race.

In the real world, ridding ourselves of the myth of race can not be severed from the politically more challenging task of changing the structural relationships among racial groups. Closely linked in practice to the goal of equality, but worth articulating as a distinct value, is the virtually forsaken nonassimilationist goal of harmony between the "races" associated with integrationism, which continues to play a role (albeit minor) in the moral cachet of the idea of color blindness. In all domains of life, from friendship and family life to work life and civic engagement, persons of different racial groups must learn a sense of kinship and connection. As equality counters the hierarchical dimension of race, harmony counters the vertical, the "othering." As the nation becomes increasingly multiracial and multi-ethnic, the twin goals of racial equality and racial harmony become increasingly urgent while increasingly complex. Were they to be achieved, however, "race" as we know it would virtually disappear, and scientific and philosophical arguments concerning the unreality of race could be integrated into everyday thought and life.

Notes

Chapter 1. "Racism": Its Core Meaning

1. David Duke, before he shed his formal ties to the Klan in order to become a politician, was criticized by a fellow Klansman for "conduct unbecoming a racist." See James Ridgeway, *Blood in the Face: The Ku Klux Klan, Aryan Nations, Nazi Skinheads, and the Rise of a New White Culture* (New York, 1990), 146.

2. Bernard Weinraub, "Stung by Criticism of Fall Shows, TV Networks Add Minority Roles," *New York Times*, Sept. 20, 1999, A1, A14.

3. "Black and White in Baltimore," *Indianapolis Star-News*, Aug. 23, 1999 (article ID no. 1999235133, on www.Indystar.com).

4. David K. Shipler, *A Country of Strangers: Blacks and Whites in America* (New York, 1997), 92.

5. Kathleen Ostrander, "Milton Board Decides to Retire Indian Logo, Name," *Milwaukee Journal Sentinel* (on line), July 20, 1999.

6. In chapter 7 I will argue that there are no races in the sense in which "race" is generally understood in popular discourse, so that it is misleading to say that someone "is of a certain race." It is more accurate to say that she has, or has been assigned, a racial designation, or that she is a member of a racial group; I will generally use the latter expression.

7. James Nuechterlein, *First Things, Chronicle of Higher Education*, Sept. 6, 1996, B9.

8. *Time*, Dec. 5, 1994, cited in *Extra!* 9, no. 2 (March/April 1996):18.

9. Robert Miles, *Racism* (London, 1989), 41–68.

10. "Police Probe Sees No Racism in Noose Prank," *Boston Globe*, May 5, 1999.

11. *Boston Globe*, Apr. 29, 1999, B1.

12. "Identifying the Face of the Enemy," *The Plain Dealer*, July 13, 1999.

13. See note 2. It was the newspaper article, rather than the NAACP itself, that framed the issue as one of racism. Kweisi Mfume, the president of the NAACP, said only that the programming was "a virtual whitewash."

14. Avishai Margalit, *The Decent Society* (Cambridge, Mass., 1996), 80–83. Michel Wieviorka reports that current usage of the term "racism" in France corresponds to something like Margalit's suggestion, "e.g. anti-worker racism, anti-women racism, anti-young people racism, anti-old people racism." "Is It So Difficult to Be Anti-racist?" in *Debating Cultural Hybridity: Multi-cultural Identities and the Politics of Anti-racism*, ed. Pnina Werbner and Tariq Modood (London, 1997), 141. Wieviorka agrees that these are misleading extensions of the term "racism."

15. Of those listed, only "sexism"—discrimination against or the denial of dignity to women, or discrimination on the basis of sex in general—has fully succeeded in attaching moral condemnation to its referent in popular thought and speech.

16. Several sources note that *Racism*, a book by the German social scientist Magnus Hirschfeld, was the first and most prominent instance of the term "racism" in this period. Trans. and ed. Eden and Cedar Paul (London, 1938, reissued Port Washington, N.Y., 1973 [orig. pub. in German, 1933]).

17. The noun "America" is best jettisoned as referring to the United States of America, as both North and South America include many nations whose existence is ignored by this terminology; I will avoid using it whenever possible. But there is no readily available adjectival form of "the U.S." or "USA," and I will follow general convention in using "American" for this purpose, except when highlighting a difference between Latin America and the United States.

18. Elazar Barkan, *The Retreat of Scientific Racism: Changing Concepts of Race in Britain and the United States between the World Wars* (New York, 1992).

19. It is telling that Gunnar Myrdal's monumental 1944 account of the pervasive inferior treatment of African Americans, *An American Dilemma* (New York, 1964 [1944]), did not use the word "racism" to describe and condemn that treatment.

20. George Mosse, *Toward the Final Solution: A History of European Racism* (Madison, Wis., 1985), ix.

21. John Rex, "Racism," *The Blackwell Dictionary of Twentieth-Century Social Thought*, ed. William Outhwaite and Tom Bottomore (Oxford, 1994), 538.

22. Charles Taylor, *Sources of the Self: The Making of Modern Identity* (Cambridge, Mass., 1989), 7.

23. Pam Belluck, "A White Supremacist Group Seeks a New Kind of Recruit," *New York Times*, July 7, 1999, A1, A14.

24. Jorge L. A. Garcia argues effectively against the view that the core of racism, as we now understand the idea, lies in a system of beliefs. "The Heart of Racism," *Journal of Social Philosophy* 27, no. 2 (Fall 1996): 5–45; "Current Conceptions of Racism: A Critical Examination of Some Recent Social Philosophy," *Journal of Social Philosophy* 28, no. 2 (Fall 1997): 5–42; and "Philosophical Analysis and the Moral Concept of Racism," *Philosophy and Social Criticism* 25, no. 5 (1999): 1–32. Garcia argues that the "heart of racism" is race-based ill will. More generally, Garcia develops a persuasive case for the centrality of morality to our current concept of racism. My own argument against belief-centered accounts of racism and for the centrality of the moral in racism is very much indebted to Garcia's work.

25. On Barzun's terminology, see Miles, *Racism*, 44. The 1999 *Encyclopedia Britannica Online*'s entry on "racism" begins, "Racism, also called 'racialism'. . . ."

26. In Britain the term "racialism" has a good deal more public currency than it does in the United States, and has come to take on some of the wider scope of the American use of "racism." In the 1970s several British theorists suggested that "racialism" be used to denote practices of racial discrimination, and "racism" be confined to racist ideologies of biological determinism and hierarchy. (Miles, *Racism*, 53, citing Sivanandan; Rex, "Racism," *Blackwell*, 149, citing Banton.) John Rex claims that this suggestion never gained wide acceptance, and that "racism" remains the term of choice in expressing general condemnation in the racial domain in Britain. John Rex, "Racism, Institutionalized and Otherwise," in *Racism*, ed.

Leonard Harris (Amherst, N.Y., 1999), 149. In chapters 3 and 6, I will discuss some other meanings that have been given to "racialism."

27. Gordon Allport, *The Nature of Prejudice* (Reading, Mass., 1988 [1954]).

28. According to Michael Banton, Oliver Cox in his important 1948 work, *Class, Caste, and Race* (New York, 1970 [1948]) did define "racism" as "a philosophy of racial antipathy." Banton, *Racial Theories*, 2d ed. (Cambridge, Eng., 1998), 171.

29. *Report of the National Advisory Commission on Civil Disorders* (New York, 1968). (Kerner was chairman of the commission.) Tom Wicker's brief introduction used the expressions "racism" and "white racism" as well (vii, ix).

30. Kwame Ture and Charles Hamilton, *Black Power: The Politics of Liberation* (New York, 1992 [1967]).

31. The *Seattle Times* received hundreds of letters and phone calls in response to the whale killing, many of which deplored it but without expressing hostility toward the tribe, or Native Americans in general. A substantial minority of callers and writers expressed distinctly racist sentiments. The subsequent debate about "racism" involved the sort of confusions I am attempting to address in this book. Many supporters of the Makah saw all opposition as racist, and some writers evidenced racism while denying it. Alex Tizon, "Whale Killing Uncovers Anti-Indian Hatred," *Boston Globe*, May 30, 1999. Tizon, a *Seattle Times* reporter, commented, "Airwaves and editorial pages across Western Washington have carried anti-Indian vitriol not heard or seen for a quarter-century."

32. Laurence Thomas draws a similar distinction to that between inferiority and antipathy racism in "The Evolution of Antisemitism," *Transition* 57 (1992): 94–108, esp. 107–8, although for Thomas the more basic character of antipathy racism is a judgment of the target group—Jews, in Thomas's discussion—as morally depraved and evil. My notion of antipathy racism does not require such a judgment; antipathy can be directed toward those thought of as inferior but not evil. People sometimes defend themselves against the charge of being racist by saying that they do not hate anyone because of their race. But they may still be inferiorizing racists.

Conflating the two forms can distort the specific character of historical forms of racism. Barbara Katz Rothman, for example, says, in relation to Nazism, "To have such a program . . . there has to be a concept of race, a separate biological group capable of infiltrating, weakening, destroying, not by military force, but by procreation, by the force of life itself. For the Ku Klux Klan, blacks were such a force; lynching was the cure." *The Book of Life: A Personal and Ethical Guide to Race, Normality, and the Implications of the Human Genome Project* (Boston, 2001), 61–62. But the Klan did not view blacks as an internal destructive agent, but as a group that needed to be kept subordinate, in accord with their inferior natures. Lynching was not a way to exterminate blacks but to keep them "in their place."

33. This typology is standard. See, for example, Louise Derman-Sparks and Carol Brunson Phillips, *Teaching/Learning Anti-racism* (New York, 1997), 10.

34. Beverly Tatum, a particularly insightful observer of race in America, echoes a widespread view in defining "racism" as a "system of advantage based on race," though she is aware that this definition does not capture all of what people mean by the term. Tatum, *"Why Are All the Black Kids Sitting Together in the Cafeteria?" and Other Conversations about Race*, rev. ed. (New York, 1999), 10.

35. For a detailed argument against the "system of advantage" definition of "racism" see L. Blum, "What Is 'Racism' in Antiracist Education?" *Teachers College Record* 100, no. 4 (Summer 1999): 860–80, and Garcia, "Current Conceptions," 11–14.

36. Inferiorizing racism is sometimes assumed to consist merely in the belief that one's own group is superior to some other group. This definition will do for practical purposes, but it does not capture the full force of inferiorizing racism in its familiar manifestations. The respect in which the group is seen as inferior must be reasonably fundamental—such as moral character, intelligence, or capacity for living a self-directed life. It is not racist to view group A as by nature better at badminton than group B. In addition, the group seen as infe-

rior must be viewed not merely as inferior to some other group but as significantly *defective*. Suppose, for example, that someone believes that Asians are intellectually superior to whites, but that whites' intelligence is more than adequate for the tasks of life. In this view, whites are not deficient; they are just less intelligent than Asians. (I am accepting this use of "intelligence" for the sake of argument only, as this alleged quality is the focus of one of the central expressions of inferiorizing racism, especially against blacks and Latinos. I do not regard intelligence is a unitary measurable characteristic.) Historically, systems of racial degradation have involved not only the belief that some groups were superior to others, but that the inferior ones were importantly deficient and thus unworthy of full human status or civic or moral equality; this is my view of inferiorizing racism.

37. *A Soldier's Story*. Written by Charles Fuller. Dir. Norman Jewison. Columbia Pictures, 1984.

38. A group of black and Latino/Hispanic sixth-graders in Washington D.C. assented to a troubling array of negative stereotypes about their own groups, such as "Blacks are poor and stay poor because they're dumber than whites (and Asians)" and "Black people don't like to work hard." Reported in Martha Minow, *Not Only for Myself: Identity, Politics, and the Law* (New York, 1997), 149–50.

39. Joel Kovel, *White Racism: A Psychohistory* (New York, 1971).

40. Opinion surveys show especially a downward trend in whites' alleging lack of innate intelligence in blacks. Schuman et al. cite National Opinion Research Council (NORC) polls that put that figure at 10 percent in 1996 (compared, for example, to 27 percent in 1977). Explanations of blacks' lower socioeconomic status in terms of inadequate motivation, by contrast, have shown a steady rise—to 52 percent in 1996 (from 34 percent in 1977). Howard Schuman, Charlotte Steeh, Lawrence Bobo, and Maria Krysan, *Racial Attitudes in America: Trends and Interpretation*, rev. ed. (Cambridge, Mass., 1997), 156–57. As the authors remind us, these figures measure only what people are willing to avow. The extent of innatist racism is surely higher. Nevertheless, the comparative drop in avowed innatist inferiorizing racism over time surely represents a genuine change in cultural attitudes.

Several scholars of race within the social sciences have seen the decline of avowed belief in black racial inferiority as calling for new theories to make sense of personal racism and racial prejudice on the contemporary scene. David Sears's and Donald Kinder's concept of "symbolic racism" and John McConahay's similar notion of "modern racism" are influential representatives of this tendency. Donald R. Kinder and Lynn M. Sanders, *Divided by Color: Racial Politics and Democratic Ideals* (Chicago, 1996); John B. McConahay, "Modern Racism and Modern Discrimination: The Effects of Race, Racial Attitudes, and Context on Simulated Hiring Decisions," *Personality and Social Psychology Bulletin* 9 (1983): 551–58. Both postulate continuing negative racial affect toward, and negative stereotypes of, blacks, disengaged from beliefs about racial inferiority but wedded to a perception of blacks as violating "cherished American values such as the work ethic, self-reliance, impulse control, and obedience to authority." David Sears, John Hetts, Jim Sidanius, and Lawrence Bobo, "Race in American Politics," in *Racialized Politics: The Debate About Racism in America*, ed. Sears, Sidanius, and Bobo (Chicago, 2000), 17. To an extent, these theories claim that antipathy racism has been sustained while inferiorizing racism has declined. But the idea of violating cherished American values is, in my view, related to inferiorizing racism. Some of these alleged violations (lack of impulse control, lack of self-reliance) seem to me an only slightly different way of seeing blacks as not fully civilized. The key question here is whether the attributed characteristics are viewed by the subject as a matter of the *culture* of African Americans, and thus as susceptible to change; or whether they are seen as inherent. (This issue will be discussed in chapter 7.) Also, one would need to know whether the allegation is merely a socially acceptable cover (perhaps adopted unconsciously) for racial antipathy, or whether, as some of the authors writing in this tradition allege, it is a fully independent factor. If the former, it remains a clear instance of racism. Even if these perceptions of blacks are not fueled by a preexisting racial hostility, if they are simply, or primarily, a product of racial stereotyping, they are objectionable on this score as well. Finally, to the extent that these beliefs are a product of independent intellectual processes, unrelated to racial animus or racist stereotypes, they seem to me not pertinent to personal racism at all, although it can be argued (as some of these authors do) that adherence to such beliefs has the effect of hindering policies that would address the historical injustices which blacks have suffered. But I have cautioned that we keep considerations pertinent to social policy regarding race and considerations relevant to attributing personal racism clearly distinct.

41. Allport, *Nature*, 9.

42. Ibid., 8.

43. Adrian M. S. Piper penetratingly articulates and analyzes this form of prejudice and discrimination, which she calls "second-order discrimination." "Higher-order Discrimination," in *Identity, Character, and Morality: Essays in Moral Psychology*, ed. Owen Flanagan and Amélie O. Rorty (Cambridge, Mass., 1990). As Piper says, one sign of the presence of such prejudice is the subject's devaluing the characteristic in question—for example, being a good dancer—only in the targeted group (e.g., blacks) but not in members of other groups. Piper discusses a further type of unacknowledged prejudice, which she also calls "second-order discrimination": when a characteristic—say wearing baggy pants and a backward baseball cap—is disliked or devalued in *anyone*, but precisely because it is associated with a specific devalued group (in this case, blacks). In the second case, blackness is devalued in general, even when it is found in nonblack groups.

44. Generally, prejudiced people adopt the common cultural stereotypes attached to the target groups. But this is not essential to prejudice. The racially prejudiced person's negative beliefs could be completely quirky and idiosyncratic (for example, thinking that Mexican Americans are emotionally closed and are scheming to take over the society, two characteristics not generally associated in the United States with Mexicans or Mexican Americans).

45. Janet Ward Schofield and H. Andrew Sagar, "Integrating the Desegregated School: Problems and Possibilities," in *Advances in Motivation and Achievement: A Research Annual*, ed. M. Maehr and D. Bartz (Greenwich, Conn., 1984), 33–36.

46. A well-developed literature in social psychology—much of it inspired by what Allport called "the contact hypothesis"—attempts to articulate the conditions under which contact between racial groups leads to understanding, acceptance, and a reduction in prejudice. A good summary of this literature can be found in Walter Stephan, *Reducing Prejudice and Stereotyping in Schools* (New York, 1999), 40–57.

47. Allport's point about the "inflexibility" of the generalization is that it must be resistant to counter-evidence. (Appiah also builds such resistance into his definition of "racism" in "Racisms," in *The Anatomy of Racism*, ed. David Theo Goldberg [Minneapolis, 1990], 5, 6–8.) If someone immediately gives up a generalization about a group upon being presented with evidence that some members of the group do not possess the characteristic in question, Allport says the generalization was a "misconception" but not an inflexible generalization, as involved in prejudice (9). Allport is certainly correct that genuine prejudices generally involve inflexible generalizations and not mere misconceptions. But I think that a person who had formed a genuine antipathy toward a group, yet one based on a misconception she abandons in the face of counter-evidence, was still prejudiced until the time she abandoned her antipathy. Her prejudice may not have been deeply-rooted, but it was still a prejudice.

48. See, for example, Paul M. Sniderman and Edward G. Carmines, *Reaching Beyond Race* (Cambridge, Mass., 1997), 15. The authors comment on their survey question "To what extent is opposition to affirmative action driven by racial prejudice?" by saying, "Racism is not the only issue, however," thereby seeming to equate "racism" and "racial prejudice."

49. Ted Golda, "A Megastar Long Buried under a Layer of Blackface," *New York Times*, Oct. 22, 2000, Arts & Leisure, 1, 34.

50. Ibid. Blackface minstrelsy is a racially complex phenomenon to which contemporary historical scholarship has devoted a good deal of attention. Its ambiguity is expressed in the

title of Eric Lott's *Love and Theft: Blackface Minstrelsy and the American Working Class* (New York, 1993). Blacks themselves came to use blackface in performance modes that, W. T. Lhamon Jr. argues, subverted the stereotypes it traded on. *Raising Cain: Blackface Performance from Jim Crow to Hip Hop* (Cambridge, Mass., 1998).

51. Ellis is interviewed in Studs Terkel, *American Dreams: Lost and Found* (New York, 1980), 200–211.

52. A further complexity is that not every genuine racist is equally psychically invested in his or her racism. The film *Remember the Titans*, although clearly somewhat sentimentalized, portrays a white football player, Gerry Bertier, who at the beginning of the film is a racist. (Several of the characters, including Bertier, are based on actual persons.) Bertier is hostile to and holds demeaning views of the black football players who join the team as part of the integration of his Virginia high school in 1971. But through forced contact with the black players and under the direction of the new black coach, Bertier fairly quickly changes and sheds his previous racism. Other white players turn out to be more resistant, and one of them finds the path to racial acceptance impossible. Prior to the team's integration Bertier was certainly a racist—he was psychically invested in racist hostilities and inferiorizing views of blacks—but this investment did not run very deep. *Remember the Titans.* Dir. Boaz Yakin. Walt Disney Pictures, 2000.

53. The flag most commonly associated with the Confederacy and generally known in contemporary culture as "the Confederate flag" is a blue cross with white stars, set on a red background. This flag is sometimes inaccurately referred to as the "stars and bars," which was the official flag of the Confederate States of America. See Sanford Levinson, "They Whisper: Reflections on Flags, Monuments, and State Holidays, and the Construction of Social Meaning in a Multicultural Society," *Chicago-Kent Law Review* 70, no. 3 (1995): 1086 n. 21.

54. Patricia Williams, *The Rooster's Egg: On the Persistence of Prejudice* (Cambridge, Mass., 1995), 29. Williams points out that the brouhaha surrounding this incident focused so much on free speech and First Amendment concerns that the issue of the cultural meaning of the flag was misrepresented. "There was a ubiquitous assumption that the white student's attribution of meaning to the Confederate flag was 'just hers,' so no one else had any 'business' complaining about it. The flag's meaning became a form of private property that she could control exclusively and despite other assertions of its symbolic power" (29–30).

55. In recent years the Confederate battle flag has become a rallying symbol for a barely disguised neo-Confederate racist movement in the South. See "Rebels with a Cause," *Southern Poverty Law Center's Intelligence Report*, no. 99 (Summer 2000): 6–12, and Ron Nixon, "Letter from South Carolina," *Nation*, May 15, 2000, 21–23.

56. Two black founders of a company called "NuSouth" have made one attempt at forging such a new symbol. They have created a logo for a line of clothing, consisting of the Confederate flag in the colors of African liberation—red, green, and black. Though these men are primarily out to make money rather than engage in a political project, this is nevertheless the sort of process that could lead to the cultural shift required for the widespread discrediting of the Confederate flag as an appropriate symbol of southern pride. See Jack Hitt, "Confederate Chic," *Gentleman's Quarterly*, Nov. 1997, 261ff. The ingeniousness of the "NuSouth" flag is that it both evokes the flag that is so meaningful to many people, yet explicitly and pointedly distances itself from its racist meanings. According to a March 1999 account, several people wore shirts with the logo to the Million Man March in 1995, but 70 percent of sales are to white customers. Curtis Wilkie, "Pair Redo Stars, Bars in Hues of Liberation," *Boston Globe*, Mar. 20, 1999, A1, A7.

57. The swastika is a particularly good example of change in the public meaning of a symbol. Although few in the Western world would deny that the swastika is, currently, a racist symbol, it has existed as a good luck (or otherwise innocuous) symbol for several thousand years and in many different parts of the world (including the United States, where it was once used as a Coca-Cola logo), having originated in India. Whether in the foreseeable future the swastika can shed the cultural meanings associated with Nazism is doubtful, though

some persons wish to attempt such a resuscitation. Sarah Boxer, "A Symbol of Hatred Pleads Not Guilty," *New York Times*, July 29, 2000, A18.

58. Tatsha Robertson, "Old Symbols, New Debates," *Boston Globe*, Aug. 7, 1999, B1, B5.

59. I am grateful to David Wong for pressing me to clarify what it is that makes a symbol racist.

60. There is no denying that children *are* often aware that their remark or joke is hurtful. Florence and Miriam Davidson report a child coming into a room and saying, "Is anyone Jewish?" so that, if the answer is no, he can tell a joke. The Davidsons' informants said that in such situations no one ever admits to being Jewish. To do so would be to spoil the good time of one's peers, and to reveal oneself as a member of an ethnic group that is ripe for insult and disdain. The children telling the joke, and those laughing at it, realize that it is offensive, and that it puts down an ethnic/racial group; it is in that sense racist. Florence H. and Miriam M. Davidson, *Changing Childhood Prejudice: The Caring Work of the Schools* (Westport, Conn., 1995).

Children may recognize that a joke is at a group's expense without really understanding *how* it insults the group. For example, someone in the group hearing the anti-Jewish joke might see that his friends are laughing at it yet not understand why it is funny; perhaps he is not aware of the anti-Jewish stereotypes the joke relies on. Later he might tell that same joke himself, remembering that it drew a laugh in non-Jewish company. As he knows the joke is hurtful, it is as important for the educator to help him see why he should not say it as it is to help the child who actually holds the stereotype of Jews that the joke is based on. The former child is on the road to developing fully racist attitudes as well. To be able to tell racist jokes and to hear them without anyone objecting legitimizes racist stereotypes and thus encourages the actual adopting (not only the purveying) of those stereotypes.

61. Lilia Bartolomé and Donaldo Macedo, "Dancing with Bigotry: The Poisoning of Racial and Ethnic Identities," *Harvard Education Review* 67, no. 2 (Summer 1997): 241–42.

62. In this section I am discussing symbols that are racist because of their content and in light of their history and cultural meaning. A symbol or epithet can be racist, however, because of the displayer's or speaker's intention in using it, not because it is in any way culturally racist. For example, in 1994, Nation of Islam lieutenant Khallid Muhammad referred to Jews as "bagel-eaters" in a speech at Keene College. This remark was antisemitic because Muhammad intended it as a racial or ethnic insult, not because "bagel-eater" is a culturally established offensive expression for Jews. Jayson Blair, "K. A. Muhammad, 53, Dies; Ex-official of Nation of Islam," *New York Times*, Feb. 18, 2001.

63. Mike Royko, "Time to Be Color Blind to All Words of Hatred," *Chicago Tribune*, Feb. 9, 1994, 3.

64. In a 1998 case, the Ninth Circuit Court of Appeals described "nigger" as "the most noxious racial epithet in the contemporary American lexicon," and asserted that the word "as applied to blacks is uniquely provocative and demeaning and there is probably no word or phrase that could be directed at any other group that could cause comparable injury." *Monteiro v. Tempe Union High School Disctrict*, 158 F. 3d 1022 (CA 9 1998), cited in Randall Kennedy, "Who Can Say 'Nigger' . . . and Other Related Questions," Tanner Lectures, Stanford University, 1999, pp. 4–5 (in manuscript).

65. An interesting perspective on the word's use by younger blacks is provided by a black student: "When T called me a 'nigger' it really made me mad. It didn't use to make me as mad when I heard that word. But now I know how my African ancestors were made slaves and it's different. I know what it means." Deborah Byrnes, "Addressing Race, Ethnicity, and Culture in the Classroom," in *Common Bonds: Anti-bias Teaching in a Diverse Society*, ed. Byrnes and Gary Kiger (Wheaton, Md., 1992), 19. It must be mentioned, however, that the use of "nigger" by blacks has been defended by many blacks—a familiar pattern of a group appropriating a term used to insult them for positive purposes. Such "reclamation," by stigmatized groups, of derogatory terms referring to them is insightfully explored in Lynne Tirrell, "Derogatory Terms: Racism, Sexism, and the Inferential Role Theory of Meaning," in *Lan-*

guage and Liberation, ed. Christina Hendricks and Kelly Oliver (Albany, N.Y., 1999). There is no inconsistency in regarding the use of racially charged symbols and language as morally asymmetrical with respect to their use by an in-group or an out-group. Indeed, I defend a similar asymmetry in chapter 2.

66. I am grateful to Jorge Garcia for pressing me to recognize racist believing as a phenomenon distinct from racist belief. Garcia explores both in "Heart of Racism" and, especially, "Current Conceptions," 14–16.

67. Anthony Appiah similarly distinguishes between "propositional racists," who abandon racist beliefs in the face of counter-evidence, and "racially prejudiced" persons, who do not (generally because they have an ideological attachment to those beliefs, perhaps because they serve to rationalize such persons' own privileged position). "Racisms," 6–9.

68. It is by no means easy to discern whether a person actually holds a belief subconsciously or acts *as if* she holds such a belief but really does not.

69. David T. Wellman, *Portraits of White Racism,* 2d ed. (Cambridge, Eng., 1993), xi. Wellman's is by no means an idiosyncratic view. The idea that racist beliefs should be understood as those whose social effect is to defend white privilege is a familiar trend in discussions of racism. See for example, Harlan Dalton, *Racial Healing: Confronting the Fear between Blacks and Whites* (New York, 1996), 93.

70. Wellman's use of "defend" in his definition of "racist beliefs" carries an implication that the belief's proponents are taking sides in a social struggle over advantage and disadvantage, an implication somewhat at odds with his phrase "regardless of the intentions involved."

71. In 1999 the U.S. Department of Education's Office for Civil Rights circulated guidelines stating that the use of any educational test that has a significant disparate impact on members of any race is discriminatory and is illegal "unless it is educationally necessary and there is no practicable alternative form of assessment." Patrick Healy, "Civil Rights Office Questions Legality of College's Use of Standardized Tests," *Chronicle of Higher Education,* May 28, 1999, A28.

72. For example, though Martin Trow concedes that the current degree of underpreparation of blacks and Latinos that results in lower scores on tests than whites is indeed rooted in historical racial injustices, he nevertheless contends that the positive value of color blindness, and of uniformity of standards are more morally compelling than the reasons in favor of admitting those black and Latino applicants. "California after Racial Preferences," *Public Interest* (Spring 1999): 64–85. For my argument that "color blindness" can not bear the moral weight that views like Trow's place on it, see chapter 4.

73. See, for example, Gertrude Ezorsky, *Racism and Justice: The Case for Affirmative Action* (Ithaca, N.Y., 1991), 9. The term "institutional racism" was coined by Ture and Hamilton in 1967, but their usage differs from more recent ones in an important respect. They use it to refer to *intentional* subordination, accompanied by antiblack attitudes. The more recent definitions, on which I have drawn, retain the idea that racially unjust outcomes can be a product of the "normal" workings of institutions and policies, but jettison Ture and Hamilton's implication that these workings are always undergirded by racial animus. Ture and Hamilton, *Black Power,* 3–6.

74. Indeed, Ezorsky recognizes these benefits. *Racism and Justice,* 24.

75. The Supreme Court, however, has ruled such a compromise between seriority and affirmative action unconstitutional. *Wygant v. Jackson Board of Education,* 106 S.Ct. 1842 (1986).

76. One could define "institutional racism" as "race-blind processes that increase, or maintain, racial injustice and that involve nothing ethically positive enough to outweigh this ethically deleterious feature." This would be an improvement over the definition offered in the text, if more cumbersome. But it would still suffer from the implication (denied by the definition but carried by the common associations with "racism") that the processes are

themselves somehow tainted with racist motives. Andrew Koppelman, *Antidiscrimination Law and Social Equality* (New Haven, Conn., 1997), 48.

77. William Julius Wilson finds this practice and motivation in some employers, in his study of employers in Chicago. W. J. Wilson, *When Work Disappears: The World of the New Urban Poor* (New York, 1996), chap. 5.

78. Such intentional exclusion might not be an entirely straightforward case of racial bias or antipathy, but rather "statistical discrimination", in which employers harbor no animus toward blacks but believe on the basis of a statistical generalization that blacks are less reliable workers than some other groups. See chapter 4.

79. My account of institutional racism as "racist institutions" or "institutionalized racism" is indebted to Garcia, "Heart of Racism," 10–11, 24–28; and "Current Conceptions," 6.

80. *Gaston County v. United States*, 395 U.S. 285 (1969). My account of the Gaston County case is drawn from Robert E. Smith, *Racism in the Post Civil Rights Era: Now You See it, Now You Don't* (Albany, N.Y., 1996), 58–59.

81. "Insurer to Pay Back $206 Million," *Boston Globe*, June 22, 2000, D2.

82. Greg Winter, "Coca-Cola Settles Racial Bias Case," *New York Times*, Nov. 17, 2000, A1, C6.

83. This development, and its wider deleterious effects on urban black communities, has been extensively documented by William Julius Wilson in two famous studies, *The Truly Disadvantaged: The Inner City, the Underclass, and Public Policy* (Chicago, 1987), and *When Work Disappears*. Wilson's arguments about the racial dimension of black poverty and their ethical implications are given nuanced scrutiny by the philosopher Bernard Boxill in *Blacks and Social Justice*, rev. ed. (Lanham, Md., 1992), 30–31, 44–46, 227–245.

84. It has been plausibly argued that the increased ideological opposition to such programs, which is harmful to low-income persons of every race, has in part been driven by their association with persons of color, and especially blacks (who indeed are disproportionately benefited by them). See Thomas Edsall and Mary Edsall, *Chain Reaction: The Impact of Race, Rights, and Taxes on American Politics* (New York, 1992). If this is so, then racial animus or disaffection would play some role in the sustaining (though not the original causing) of both the race and the class injustices described in the text.

85. Wilson, *When Work Disappears*, 208.

86. One shortcoming I see in Jorge Garcia's theory of racism (see note 24) is a failure to explain why contemporary reflective attitudes accord different moral valences to different forms of ill will or unconcern—and in particular why race-based ill will is more vicious than other forms. In Garcia's view race-based ill will is simply one subspecies of ill will (or, perhaps, of unjustified ill will), distinguished from other forms by its object and cause (the other's [assigned] race), but not by its moral weight or significance. (This viewpoint is implied rather than explicitly stated.) Although in his articles on this subject Garcia occasionally mentions the sorts of historical and social considerations I argue are central to the distinctive moral opprobrium of "racism," he never builds these into his account of racism.

87. To say that these systems were "race-based" is to say that they were understood, especially by their perpetrators, to be appropriate and justified because of the racial character of the subjugated group. It is not to say they were motivated in their fundamental character by racial animus or an intrinsic desire to subjugate a racial group. On the contrary, as will be discussed further in chapter 6, most were motivated largely by greed for power and financial gain. (Nazism is an exception, in its relation to Jews.)

88. Consider the following want ad in the New York Evening Post, from 1830: "Wanted, A Cook or Chambermaid . . . must be American, Scotch, Swiss, or African—no Irish." Cited in Roger Daniels, *Coming to America: A History of Immigration and Ethnicity in American Life* (New York, 1990), 131. On the lowly status of Irish Americans during this period, see David Roediger, *The Wages of Whiteness: Race and the Making of the American Working Class* (New York: Verso, 1991), and Noel Ignatiev, *How the Irish Became White* (New York: Routledge, 1995).

89. Discrimination against the Irish was never given the force of law, as it was in respect to blacks, who were deprived of suffrage rights, could not intermarry, and were subject to other restrictions. (See chapter 7.) In this vital respect no "white" immigrant group faced legally enforced barriers comparable to those endured by blacks or, indeed, by Asians. (See chapter 7 for more on differential treatment of racial groups.)

90. Racism in the slavery and segregation eras was more likely to function in this all-or-nothing way. Nevertheless, there is much evidence that, even in such contexts, white attitudes toward blacks were often vary ambivalent. Thomas Jefferson is a particularly striking example. See Lott, *Love and Theft,* and Grace Hale, *Making Whiteness: The Culture of Segregation in the South, 1890–1940* (New York, 1998).

91. Bob Blauner, "'Talking Past Each Other': Black and White Languages of Race," in *Race and Ethnic Conflict: Contending Views on Prejudice, Discrimination, and Ethnoviolence,* ed. Fred L. Pincus and Howard J. Ehrlich (Boulder, Colo: Westview Press, 1994).

92. Confining the opprobrium of "racism" to particular categories requires more fine-tuning than I am able to give of what counts as a distinct "category." Verbally insulting someone with a racist epithet is not morally worse than murdering him for personal gain (a nonracist reason) even though both are instances of "behavior." One can avoid this problem formally by saying that the types in question must all be morally comparable, *in the absence of racial considerations.* So racist insults would be compared to (and would be worse than) nonracist insults; racist murders worse than nonracist murders. The latter intuition is recognized legally in the idea of a "hate crime": a crime otherwise of the same type (e.g., violent assault) is rendered worthy of more severe punishment if it is motivated by hatred for certain categories of person.

93. This section is indebted to a discussion of an earlier draft with David Wilkins, Lani Guinier, Martha Minow, and especially David Wong and Jorge Garcia, and to subsequent comments from Garcia, to whom I am also grateful for his suggestion of the name of the section ("Selective Racism"), and of the type of racism or prejudice discussed therein.

94. A form of selective prejudice well known to social psychologists is that wherein attitudes toward individual members of a group do not always translate into comparable attitudes toward the group as such. Thus cooperative learning in schools, in which members of racial group A get to know, like, and respect members of racial group B, does not always result in a reduction of prejudice toward or stereotypes of group B itself. See Stephan, *Reducing Prejudice and Stereotyping,* 42.

95. Someone who is hostile toward young males in general, not specifically black males, presents a different case, which is not racial prejudice but some combination of age and gender prejudice.

96. This form of selective racial prejudice is also manifest in white persons who say to a black person with whom they are friendly or toward whom they have positive feelings, "I don't think of you as black," wrongly thinking this remark to be a compliment and a demonstration that they lack prejudice. A similar phenomenon involves Christians saying "But some of my best friends are Jews" as evidence that they lack prejudice, failing to recognize that, as in the former case, seeing some individuals as *exceptions* to negative group-targeted affect or generalizations leaves those negative sentiments fully in place. This is a slightly different form of the phenomenon discussed in note 94.

97. Shipler reports a subtle but no doubt fairly common form of veiled animus toward blackness. A young light-skinned mixed-race woman said of her white employer who liked the *Cosby Show* that she "became very irate when one of the daughters named her twins Winnie and Nelson [after the Mandelas] because then the show became too black." Shipler, *Nation of Strangers,* 134–135. It is as if many white people took the *Cosby Show* to be making a deal with them that they would warmly accept this black family-centered show as long as it did not mark itself as being "too black." This form is in certain ways akin to what Adrian Piper called a form of "higher-order discrimination" (see note 43), in being directed toward blackness itself.

98. A modification of this form of selective prejudice—a common form, I would sug-

gest—involves the subject being prejudiced against blacks in general, with the prejudice against young black males being especially intense; such prejudice cannot be accounted for as a summing of prejudice against young people and males. The confluence of identity categories is necessary to trigger the (given level of) prejudice.

99. I wish to thank the Francis Villemain Memorial Lecture series at San Jose State College, at which material from this chapter (and chapter 3) were presented in something like its present form.

Chapter 2. Can Blacks Be Racist?

1. The schema of "white" vs. "people of color" does not exactly apply to the Nazi philosophy, as both the superior groups ("Aryans") and the inferior groups (Slavs, Jews) were primarily distinct Europeans subgroups who were conceived of as distinct races. Yet even in Nazism the superior "races" were viewed as lighter and the inferior as darker. Moreover, the Nazis did regard all the groups we now think of as "people of color" as inferior, though the Nazi alliance with the Japanese forced them to temper their view in that case. Neo-Nazism within the United States has tended to drop the "Aryan" emphasis and call the superior group "whites"; Jews are distinctly regarded as "nonwhite."

2. Other ethnoracial groups were not included in these surveys, in part because all the studies have a historical dimension reaching back at least several decades, when the numbers of Asians and Latinos were much smaller, but also because the race problem has been standardly defined as "black and white."

3. Jennifer Hochschild, *Facing Up to the American Dream: Race, Class, and the Soul of the Nation*, with a new preface by the author (Princeton, N.J., 1996); Kinder and Sanders, *Divided by Color;* Schuman, Steeh, Bobo, and Krysan, *Racial Attitudes.*

4. Blauner, "Talking Past."

5. Hochschild, *Facing Up,* 63 (1991 figures).

6. Blauner, "Talking Past," 20. Admittedly, Blauner's article was originally published in a general-circulation rather than scholarly publication. That form of writing can discourage qualification and nuance. Nevertheless, precisely because it will be read by a wider public, the author has a particular responsibility to guard against this sort of overstatement.

7. Navarette, *Darker Shade of Crimson,* 107–8.

8. Apache, *Apache Ain't Shit,* Tommy Boy Music, Time Warner, 1993. Cited in "Lyrics by Black or Latin Artists Who Put out Violent Racism and Who Were Either Awarded Grammy's or Were Promoted by Artists Who Won Grammy's," July 26, 1999, at www.home.att.net/ *~phosphor/introtogrammys.html. This website has many examples of similar lyrics; whites are frequently referred to as "devils."

Singing these lyrics does not make the performer or the writer "a racist" nor someone who harbors racist attitudes. Nevertheless, such performers are certainly purveying racist sentiments, even if they are just out to make a buck and do not expect to be taken seriously.

9. "'Racial' prejudice is severe against the roughly 700,000 Koreans who remain in Japan from among those imported for forced labor there during World War II. Despite the fact that more than forty years have passed and most of these so-called Koreans have become Japanese in language and living style, they are prevented as much as the laws permit from acquiring Japanese citizenship. Most Japanese still feel that marriage with the child of a Korean or Chinese immigrant, as with the surviving 2 percent of Japanese irrationally designated as outcasts (*burakumin*), would sully their 'pure' Japanese blood." Edwin O. Reischauer, "Race Prejudice Pervades the World," in *The Japanese Today: Change and Continuity* (Cambridge, Mass., 1988), reprinted in *On Prejudice: A Global Perspective,* ed. Daniela Gioseffi (New York, 1993), 183. An article in the *New York Times* details the continuing devaluation of ethnic Koreans in Japan. Howard French, "Forever Korean: Once Scorned, Always

Scorned," *New York Times*, Nov. 20, 2000. On the *burakumin*, see Claude Fischer et al., *Inequality by Design: Cracking the Bell Curve Myth* (Princeton, N.J., 1996), esp. chap. 8. On more general racism within Japanese society, especially in connection with the explicitly racial discourse circulating in Japan during World War II, see Charles Mills, *The Racial Contract* (Ithaca, N.Y., 1997), 127–28. A particularly poignant and horrible example of transnational racism is that of a Mauritanian black man who was expelled by Arab authorities because he was black, then immigrated to the United States, where he was murdered eight years later by a white skinhead in Denver, Colorado. James Brooke, "Killing Wasn't Much, Skinhead Says," *New York Times*, Nov. 22, 1997, 47.

10. Ghassan Hage, *White Nation: Fantasies of White Supremacy in a Multicultural Society* (Annandale, Australia, 1998), 34.

11. "Friends Helped Labor Nominee Move Up, Then Almost Brought Her Down," *New York Times*, Mar. 12, 1997. (The article is about Alexis Herman, then President Clinton's secretary of labor; Godwin was a classmate and friend of Herman's.)

12. *The New Republic*, Nov. 6, 1995, 27.

13. I remember reading and being impressed with this point years ago in Bernard Boxill's first edition of his pioneering work, *Blacks and Social Justice*, but am unable to find the reference in the more recent edition. Boxill, *Blacks and Social Justice*, rev. ed.

14. Ibid., 51.

15. Joseph Barndt, *Dismantling Racism: The Continuing Challenge to White America* (Minneapolis, 1991), 28.

16. Studs Terkel, *Race: How Blacks and Whites Think and Feel About the American Obsession* (New York, 1992), 205.

17. This example, and much of the accompanying argument in the remainder of this chapter, is taken from Lawrence Blum, "Moral Asymmetries in Racism," in *Racism and Philosophy*, ed. Susan Babbitt and Sue Campbell (Ithaca, N.Y., 1999), 79–97. The example itself is adapted from Valerie Ooka Pang, "Racial Prejudice: Still Alive and Hurtful," in Nitza Hidalgo, Emilie Siddle, and Ceasar McDowell, *Facing Racism in Education* (Cambridge, Mass., 1990), 29.

18. I am not saying, however, that white dominance in the major institutions in the society is entirely irrelevant to the harm caused by nonwhites in subinstitutions in which they hold power. In the example earlier, the white student, though a minority in the school and thus vulnerable to the prejudices of his classmates, is "buffered" from the more extreme pain of a black student who knows that he is not only a minority in the school but subordinated and stigmatized in the larger society.

19. Michael Omi and Howard Winant's influential account of race and racialization in the United States rejects the "racism equals prejudice plus power" view and asserts that blacks can be racist. *Racial Formation in the United States: From the 1960s to the 1990s*, 2d ed. (New York, 1994), 69–73. Garcia, however, points out in his perceptive assessment of their account that Omi and Winant retain a definitional link between racism and systems of domination. They see racism as an attempt to impose domination on another racial group. Racism does not require an actually existing structure of domination in the society, but does require an intention to dominate on the part of the racist. Garcia agrees with my rejection of this view on the grounds that racial antipathy is racism independent of any attempt to dominate. Garcia, "Philosophical Analysis," 10–12.

20. "*Playboy* Interview—Spike Lee—Candid Conversation," *Playboy*, July 1991, 51.

21. Andrew Hacker, *Two Nations: Black and White, Separate, Hostile, Unequal*, expanded and updated (New York: Ballantine Books, 1995 [1992]), 33.

22. McCall describes a form of antiwhite hatred shared by his black ninth-grade peers, which led to violence against whites: "We all hated white people. . . . We walked through secluded areas of the building after classes on Fridays. When we came upon a white boy, somebody would light into him, then everybody sprang and we'd do him in." Nathan McCall, *Makes Me Wanna Holler* (New York, 1994), 58.

23. For examples, see "For the Record," in the Southern Poverty Law Center's *Intelligence Report* (published by Klanwatch, Spring 1997), 31: "A white woman was allegedly assaulted and robbed by a black man who used racial epithets." "A white man was allegedly attacked by two Hispanic men who used racial slurs."

24. Garcia makes this point about the powerless bigoted racist very convincingly. "Some Current Conceptions," 13.

25. "*Playboy* Interview."

26. Spike Lee's portrayal of racism in his superb film *Do the Right Thing* (Universal Pictures, 1987) belies his cavalier remarks about individual racial prejudice on the part of persons of color. In one powerful montage scene, Lee displays five characters—a Korean, an African American, an Italian, a Jew, and a Latino—spewing out racial epithets at one of the other groups. The audience is clearly meant to react to this scene not as a universal condition of innocuous prejudice but rather as a disturbingly widespread manifestation of racism, which the film implies is in some form responsible for the serious racial divisions and troubles explored therein.

27. That racism is ideology is an argument much less frequently made, however, than that racism is prejudice plus power. Outside of some academic circles, "racism" has long since broadened its reach beyond ideology.

28. Miles's understanding of "ideology" seems too expansive to me; it jettisons whatever advantage is gained by using the connection to the original Nazi ideology as leverage to prevent conceptual inflation.

29. This theory of white inferiority is derived from a book by Michael Bradley, *The Iceman Inheritance: Prehistoric Sources of Western Man's Racism, Sexism, and Aggression* (Toronto, 1978). Frank Dikötter argues that around the middle of the last century, a racial consciousness emerged in China in relation to Westerners, as a result of first contacts and a need to defend Chinese civilization. "The Idea of Race in Modern China," in *Ethnicity*, ed. John Hutchinson and Anthony Smith (Oxford, 1996), 245ff.

30. Miles would not be unhappy with the consequence that blacks can be racist; he rejects the view that only whites can be racist. *Racism*, 6.

31. Appiah makes a similar point when he says that certain racially prejudiced persons may not be morally responsible for their prejudices and so might be bad people yet not be responsible for being bad. "Racisms," 9.

32. Muhammad explains to Baldwin an elaborate theory of history premised on the idea that the white man is a "devil" whose reign on earth is soon coming to an end, when he will be totally destroyed. James Baldwin, *The Fire Next Time* (New York, 1988 [1963]), 90–93.

33. Marilyn Friedman suggests that it might sometimes be of value, and in any case justified, for the racially victimized to be racist toward, though not physically harm, their victimizers. Without engaging all of her quite interesting arguments on this point, I suggest that the most she shows is that it might make someone feel good to be racist, not that it would be genuinely empowering or enhance a worthy form of self-respect. The initial plausibility of her argument lies in conflating the targeting of one's actual victimizer with targeting "a member of the group that systematically perpetrates the primary racism." Friedman, "Racism: Paradigms and Moral Appraisal (A Response to Blum)," in Babbitt and Campbell, *Racism and Philosophy*, 102–7. Bernard Boxill seems to me correct on this matter when he argues that while it generally expresses and enhances self-respect to protest and defend oneself against racial wrongs, the form of that protest is not a racist attack on one's victimizer but an assertion of one's dignity and a challenge to the perpetrator's view of oneself. (Boxill cites W. E. B. Du Bois and Frederick Douglass in support of this view.) Boxill, *Blacks and Social Justice*, 187–88.

34. Some dimensions of this asymmetry argument will apply to racist practices and institutions as well; but I am concerned here only with personal racism.

35. In an insightful critique of the article on which this chapter is based, Marilyn Friedman raised two objections. One is that my discussion of moral asymmetry seemed to imply

that racial victimization of whites by persons of color was the paradigmatic form of racism, so that the sources of asymmetry involved in forms of racism against persons of color appeared as "extra" factors over and above the core meaning of racism as it occurred in antiwhite racism. I think Friedman may have been right about this, and through my account of the historical sources of the moral opprobrium attached to racism in chapter 1 I have tried to make it clear that our sense of what racism is derives primarily from the racism of whites. At the same time, the contemporary meaning of "racism" certainly does include antiwhite racial antipathy and inferiorization.

Friedman's second criticism was that I seemed to regard single acts as the fundamental unit of racism, rather than patterns or structures. I have tried to make clear in chapter 1 that what is conceptually fundamental in racism are two themes—antipathy and inferiorization—and that no specific category in which those themes are manifest (acts, beliefs, symbols, statements, persons, structures, institutions, societies) is more fundamental than any other. Friedman, "Racism: Paradigms," 98–107.

36. Shipler, *Nation of Strangers*, 150.

37. Examples of violence against vulnerable but nonsubordinate groups: the murder of Vincent Chin, a Chinese American, in 1982, and the murder of Asian American children in an elementary school in Stockton, California, in 1989, both discussed in Yen Le Espiritu, *Asian American Panethnicity: Bridging Institutions and Identities* (Philadelphia: 1992), 134–60. Others include violence against Jews and Asian Americans by Benjamin Smith previously noted, and Buford Furrow. Furrow, an emotionally disturbed man with a history of involvement with anti-Semitic groups, declared he had intended his shootings at a Jewish community center to send "a wake-up call to America to kill Jews." Linda Deutsch, "Gunman at Jewish Center Gets Life Term," *Boston Globe*, Mar. 27, 2001, A3.

38. "Asian Americans" do not constitute a unified group from the point of view of positional inferiority. Groups present in the United States for several generations, such as Korean Americans, Japanese Americans, and Chinese Americans, are not positionally inferior, while newer immigrant groups from Southeast Asia (Vietnam, Cambodia, and Laos, for example) are.

39. Differences in European and American relationships to anti-Semitism and the Holocaust are not the only factors accounting for the presence of such laws in Europe and their absence in the United States. A stronger emphasis in the United States on protecting speech independent of content is another factor.

40. Laurence Thomas insightfully explores several other moral and epistemological asymmetries between subordinate groups (which he calls "diminished social categories") and nonsubordinate groups. "Moral Deference," *African-American Perspectives and Philosophical Traditions*, ed. John P. Pittman (New York, 1997).

41. Hochschild, *Facing Up*.

42. Dalton, *Racial Healing*, 206–10.

Chapter 3. Varieties of Racial Ills

1. This was reported to me by one of my high school students, and it is a common complaint among college students of color. Vivian Paley reports a similar incident. A black high school student says, "Yes, the teachers always turn to me when anything about black people comes up and I don't like that." Vivian Gussin Paley, *Kwanzaa and Me* (Cambridge: Mass., 1995), 135.

2. Thomas Morgan, "The World Ahead: Black Parents Prepare Their Children for Pride and Prejudice," *New York Times Magazine*, Oct. 27, 1985, 2.

3. Charles Taylor, "The Politics of Recognition," in *Multiculturalism*, ed. Amy Gutmann (Princeton N.J., 1994).

4. Taylor's essay has lent support to a commonly held view that the ethnic dimension of personal identity is the primary appropriate object of recognition, although the argument Taylor actually proffers for the good of recognition is much less particularized in scope. (The Haitian American student did, indeed, care about her ethnic identity; but she needn't have.) Taylor also assumes (again, echoing a widely held view) that everyone who is attached to her ethnic identity must be steeped in the culture that is connected to that ethnicity; but someone could care about her Japanese American identity without having grown up in or adopted anything like a distinctive Japanese American culture. It is the importance of the ethnic identity feature to the student, not the presence or absence of an ethnoculture, that triggers the need for recognition. For further critique of these assumptions in Taylor's work, see Lawrence Blum, "Recognition and Multiculturalism in Education," presentation to the Philosophy of Education Society of Great Britain, April 2001; "Ethnicity, Identity, Community" in *Justice and Caring: The Search for Common Ground in Education*, ed. Michael Katz, Nel Noddings, and Kenneth Strike (New York, 1999); and K. Anthony Appiah, "Identity, Authenticity, Survival: Multicultural Societies and Cultural Reproduction," in *Multiculturalism*, ed. Amy Gutmann.

5. *Skin Deep*, Dir. Frances Reid. Iris Films, 1991.

6. Racial groups generally wish recognition not only for the distinctness of their identities, but also as equals. For a view that Taylor fails adequately to distinguish between these forms of recognition—and, more generally, fails to appreciate how issues facing racial groups are different from those facing ethnocultural groups—see L. Blum, "Recognition, Value, and Equality: A Critique of Charles Taylor's and Nancy Fraser's Accounts of Multiculturalism," in *Theorizing Multiculturalism: A Guide to the Current Debate*, ed. Cynthia Willett (London, 1998), 73–99, and L. Blum, "Multiculturalism, Racial Justice, and Community: Reflections on Charles Taylor's 'The Politics of Recognition,' " in *Defending Diversity: Contemporary Philosophical Perspectives on Pluralism and Multiculturalism*, ed. L. Foster and P. Herzog (Amherst, Mass., 1994), 175–206.

By tying the form of recognition involved here to the individual's relationship to her group identity, I deliberately avoid having to take a position on the complex matter of the character of the group identity in its own right. In the context of "identity politics," conceptions of these group identities are often, and rightly, criticized for being too narrowly construed, thereby constricting individual members; for pretending that clear and sharp boundaries can be drawn around group identities; and for encouraging a narrow group-focused concern. By focusing on the individual, my account takes the identity as the individual himself construes it; it is *that* identity that warrants recognition, not the group identity as construed by some subgroup (for example, a traditionalist or conservative one).

7. A further dimension of this situation involves the white friends' failure to see the importance of celebrating King's birthday *in its own right*, not its importance to the friend. The former might involve an ignorance of or, worse, a resistance to crediting King as an important national leader and to acknowledging the centrality of race and racism in American history.

8. Sometimes the demand, or plea, to be seen as an individual is a way of denying group-based identities that one would rather not acknowledge. For example, it can be a way for white persons to deny that, like it or not, they are seen as white, and that certain privileges come with that status. (See "White Privilege," below.) But appreciation of individuality is only one value in the general domain of race and culture, and should not be understood as a necessarily overriding one.

9. Race and skin color are not the same thing, as we shall see in chapter 4, but "skin color" is sometimes used, as here, to mean "race."

10. Martin Luther King Jr., "I Have a Dream (1963)," in *Testament of Hope: The Essential Writings and Speeches of Martin Luther King Jr.*, ed. James M. Washington (San Francisco, 1991), 219.

11. Letter from John Ciccone, director of the South Boston Information Center, to *Boston Globe*, Nov. 12, 1998.

12. *Chronicle of Higher Education*, Jan. 5, 1994, B4.

13. Jim Sleeper, *Liberal Racism* (New York, 1997), 5.

14. David Hollinger, *PostEthnic America: Beyond Multiculturalism* (New York, 1995), 171.

15. Sleeper, *Liberal Racism*, 9.

16. Values involved in the affirmative action dispute are, for example, the principle of "selection by merit"; procedural fairness; race blindness; correcting historical injustices; educating future leaders of major racial groups; the value of racial diversity to education; and the like. Affirmative action will be discussed in more detail in chapter 4.

17. Sleeper, *Liberal Racism*, 4.

18. In chapter 6 I will appropriate the term "racialism" for a different use.

19. A countervailing argument is that one should select the white instructor precisely in order to break down the very social division that makes the Asian and Asian American students uncomfortable with the white instructor.

20. Nor need a racialist think of racial identity as "primordial" in order to be a racialist. She might well recognize the socially formed and contingent character of racial identities, yet still give them too much importance. This point will be discussed further in chapter 8.

21. See Dinesh D'Souza, *Illiberal Education*, chap. 2.

22. Navarette, *Darker Shade*, 81.

23. On reasons for and values of in-group socializing, especially among black students, see Tatum, "*Why Are All the Black Kids.*" Tatum is particularly sensitive to the developmental dimensions of same-race socializing—how different students' needs are dependent on their stages of racial identity development.

24. The freedom that student groups sometimes seek for cultural expression is a further value, different from the value of recognition of the ethnocultural group. Here students seek only the freedom to express their culture, whether anyone else recognizes the culture (or cultural identity) or not. In practice these two values are not always easy to distinguish, since both the freedom and the recognition have to be granted by the wider institution, and granting the freedom does itself involve a kind of recognition. Yet what one desires from recognition depends on other persons in a way that desiring freedom of cultural expression does not. In "Politics of Recognition," Taylor argues that the Quebecois desire freedom to maintain their distinctive ethnoculture but also (what they do not always admit) acknowledgment from the Anglo-dominated Canadian society as a whole (64).

25. Shipler, *Country of Strangers*, 45 (drawing on interviews with black college students).

26. Tatum argues that the healthiest form of racial identity among minorities involves a security about one's racial identity that permits friendships with members of other races who respect one's own race and racial identity. "*Why Do All the Black Kids,*" 76. Tatum draws her scheme of racial identity development from William Cross Jr., *Shades of Black: Diversity in African-American Identity* (Philadelphia, 1991).

27. In describing the experiences of Cedric Jennings, a black student at Brown University from a poor, urban background, the writer Ron Suskind says, "He feared that if he got close to Harambee [a residence hall for black students and students interested in Afro-American studies], the undertow would be irresistible and his oaths about integration, about taking the toughest path, mixing with kids from all races and creeds, would give way to a separatist compromise." (Suskind adds his own comment: "At Brown, that's the path of least resistance almost everyone takes.") Ron Suskind, *A Hope in the Unseen: An American Odyssey from the Inner City to the Ivy League* (New York, 1998), 332.

28. "Liberal" and "conservative" were determined by listings of members of the Liberal and Conservative parties in New York.

29. The liberals also hung up on the black caller more frequently than did the conservatives, although the conservatives were less likely to help the blacks than to help the whites.

Thus the conservatives could be accounted more prejudiced than the liberals; but it was the liberals' particular form of prejudice in which Gaertner and Dovidio were interested.

30. On this and the other experiments, see Samuel Gaertner and John F. Dovidio, "The Aversive Form of Racism," in *Prejudice, Discrimination, and Racism*, ed. Gaertner and Dovidio (Orlando, Fla., 1986).

31. Gaertner and Dovidio draw the term "aversive racism," the idea of a conflict between racist feelings and an egalitarian conscience, and the centrality of avoidance (rather than a desire to dominate the racial other), from Kovel's *White Racism*.

32. Gaertner and Dovidio, "Aversive Form," 63.

33. In an article published in 1997, Gaertner and Dovidio (in concert with other authors) reassess their "aversive racism" hypothesis and the experiments on which it was based. They say that the differential treatment of blacks and whites need not have stemmed from an animus toward blacks but from a "prowhite" sentiment analogous to favoring members of one's family in invitations to a holiday dinner. (Both the new analysis, and the analogy on which it draws, seem faulty to me.) Abandoning the idea of an antiblack animus seems to me akin to acknowledging that a more benign sentiment such as racial discomfort might be operating. Nevertheless, Gaertner and Dovidio continue to refer to the subject as an "aversive racist." This seems even more conceptually misleading than in their original hypothesis, since they now much more definitively deny that any racial animus is involved. Samuel L. Gaertner, John F. Dovidio, Brenda S. Banker, Mary C. Rust, Jason A. Nier, Gary R. Mottola, and Christine M. Ward, "Does White Racism Necessarily Mean Antiblackness? Aversive Racism and Prowhiteness," in *Off White: Readings on Race, Power, and Society*, ed. Michelle Fine, Lois Weis, Linda C. Powell, and L. Mun Wong (New York, 1997), 167–78.

34. Gaertner and Dovidio would not call such children aversive racists either, since their view thereof involves a self-conception as a racial egalitarian. It is this self-conception that drives the aversions from consciousness. But it is the alleged aversions themselves that my example of the children is meant to question.

35. Walter and Cookie Stephan examine several forms and sources of "intergroup anxiety" that would apply specifically to racial anxiety yet would not count as racism or racial prejudice (though they do count prejudice as one source of such anxiety). Walter G. Stephan and Cookie White Stephan, "Intergroup Anxiety," *Journal of Social Issues* 41, no. 3 (1985): 157–75.

36. At the same time, racial anxiety can certainly mask an unconscious hostility or animus. Perhaps we should read Gaertner and Dovidio's concept of aversive racism as implying that it *always* does.

37. On the civic value of racially mixed schools in which students learn to become more comfortable with members of different racial groups, see Lawrence Blum, "Racial Integration in a Multicultural Age," in *NOMOS* XLIII: *Moral and Political Education*, ed. Stephen Macedo and Yael Tamir (New York, 2002).

38. Walter Stephan, *Reducing Prejudice and Stereotyping in Schools* (New York: 1999), provides a wealth of information about how to improve intergroup relations in schools.

39. Shipler, *Nation of Strangers*, 448.

40. "The over-readiness to make blanket charges of racism—against people, points of view, institutions—has had an effect very nearly the opposite of the one intended. How seriously can one take the idea of racism if everyone is said to be a racist?" Paul M. Sniderman and Thomas Piazza, *The Scar of Race* (Cambridge, Mass., 1993), 6–7, 66.

41. Sniderman and Piazza seldom cite particular authors as espousing the views they oppose; here, however, they appear to have in mind theorists such as Sears and McConahay (discussed in chapter 1, note 40), who tend to see current racism as bolstered by core American values.

42. Sniderman and Piazza, *Scar of Race*, 92–97.

43. Ibid., 108–9.

44. Part of the reason Sniderman and Piazza may be equivocal about counting some white stereotyping of blacks as racial prejudice is that they seem ambivalent about whether the stereotyping is, in some sense, warranted. On the one hand they repeatedly refer to the stereotypes as "one-sided," "moralistic," "oversimplified"; on the other hand they say the stereotypes (even the "nasty" ones) "capture real features of everyday experience" or have "an element of reality." Ibid., 42–44.

45. Ibid., 109.

46. I want to clarify that I am taking no stand on the empirical links between personal racism (in any of its forms) and stances on race-related policy matters. I am concerned only to recognize that these are two different issues, and that different moral vocabularies apply to each. I do, therefore, agree with Sniderman and Piazza as against "new racism" theorists that policy stances that amount to opposition to black interests are not automatic, or criterial, indicators of personal racism. But this still leaves it open whether *in fact* much opposition to policies that benefit blacks is driven by personal racism.

47. Ibid., 176–77.

48. The authors' particular concern to demonstrate shortcomings in affirmative action is part, I think, of what leads them to this normatively unwarranted, morally neutral stance toward historical racial injustices.

49. Sniderman and Piazza themselves imply, at several places, that a central cause of continuing racial inequality is a legacy of institutionalized racism with roots in the slavery and segregation eras. But they refuse to take the next step—coming to grips with this legacy as a core moral response to contemporary racial injustice. The following passage illustrates some of the confusion here: "All this further strengthens the argument that the central problem of racial politics is *not* the problem of prejudice. Bigotry provides a temptingly simple cause for a complex problem; it underlines the moral appeal of working to overcome the legacy of slavery and discrimination by fixing attention on the evil originally responsible for it. And not least, it fixes responsibility for the persistence of the problem on 'them'—on the out-and-out bigots—in the process diverting attention from 'us.'" Ibid., 107. Overcoming the legacy of slavery and discrimination is precisely *not* a way of putting the blame on "bigots," especially not current ones. Instead, it is a way of calling attention to ongoing processes and structures that operate independent of bigotry. It is also quite misleading to speak of the cause of slavery and segregation as being "bigotry." The causality is, if anything, in the other direction; bigotry arose as a rationalization for slavery and segregation, themselves founded on power, status, and economic gain. (See below, chapter 6.)

For an excellent critique of other errors of historical analysis in *The Scar of Race*, see George Lipsitz, "'Swing Low, Sweet Cadillac': White Supremacy, Antiblack Racism, and the New Historicism," *American Literary History* 7, no. 4 (Winter 1995): 700–25, esp. 705–10. (Lipsitz is blind, however, to the genuine interest and merit in Sniderman and Piazza's arguments.)

50. Dalton, *Racial Healing*, 7.

51. Charles Mills explains the "invisibility" of white privilege as an epistemologically deep dimension of its character: "In a racially structured polity, the only people who can find it psychologically possible to deny the centrality of race are those who are racially privileged, for whom race is invisible precisely because the world is structured around them, whiteness as the ground against which the figures of other races—those who, unlike us, are raced—appear." Mills, *Racial Contract*, 76.

52. Peggy McIntosh's 1988 article, "White Privilege and Male Privilege: A Personal Account of Coming to See Correspondences through Work in Women's Studies," is generally credited with bringing the idea of white privilege to the attention of a wide academic audience. In *Race, Class, and Gender: An Anthology*, ed. Margaret L. Andersen and Patricia Hill Collins (Belmont, Calif., 1992), 70–82. The article is widely reprinted and still frequently referred to. McIntosh listed forty-six unearned advantages or "privileges" (having introduced

the term, McIntosh goes on to question it) that accrue to white persons in relation to persons of color.

53. Beverly Tatum defines racism as "a system of advantage based on race." "*Why Do All the Black Kids,*" 7 (drawing from David Wellman). Dalton says racism is "culturally acceptable ideas, beliefs, and attitudes that serve to sustain the racial pecking order." *Racial Healing*, 92.

54. White privilege is more closely tied to structures of racial injustice, discussed in chapter 1, in connection with institutionalized racism.

55. W. E. B. Du Bois, *Black Reconstruction in the United States, 1860–1880* (New York, 1992 [1935]).

56. Derman-Sparks and Phillips, *Teaching/Learning Anti-racism*, 24.

57. One problem I see in Charles Mills's excellent and compelling argument for the pervasiveness and invisibility of white privilege in Western society is a conflation of racial and national privilege. Mills is correct to say that being born in the West grants unearned privilege; and that, within Western nations, being white is privileged. But he fails to note, and implies the contrary, that being born black or otherwise "of color" in the West also garners national privilege. Blacks may, on the average, benefit less than whites from national privilege; but simply being born in the United States gives them unearned advantages over black persons born in the "Third World." Mills, *Racial Contract*, 19–40.

Chapter 4. Racial Discrimination and Color Blindness

1. David Wasserman points out that the concept of discrimination encompasses distinct, morally significant features. "Discrimination, Concept of" in *Encyclopedia of Applied Ethics*, vol. 1 (San Diego, 1998), 805–814. My view of what those features are differs from Wasserman's in certain respects.

2. Whether the difference between effort and ascription is morally relevant (to injustice or discrimination in selection) for some reason other than what it is to be treated as an individual is a different matter. For example, it could be argued that *only* those characteristics reflecting the applicant's effort are fair to use in college admissions. (As far as I know, however, no colleges operate with such a principle, which would disallow legacy status, geographical location, class background, and other ascriptive factors standardly taken as pertinent.)

3. To be precise, what is described here is the structure of "reward goods"—goods to be allocated selectively—and the form of discrimination applicable to them. "Equality goods" involve a different form of discrimination. This distinction will be discussed below.

4. The judgment of wrongful discrimination on the basis of arbitrary and irrelevant characteristics depends on a further tacit assumption—that the goals of the institution are worthy, or at least morally acceptable. We would not say that it was "wrongful discrimination" for a neo-Nazi group to refuse admission to an aspirant because she was too short. We simply do not apply the morally negative concept of discrimination when the goals of the organization are unworthy, though we might say that it is *irrational* of such a group to distinguish among aspirants on the basis of certain qualities.

5. This account of the conceptual and empirical substructure of discrimination as arbitrariness involves some oversimplification; it assumes that determination of the legitimate goals of an institution is logically prior to, and entirely distinct from, a determination of "relevant qualities." But we sometimes judge an institution's goal as unworthy, at least in part, because countenancing it will yield a determination of relevance that we find objectionable. Robert Post describes a case in which a court ruled that it was illegitimate for an airline to utilize its "sexy image" as a basis on which to hire only "attractive female flight attendants," on the grounds that doing so played into unfortunate gender stereotypes. Robert Post, "Prej-

udicial Appearances: The Logic of American Antidiscrimination Law," *California Law Review* 8, no. 1 (Jan. 2000): 23. Post's article details the intricate and complex relationships between determination of legitimate institutional goals and judgments of the legitimacy of treating certain characteristics as relevant (primarily with regard to gender-related characteristics in employment contexts). Post's argument also suggests that our considered judgments about morally legitimate institutional goals and relevant characteristics is affected by whether the institution is public or private. See also Deborah Rhode's discussion of "bona fide occupational qualifications" in *Justice and Gender: Sex Discrimination and the Law* (Cambridge, Mass., 1989), 92ff.

6. Susan Sturm and Lani Guinier, "The Future of Affirmative Action: Reclaiming the Innovative Ideal," *California Law Review* 84, no. 4 (July 1996): 953–1036, esp. 969–970.

7. See David Wilkins, "Introduction: The Context of Race," in Gutmann and Appiah, *Color Conscious*, 18: "The looser the fit between these 'color blind' criteria and the social purposes of the job, the less force there is to the claim that departing from these criteria to achieve some other social purpose (for example, breaking racial stereotypes) violates the rights of either those who are not selected or, more important, those who ultimately use the service." Wilkins's stance suggests a slightly different way of framing the normative structure underlying "discrimination": to regard some of the goals guiding the selection procedure not as goals of the institution itself but as more general social goals (correcting for historical racial injustice, for example, or breaking racial stereotypes) that are appropriate for the institution to pursue. It will become legitimate for the institution to make use of those goals in its selection procedure when the institution's own goals underdetermine the criteria to be used in selection, that is, when there is a looseness of fit between the institution's goals and currently utilized selection criteria (for example, SAT scores). (This point is similar to that made by Robert Post above, note 5.)

8. Wilkins, "Context of Race," 18.

9. *Regents of the University of California v. Bakke*, 438 U.S. 265 (1978). The other justices forming the majority did not concur with this "diversity" rationale, though they did concur in upholding certain forms of affirmative action admission practices that Powell saw as in accord with that rationale.

10. In fact, *Bakke* yields a fairly weak diversity-based rationale for singling out racial identity, as the First Circuit Court of Appeals pointed out in its rejection of the Boston Latin School's affirmative action admissions policy. *Wessmann v. Gittens*, 98–1657 (1st Cir. 1998). There are many forms of diversity of opinion and experience relevant to education; why, then, should race be privileged over other dimensions of diversity? See Elizabeth Anderson, "Integration, Compensation, and Affirmative Action,"presentation to Harvard Colloquium in Constitutional Law and Political Theory, Nov. 2000. A step toward putting the *Bakke* diversity rationale on a stronger footing was taken in a U.S. District Court case, concerning affirmative action in the University of Michigan's undergraduate admissions, in December 2000. In that case, the judge found that the university had provided empirical support for the view that racial diversity promoted educational goals that (in contrast to some of the civic goals mentioned in the text) had no intrinsic bearing on race—goals such as "engagement in active thinking processes, growth in intellectual engagement and motivation, and growth in intellectual and academic skills." *Gratz v. Bollinger* (case # 97-CV-75231-DT), Dec. 13, 2000 (United States District Court, Eastern District of Michigan, Southern Division), 23.

11. See a recent reiteration of the argument that the mere taking account of race (to favor blacks and Latinos) automatically constitutes discrimination against whites in Roger Clegg, "Photographs and Fraud over Race," *Chronicle of Higher Education*, Nov. 24, 2000, B17.

12. Johanna Schneller, in "Drama Queen," *Premier*, Aug. 2000, 59, uses "golden" and "tawny" to describe Jennifer Lopez's skin color.

13. *Skin Deep*, dir. Reid.

14. See for example Peter Wade, *Race and Ethnicity in Latin America* (London, 1997), 14,

and F. James Davis, *Who Is Black? One Nation's Definition* (University Park, Pa., 1991), 99–105.

15. William Julius Wilson reports a study finding that even after education, income, family background, and place of residence were taken into account, "dark-skinned black men were 52% less likely to be working than light-skinned black men." W. J. Wilson, *When Work Disappears*, 136.

16. See Kathy Russell, Midge Wilson, and Ronald Hall, *The Color Complex: The Politics of Skin Color Among African Americans* (New York, 1993).

17. Yvonne treats skin color as analogous to eye color—a nonracial characteristic that happens to partially correlate with race (although Yvonne is not affected by the correlation). On eye color, see chapter 5.

18. The idea of immutable characteristics has played a role in the rationale for antidiscrimination law. "Since sex, like race and national origin, is an immutable characteristic determined solely by the accident of birth, the imposition of special disabilities upon the members of a particular sex because of their sex would seem to violate 'the basic concept of our system that legal burdens should bear some relationship to individual responsibility.'" *Frontiero v. Richardson*, 411 U.S. 677, 686 (1973) (plurality opinion), cited in Andrew Koppelman, *Antidiscrimination Law*, 64. Koppelman makes a compelling case that immutability is not properly seen as so fundamental to the wrong of discrimination as this quote states (64–67).

19. *Hopwood v. State of Texas* 78 F. 3d 932 (5th Cir. 1996).

20. To acknowledge that race and racial identity are pertinent to educational goals is not to address the question of whether such goals are *constitutionally* legitimate, or, if they are, whether they carry sufficient weight to trump what the Fifth Circuit Court and other courts have regarded as discrimination against whites that attends the use of racial diversity as a factor in admissions. Justice Powell's majority opinion in the *Bakke* case argued in the affirmative on this question; the Fifth Circuit, in the *Hopwood* case, explicitly ruled in the negative.

Moreover, my discussion of the *Hopwood* case is not meant as a critique of the full scope of the court's legal reasoning in the case, but only of the portion that confuses skin color with racial identity. As I argue below I also think the court has misunderstood the character of discrimination, and racial discrimination in particular. But I am not in a position to say whether my criticism is legally, as well as morally, pertinent. For extended critiques of the court's legal reasoning in *Hopwood* (and similar reasoning in comparable cases), see Reva Siegel, "The Racial Rhetorics of Colorblind Constitutionalism: The Case of *Hopwood v. Texas*," in *Race and Representation: Affirmative Action*, ed. Robert Post and Michael Rogin (New York, 1998), 29–72, and Anderson, "Integration."

21. As of November 2000, Michigan, Washington, D.C., Santa Cruz, California, and San Francisco were the only jurisdictions with laws against weight-based discrimination. Carey Goldberg, "Fat People Say an Intolerant World Condemns Them on First Sight," *New York Times*, Nov. 5, 2000, 28.

22. White in *Cleburne v. Cleburne Living Center, Inc.*, 473 U.S. 432 (1985), cited in Post, "Prejudicial Appearances," 9–10.

23. I take the importance of stigma from Koppelman, *Antidiscrimination Law*, and Glenn Loury, *The Anatomy of Racial Inequality* (Cambridge, Mass., 2002). Loury utilizes this idea primarily in regard to race. Both Koppelman and Loury cite Erving Goffman's pioneering work in this area, *Stigma: Notes on the Management of Spoiled Identity* (New York, 1986 [1963]).

24. This view of group harms is drawn from Owen Fiss, "Groups and the Equal Protection Clause," in *Equality and Preferential Treatment*, ed. M. Cohen, T. Nagel, and T. M. Scanlon (Princeton, N.J., 1977), as described in Koppelman, *Antidiscrimination Law*, 81–82.

25. Subordination is not necessarily or even typically recognized as such, since to do so would imply recognizing it as morally wrong. Typically the dominant society regards the inequality as natural or deserved. It is this attitude that spawns inferiorizing or stigmatizing.

26. Koppelman, *Antidiscrimination Law*, 84.

27. Dinesh D'Souza cites a report in 1993 by the Lawyers' Committee for Civil Rights based on an informal survey indicating that one-third of taxi drivers refuse to stop for black customers. Dinesh D'Souza, *The End of Racism: Principles for a Multiracial Society* (New York, 1995), 250–51.

28. Economists refer to this as "statistical discrimination" when the costs of acquiring the information necessary to make a fully-informed decision are too high or outweigh the costs and risks of making the decision based on the available, incomplete information.

29. D'Souza, *End of Racism*, 252.

30. Jody David Armour, *Negrophobia and Reasonable Racism: The Hidden Costs of Being Black in America* (New York, 1997), 20–21, 39–40. Armour's book is an indispensable discussion of the moral character of rational discrimination, to which my own account is indebted.

31. Ibid., 38.

32. Charges of various sorts of bias in the criminal justice system more generally have been rife since the 1990s. One particularly troubling example is a report that at every point in the juvenile justice system, black and Latino youth are more harshly treated than their white counterparts. They are arrested more often and are much more likely to be held in jail, sent to juvenile prison, sent to adult prison, and given longer prison terms. "Among young people who have not been sent to a juvenile prison before, blacks are more than six times as likely as whites to be sentenced by juvenile courts to prison." Fox Butterfield, "Racial Disparities Seen as Pervasive in Juvenile Justice," *New York Times*, April 26, 2000, A1, A18. By comparing similarly situated youth at each stage, the study, sponsored by the Justice Department, shows the magnifying of racial disparities at each successive stage in the process.

33. Fred Kaplan, "Meter Is Running on Giuliani's Crackdown on Cabbies," *Boston Globe*, Nov. 12, 1999, A3. Mayor Giuliani has raised the penalty to suspension, pending a hearing. Previously drivers were only fined. The article points out that almost all cabdrivers in New York are immigrants, and some are black. This fact might suggest that straightforward antiblack prejudice is not involved, but it cuts no ice against the idea that racial stereotyping is operating; one respondent, a professor who has studied black immigrant groups in New York, says, "A lot of West Africans or Haitians or Jamaicans who come here—they don't know they're 'black' yet." At the same time, an instructor in a mandatory course in "racial sensitivity" for all new cabdrivers says, "The irony is, our drivers are victims of racism themselves. Some of them say the only way they can get a cab when they're off duty is to wave their hack licenses in the air."

34. Armour, *Negrophobia*, 56–57.

35. Although both cases involve race, they are not entirely comparable, since in the black case the women's activity, justified though it is, plays into an existing and hurtful stereotype of the black rapist, while in the other there is no comparable race-specific stereotype.

36. Suppose, for example, that cabdrivers were permitted to ask prospective customers where they were going, and, if the driver had reason to be fearful of the location, to negotiate a compromise location.

37. As David Wasserman points out, such a group would be partly analogous to those regarded by eugenicists in the early twentieth century as "undesirables" whose numbers should be reduced through control of their reproduction. Wasserman, "Discrimination," 809b. Wasserman claims that this argument depends on drawing an analogy with blacks, who are seen as the paradigmatic victims of stigmatizing discrimination. I am not certain of this; but in any case, the analogy does not necessarily depend on seeing eugenics as racist. Not all eugenicists were racists; E. A. Hooton, for example, thought some members of every group were biological undesirables. The opprobrium attached to eugenics, plausibly regarded as carrying over to discrimination against those with propensities to diseases or disabling conditions, is at least partly independent of the opprobrium of racism.

38. To say that everyone is entitled to a certain equality good is not to say who is morally bound to provide the good. In the case at hand, a teacher is plausibly regarded as one, al-

though only one, of several agents (schools, principals, school systems) charged with providing equal education. Cabdrivers are transportation agents charged with providing equal access to public transport.

39. Glenn Loury identifies discrimination with "reward bias"—by which he means bias in job selection and compensation—and argues that discrimination is a less important factor in accounting for blacks' unequal position in society, than others, such as exclusion from social networks of dominant groups. *Anatomy of Racial Inequality.* This interpretation of "discrimination," perhaps corresponding to economists' use of the term, seems to me unnecessarily narrow. We customarily speak of discrimination in regard to certain equality goods as well.

40. Some would object to the inclusion of gays and straights on this list, arguing that those who engage in homosexual activity violate moral norms governing behavior, just as do liars and cheats; stigmatizing of them would therefore be justified. By contrast, blacks, Latinos, and women are unjustifiably stigmatized because of unchosen attributes, not what they do. By including gays and lesbians in the category of the unjustifiably stigmatized, however, I am rejecting that point of view. For a thoughtful defense of my viewpoint, which is sensitive to the religiously based arguments on the other side, see Patricia Beattie Jung and Ralph F. Smith, *Heterosexism: An Ethical Challenge* (Albany, N.Y., 1993).

41. In accord with customary usage, by "color blindness" I will mean race blindness rather than skin-tone blindness. Conflating race with skin tone, as the court did in the *Hopwood* decision, suggests the idea that we should be "blind to skin color" because skin color is a superficial characteristic (as well as an immutable one), indicating nothing of substance about a person. But race blindness arises from an entirely different source, presupposing that race is, or has been made to be, a deeply important characteristic.

42. See the argument in chapter 1 that the moral power of the term "racism" derives in part from the historical abuses perpetrated in the name of race.

43. I think an argument can be made that obesity is currently a more stigmatized characteristic than blackness. It has not, however, been nearly the source of political and economic inferiorization that blackness has been. Similarly, gays and lesbians have, until recently, been seen and treated as a pariah caste, evil or sick, and in any case barely worthy of human respect. But since gays and lesbians are not visible as such in the way racial groups are (though a person's "race" is not always visible either [see chapter 6]), as a group they have not suffered the economic and political disabilities attending the stigma attached to blackness.

44. *Regents of the University of California v. Bakke*, 438 U.S. at 303, quoted in Laurence Tribe, *Constitutional Choices* (Cambridge, Mass., 1985), 224. The other major cases are *City of Richmond v. J. A. Croson Co.*, 488 U.S. 469 (1989) (striking down municipal minority set-aside program, holding state and local government to a "strict scrutiny" standard that the opinion implied was difficult to meet) and *Adarand Constructors, Inc., v. Pena*, 515 U. S. 200 (1995) (ruling that federal race-based set-aside programs also had to satisfy a "strict scrutiny" standard). See Anderson, "Integration."

45. The distinction between "race neutrality" and "race egalitarianism" is drawn from Glenn Loury, foreword to William G. Bowen and Derek Bok, *The Shape of the River: Long-term Consequences of Considering Race in College and University Admissions* (Princeton, N.J., 2000). Actually Loury uses "race blindness" for my "race neutrality." I do not follow Loury's usage since I am taking these three distinct meanings *all* to be candidates for color or race blindness. My discussion of the first two meanings of "color blind" is, however, indebted to Loury's account.

46. The percentages differ in different states. As of this writing Texas has guaranteed places to those within the top 10 percent, Florida is talking about 20 percent, and California 4 percent.

47. Mary Frances Berry, "How Percentage Plans Keep Minority Students Out of College," *Chronicle of Higher Education,* Aug. 4, 2000 (on line: http://chronicle.com/weekly/v46/i48/48a04801.htm). Berry argues that despite these figures the percentage plans do a dis-

service to black and Latino students in comparison to traditional affirmative action programs.

On the history of the Texas legislature's adoption of the 10-percent plan, see David Montejano, "Maintaining Diversity at the University of Texas," in *Race and Representation*, ed. Post and Rogin, 362–67. On other states' rejection of such plans (for example because their high schools are not sufficiently segregated for the plans to generate what they regard as adequate diversity at the college level), see Patrick Healy, "Texas Plan for College Diversity Draws Fire," *Boston Globe*, Aug. 22, 2000, A1, 17.

48. Montejano says, "A final advantage of the ten percent plan was that it was easy to present and defend rhetorically: it was simple, fair, predictable, and, most importantly, it did not use race-specific criteria. This rhetorical advantage became evident in the various public forums where the ten percent plan was discussed." "Maintaining Diversity," 364. Glenn Loury points out that the plan's acceptability also relies on an at least tacit recognition that substantive issues of racial justice are pertinent to race-related policy. If the Texas legislature had crafted a race-neutral plan that nevertheless had the effect (and aim) of admitting a higher percentage of white applicants, the public would no doubt have rejected it. Glenn Loury, foreword to *Shape of the River*, xxiv.

49. The scores of admittees under percentage plans are lower than they were under affirmative action. For example, "About 250 had scores below 1000 last year [1999], compared with 133 in 1997." Healy, "Texas Plan," 17.

50. My argument here does not endorse the notion of standards or "qualifications" employed by either traditional affirmative action or the percentage plan. Indeed, I entirely agree with Susan Sturm and Lani Guinier's thoroughly documented argument that qualification as grades and test scores is deleterious both to appropriate educational purposes and to fairness. I utilize the traditional notion of qualification only to show the irrationality of countenancing the percentage plans while rejecting affirmative action. Sturm and Guinier, "Future of Affirmative Action".

51. Justice Brennan's majority opinion in the *Weber* affirmative action case argued that the legislative intent behind Title VII of the 1964 Civil Rights Act (prohibiting employment discrimination) included remedying the consequences of past discrimination so as to integrate previously discriminated-against racial minorities into the economic mainstream. *United Steelworkers of America, AFL-CIO-CLC v. Weber*, 443 U.S. 193 (1979). See discussion in Anderson, "Integration."

52. See discussion in Ronald Dworkin, *A Matter of Principle* (Cambridge, Mass., 1985), 316–18.

53. Again, my argument here has been a moral rather than a legal one although the courts may have been influenced by a misunderstanding of the moral ideal of color blindness, or of the moral character of discrimination. Legal scholars have disagreed about whether the Constitution (especially the thirteenth and fourteenth amendments) supplies an understanding of discrimination that locates its central wrongfulness in the subordinating of groups, in prejudice, or in distinctions made on the basis of characteristics that bear no relation to legitimate purposes. My argument for the greater moral weight of the first two of these has no bearing on this constitutional dispute, though my sympathies are of course with those who seek to find constitutional bases for these moral intuitions. See Siegel, "Racial Rhetorics," Fiss, "Groups," and Anderson, "Integration."

54. "Racial integration" is perhaps a more accurate expression of the ideal of race harmony, but that term too has lost public favor, and I think "color blindness" has taken up the slack and become a kind of repository of the various ideals intermixed in the civil rights and antidiscrimination struggles of the past several decades, including racial harmony. On racial integration and racial harmony, see also chapter 3.

55. It might be thought that the idea of "race neutrality" best captures the idea of race as something not seen at all. But this is so only in a superficial sense. Race neutrality forbids race to be used in policy contexts; but there is little reason to think that such proscription

would have the effect of reducing actual awareness of race. Indeed, I will argue in chapter 9 that race equality is empirically more likely to diminish a destructive racial consciousness than is a ban on the public use of racial categories.

56. Siegel asks, "Is every act of racial differentiation an act of race discrimination or does race discrimination involve a systematic practice of group subordination?" "Racial Rhetorics," 38. Why are these the only two choices? Why can't there be unjustified racial differentiation that does not involve subordination? (To be fair to Siegel, she is concerned with a legal context in which the two choices she cites are in fact the two understandings of "discrimination" in the context of equal protection doctrine; and she is arguing that in law the racial differentiation has unjustifiably come to overshadow subordination.)

57. Garcia draws a distinction similar to mine by saying that discrimination "on the basis of" is not always immoral, while discrimination "against" is. "Heart of Racism," 14. In "Philosophical Analysis," Garcia calls the latter "racist discrimination" (16). I would supplement Garcia's view by including non-animus-based discrimination against an inferiorized group as a morally wrong form of discrimination. (I would, however, agree with Garcia in not calling this "racist discrimination," since it lacks a racist motive.)

58. If such benignly motivated but still wrongful discrimination against whites does not count as 'racial discrimination,' how shall we refer to it? It has something of the force of discrimination based on an irrelevant characteristic (supposing race to be irrelevant in the hypothetical example in which race-sensitive aims can be achieved without use of race-sensitive admissions practices). Yet that expression could be misleading, since racial identity would still remain relevant to various institutional goals. Perhaps 'discrimination based on an inappropriate characteristic' would be a more accurate expression, as a way of saying that race would be inappropriate at the admissions stage, yet still pertinent to institutional goals.

59. Some might argue that it is appropriate for any educational institution to continue to favor black and Latino applicants as long as racial egalitarianism has not been achieved in the society as a whole, even if it has been achieved locally. My argument requires only that the scenario described provide a plausible reason that affirmative action is no longer appropriate.

Chapter 5. "Race": What We Mean and What We Think We Mean

1. *Blackwell Dictionary of Twentieth-Century Social Thought*, 536. Lawrence Bobo, a prominent political scientist in the field of racial attitude analysis, reports a comparable account: "Common usage tends to associate 'race' with biological based differences between human groups, differences typically observable in skin color, hair texture, eye shape, and other physical attributes." Lawrence Bobo, "Racial Attitudes and Relations at the Close of the Twentieth Century," *America Becoming: Racial Trends and Their Consequences*, vol. 1, ed. Neil Smelser, William Julius Wilson, and Faith Mitchell (Washington, D.C., 2001), 267.

2. Lothrop Stoddard, the influential early twentieth-century racist propagandist, said, "Race is what people physically really are. Nationality is what people politically think they are." Matthew Frye Jacobson, *Whiteness of a Different Color: European Immigrants and the Alchemy of Race* (Cambridge, Mass., 1998), 68–69. In the popular account of race this statement may not seem far off the mark, even if its adherents would typically reject the racist use to which Stoddard put it.

3. Ashley Montagu, *Man's Most Dangerous Myth*, 4th ed., rev. and enl. (Cleveland, Ohio, 1964), 24.

4. Most Americans now know that the more definitively racial terms "Mongoloid" or "yellow" are no longer acceptable for people of east (and perhaps southeast) Asian extraction; so they use the seemingly geographical term "Asian," but still think of the group thus designated as a race. (To the extent that South Asians succeed in becoming included in the

"Asian American" rubric, "Asian" and "Asian American" are likely to become less racial and more panethnic categories [see chapter 8], although this development would by no means guarantee the weakening of a "racial" way of viewing East Asians.) "Red" has similarly lost favor as a designation of Native Americans, although, again, this linguistic shift does not signal the disappearance of a racialized view of this group. I have intentionally omitted Latino and Hispanics from this list of racial groups because, as I will discuss in chapter 8, racial designation for this group is problematic. The scientific counterpart of "Caucasian" (or "Caucasoid") for blacks is "Negroid." Unlike "Caucasian," which is now used fairly frequently, "Negroid" is almost never employed in common parlance, perhaps because of its likeness to "Negro," which is now seen as an outdated and disrespectful term (although it is still preferred by 2 percent of African-Americans (see note 22). In order to preserve the symmetry with "black," I will generally use "white" rather than "Caucasian." For a historically informed discussion of the significance of popular usage of "white" and "Caucasian," see Jacobson, *Whiteness of a Different Color.*

5. I will use "somatic" characteristics to mean external, visible, bodily ones. Occasionally I will use "phenotypic" to indicate that such characteristics are the external expression of a person's genetic makeup ("genotype").

6. The way we think about eye color in relation to race is interestingly indicative of an arbitrariness in the somatic characteristics taken to count as "race." Different eye colors are taken to correlate with different races, at least in part, but eye color is not itself viewed as a racial characteristic. This feature of the popular account of race is strikingly illustrated in a famous classroom intervention carried out in 1968 by Jane Elliott, a third-grade teacher in Iowa. All of her students were white, and to teach them something about race and racism, Ms. Elliott divided the class into two groups, brown-eyed and blue-eyed. She then proceeded to treat the brown-eyed group as if they were inferior, and deserved inferior treatment. (She subjected the blue-eyed group to the same treatment the next day.) Ms. Elliott's exercise with her class had the effect, and intention, of conferring a racial significance on eye color. Her ability to do so depends on the fact that ordinarily eye color does *not* have such significance. (Elliott's experience, and its impact on the children in her class, then and fifteen years later, is described in William Peters, *A Class Divided, Then and Now,* rev. ed. [New Haven, Conn., 1987].)

7. In Britain, by contrast, Indians have sometimes been thought of as blacks, and in Australia aboriginals are sometimes called "blacks," although they themselves prefer the designation "indigenous Australians."

8. Robb Armstrong, "Jump Start," United Feature Syndicate, 1997 (in *Boston Globe*).

9. Rainier Spencer points out how race makes us see "a khaki-colored person with a narrow nose and slightly kinky hair" as "*obviously* more black than white" even though such a person, as described, is clearly something like an equal mixture of African and European ancestry. Rainier Spencer, *Spurious Issues: Race and Multiracial Identity Politics in the United States* (Boulder, Colo., 1999), 17. Jacobson too emphasizes the way that racial thinking shapes perception: "The American eye sees a certain person as black, for instance, whom Haitian or Brazilian eyes might see as white. Similarly, an earlier generation of Americans saw Celtic, Hebrew, Anglo-Saxon, or Mediterranean physiognomies where today we see only subtly varying shades of a mostly undifferentiated whiteness." *Whiteness*, 10.

10. Perhaps an exception would be persons who change the relevant features of physical appearance, as John Howard Griffin, a white reporter, did when he treated his skin in order to live as a black man in the South in the early 1960s. John Howard Griffin, *Black Like Me* (New York, 1976 [1960]).

11. Janet Ward Schofield, *Black and White in School: Trust, Tension, or Tolerance?* (New York, 1989), 39–74. Blacks and whites were the only racial groups present in the school; the study was done in the Northeast in 1979.

12. Mary Waters, *Ethnic Options: Choosing Identities in America* (Berkeley, Calif., 1990). Waters is concerned to show how whites' privileging ethnic over racial identity, with regard to

both themselves and others, can blind them to racial inequities. In the 1940's and 1950's, ethnicity did not carry such unequivocally positive connotations but rather suggested "outsiderhood." Werner Sollors, "Foreword: Theories of American Ethnicity," *Theories of Ethnicity: A Classical Reader*, ed. Werner Sollors (New York: New York University, 1996), x–xi. Sollors claims that the word "ethnicity" was first used in the United States in 1941. British scholars John Hutchinson and Anthony D. Smith say it was the 1950's. "Introduction," in *Ethnicity*, 4.

13. The development of the idea of "people of color"—an umbrella identity for nonwhite panethnic or ethnoracial groups—may seem like a counter-example, as it expresses a sense of identification across racial groups. But in this case it is not racial belonging or classification itself, but rather the experience of being discriminated against, excluded, or stigmatized on account of one's race that provides the bond. Also, obviously, "people of color" is not a fully inclusive commonality since it excludes whites.

14. Reluctance to use racial designations is not equal across racial groups. In general, blacks are much less reluctant than other groups. I speculate about the reasons for this later in this chapter.

15. Audrey Smedley emphasizes this comprehensive nature of race as a form of consciousness in *Race in North America: Origin and Evolution of a Worldview*, 2d ed. (Boulder, Colo., 1999).

16. Let me guard against some possible misunderstanding of what I am claiming to explain in my proffered account of "racial thinking." First, the use of racial labeling is not a fully reliable indicator of racial thinking; it is neither necessary nor sufficient for it. Someone—especially black persons themselves—may use the racial label "black" with more of a cultural than a racial significance (although, as we will see in chapter 8, its use can have *both* a fully racial and a fully cultural significance). On the other side, persons may use an ethnic or panethnic expression such as "European American," "African American," or "Latino" yet still *think* of the group referred to as a race.

Nor am I claiming that my account of race is meant to capture every form of racial consciousness on the contemporary American scene. For example, I believe that it is at least *possible* for persons to use racial terms in a purely classificatory and evaluatively inert sense, as akin to what the "popular account" wrongly takes to be the most common one. This purely classificatory sense is likely to involve some combination of phenotypic characteristics, ancestry, and geographical origins. As I argued earlier, however, I think people are able to accomplish this morally neutral use of race much less than they may say or think they do. Nevertheless (as I will explain in detail in chapters 7 and 8), because the sciences have by and large delegitimized race and racial thought, some persons who are particularly influenced by scientific perspectives but who continue to employ racial terminology may do so in a "scare quote" sense—that is, distancing themselves from the meanings commonly attached to racial labels.

17. See Smedley, *Race in North America*, 22 ff.

18. This general point about common humanity is well made by Anthony Skillen, "Racism," *Encyclopedia of Applied Ethics*, vol. 3 (San Diego, Calif., 1998), 779. Paul Gilroy gives it eloquent expression in a recent book: "The term 'race' conjures up a peculiarly resistant variety of natural difference. It stands . . . in opposition to most attempts to render it secondary to the overwhelming sameness that overdetermines social relationships between people and continually betrays the tragic predicaments of their common species life." Paul Gilroy, *Between Camps: Nations, Cultures, and the Allure of Race* (London, 2001), 29. (The American title of this book is *Against Race*.)

19. The impact of race thinking on individual human connection is poignantly and powerfully described in a *New York Times* article about two Cuban American friends, a darkskinned and a light-skinned man. In Cuba the friends' somatic differences did not seem important to them; but when both immigrated to Miami, the segregated social space, assumptions pervasive in the society, and expectations in their peer groups all had the effect of making the two friends drift apart. The article shows two people being subjected to a

"racializing" of their consciousness and their interaction. It is more difficult to see racialization as a created process, rather than a mere reflection of a preexisting human reality, in persons who have grown up with racial consciousness, since they take this racial distancing for granted. The two Cuban-American friends did not have such a consciousness in Cuba, but then they did in the United States. Mirta Ojito, "Best of Friends, Worlds Apart," *New York Times*, June 5, 2000, A1, A16–17.

20. A website called "National Forum on People's Differences" invites users to post questions they have "always been too embarrassed or uncomfortable to ask." The responses, reported in *Harper's Magazine*, testify to a revealing but unsurprising willingness to overgeneralize and stereotype groups in explicitly racial terms. Some examples: "Why do white people smell like wet dogs when they come out of the rain?" "Why do most black people wear their hats backwards? I have tried this many times, and I do not think this is comfortable." "It seems to me that the majority of white people are overly stuffy and stiff. Why can't they relax?" "Race, the Final Frontier," *Harper's Magazine*, July 2000, 24, 26.

21. For this reason I think Appiah is incorrect when he implies that we can have a concept of race (used in ascribing and claiming racial identities) independent of, and logically prior to, racism. Appiah, "Race, Culture, Identity; Misunderstood Connections in A. Gutmann and K. A. Appiah, *Color Conscious* (Princeton, N.J., 1996), 82. Nevertheless, as we will discuss in chapter 7, the contemporary implication of differential value among races is much weaker than it was in the classic nineteenth-century conception of race.

The modes of thinking, perceiving, and experiencing of racial others that I am alleging should not be thought of as absolutely inevitable, but rather as strong tendencies. For example, it is hardly impossible to empathize with someone of a different racial group; but thinking of her as of a different race tends to inhibit that empathy. Moreover, fully empathizing with a racial other has the effect of partially deracializing her in one's eyes.

Similar considerations apply to overgeneralizing and racial fate. It is not impossible to generalize about a racial group without overgeneralizing; but there is a strong tendency toward the latter. And it is not impossible to think about the characteristics of a racial group without thinking of them as inescapable; but there is a strong tendency to do so.

22. A survey conducted in 1990 found 78 percent of black Americans preferring "black," 20 percent "African American," and 2 percent "Negro." Andrew Hacker, *Two Nations*, 48. Yet the meanings of the apparently racial and ethnocultural associations of "black" and "African American" may be in some dispute, as suggested in a *New York Times* article from June, 2000. A girl is reported as responding to a black friend's asking her "What are you?" by telling him that she is half Puerto Rican and half white. The friend says, "But you act black." The girl comments, "I told him you can't act like a race. I hate that idea. He defended it, though. He said I would have a point if he'd said African-American, because that's a race, but black is a way of acting. I've thought about it, and I think he's right." Tamar Lewin, "Growing Up, Growing Apart," *New York Times*, June 25, 2000, 12. These teenagers' reflective assurance that "African American" is a race—which they correctly understand is not the sort of thing that can have a culture, while "black" refers to a cultural style—shows the presence of racial consciousness but in a seemingly reversed language in which to express its contrast with culture.

23. Mia Bay, *The White Image in the Black Mind: African-American Ideas about White People, 1830–1925* (New York, 2000), 219–29.

24. Appiah, *In My Father's House: Africa in the Philosophy of Culture* (New York, 1992), 13–14; "Racisms," 4–5. "Race, Culture, Identity," 54–56. The idea of "racialism" is useful in capturing a belief in race without what is generally regarded as its most odious feature, the belief in a hierarchy of worth. This use of "racialism" differs from that employed in chapter 3, where it meant "conferring too much importance on race." That use was moral, this one doctrinal.

25. Moreover, although "black" has been used for several centuries to refer to African Americans, its revival in the 1960s to replace "Negro" as the most common self-designation was prompted by the Black Power movement. At that time, and to some extent since then,

"black" has connoted group pride, in addition to any other connotations it might have carried. It has become a term reappropriated, or reclaimed, by the black community, not one simply foisted upon them. See Lynne Tirrell's discussion of reclamation in "Derogatory Terms: Racism, Sexism, and the Inferential Role of Meaning." In *Language and Liberation*, edited by Christina Hendricks and Kelly Oliver, 41–79 (Albany, N.Y., 1999). This seems a third reason why blacks may prefer "black" to "African American."

A different, but not unrelated, reason for that preference is expressed by Gwen Tomalson, in an interview with Lillian Rubin. Replying to Tomalson's saying "I'm black of course" when asked about her ethnicity, Rubin comments, "Many black people now prefer to think of themselves as African-American." Tomalson replies, "Yeah, well that's a little fancy for me . . . Maybe I'm African-American too. I guess I am. My people were dragged here from Africa, so that makes me African-American, but it doesn't mean anything to me." Lillian Rubin, *Families on the Fault Line: America's Working Class Speaks about the Family, the Economy, Race, and Ethnicity* (New York, 1994), 151.

26. Thus a further reason whites might be reluctant to go in for racial designation is that they are, at least tacitly, aware of connotations of their own superiority, and reject that implication or do not wish to publicly avow it, as racial superiority is inconsistent with the belief in equality which most whites, in the past 50 years or so, have come to hold, try to hold, or at least think they should hold.

Chapter 6: "Race": A Brief History, with Moral Implications

I am grateful for Judith Smith's wisdom and insight on the historical matters dealt with in this and other chapters, and her feedback on various drafts.

1. This account of the ancient Greeks (and to some extent Romans) is drawn from Frank M. Snowden, *Before Color Prejudice: The Ancient View of Blacks* (Cambridge, Mass., 1983). I am grateful to Marcia Homiak for assistance with this section.

2. Miles, *Racism*, 15. See also Frank Snowden, "Europe's Oldest Chapter in the History of Black-White Relations," in *Racism and Anti-racism in World Perspective*, ed. Benjamin Bowser (London, 1995).

3. In his comprehensive and important *Race: The History of an Idea in America* (New York, 1963), Thomas Gossett summarizes a similar range of observations about the Greeks and Romans: "In neither Greece nor Rome does there appear to have been much prejudice against Negroes because of their race" (7). Gossett implies that though the Greeks and Romans lacked prejudice against them, they did regard "Negroes" as a "race." Unfortunately throughout his book Gossett equates "race" with the possession of certain somatic characteristics.

4. Bernard Williams makes these points in his discussion of Greek slavery and Aristotle's defense of it in *Shame and Necessity* (Berkeley, Calif., 1993), esp. 106–17. Aristotle's discussion of slavery is in the first book of his *Politics*, 1253b23–1255b39.

5. Slavery that is *not* based on race or ethnicity is no more morally acceptable than slavery that is. My point is that racism is not the inevitable concomitant of slavery.

6. Smedley, *Race in North America*, 37–41. Smedley says that though there is not conclusive evidence for the origin of the term, it appears to involve reference to a "breeding line or stock of animals"; the *Oxford English Dictionary* continues to list this as one of the five meanings of the word "race." *OED* on-line, Aug. 4, 1999, http://dictionary.oed.com/entrance .dtl/. My account of the development of the idea of "race" is indebted to Smedley's remarkable work of historical and scientific synthesis.

7. Smedley does suggest that the word's origin in the idea of breeding for a purpose supplied the potential for its being used to denote hierarchy, and also that, more than the concepts of "nation," "people," "variety," and "kind," it implies an innate nature. These associa-

tions, which became firmly attached to the idea of race by the nineteenth century, were only dimly present in its earliest uses.

8. Gary B. Nash, *Red, White, and Black: The Peoples of Early North America*, 4th ed. (Upper Saddle River, N.J., 2000), 49.

9. Carl Sauer, *Sixteenth-Century North America* (Berkeley, Calif., 1971), 252, cited in Smedley, *Race in North America*, 74.

10. Edmund Morgan, *American Slavery, American Freedom* (New York, 1975), quoted in Smedley, *Race in North America*, 73.

11. Winthrop D. Jordan, *White over Black: American Attitudes Toward the Negro, 1550–1812* (Chapel Hill, N.C., 1969), 26. Jordan adds: "Initially . . . English contact with Africans did not take place primarily in a context which prejudged the Negro as a slave, at least not as a slave of Englishmen" (4). On the level of civilization of various African kingdoms of which Europeans became aware, see also Nash, *Red, White, and Black*, 145–47.

12. Basil Davidson, *The Search for Africa: History, Culture, Politics* (New York, 1994), 43.

13. "White" was occasionally employed, along with "Christian," but its full racial meaning had not yet developed.

14. Native Americans in the United States never became as fully racialized a group as did Africans and Europeans. Alden Vaughan, a colonial historian, argues that "red" was not widely used until the nineteenth century, and that early European colonizers viewed the cultural practices but not the somatic characteristics of Native Americans as inferior. "From White Man to Redskin: Changing Anglo-American Perceptions of the American Indian," in *Roots of American Racism: Essays on the Colonial Experience* (New York, 1995), 3–33. Vaughan summarizes: "Anglo-America's fundamental contempt for Indian culture remained relatively constant throughout the history of British America and beyond. What changed under the influence of the new perception of Indians as innately dark-skinned were expectations of the Indians' civil and theological redemption" (19).

15. On interracial mating, see Gary B. Nash, "The Hidden History of Mestizo America," in *Sex, Love, Race: Crossing Boundaries in North American History*, ed. Martha Hodes (New York, 1999), 10–32.

16. For further exploration of the differences between Latin America and the United States regarding slavery and conceptions of race or race-like groupings, see Smedley, *Race in North America*, chap. 6. "In summary, the documented evidence from a variety of sources suggests that [in the Spanish and Portuguese colonies] whereas minute physical variations and admixtures were recognized and utilized to create an ideology of social inequality, they were not homogenized and translated into specific, exclusive, and distinct groupings [as in the British colonies of North America]. And even the names and categories invented to try to represent every possible ancestral combination were not associated explicitly with stereotyped behavior or institutionalized as dogma about innateness" (136). See also F. James Davis, *Who Is Black?* esp. 99–105.

The experience of the French in the New World provides further evidence of significant differences among the European colonial powers in their treatment of subject peoples, and of the role of demographic, economic, and religious factors rather than inherent moral propensities in accounting for these differences. The French, concentrating their colonizing activities in the area of Canada, engaged in a very profitable fur trade, which required the cooperation, not military subjugation, of indigenous peoples. The small numbers of French also provided an incentive for amicable rather than hostile relations. Like the Puritans in New England, French Jesuits attempted to convert the "natives," but their conception of conversion directed them to show regard for the religions and ways of life of the indigenous peoples (especially the Hurons), and to work within their indigenous religions to bring them gradually toward Catholicism. Gary Nash summarizes: "The French coexisted fruitfully with native societies to a degree unprecedented elsewhere in North America." *Red, White, and Black*, 46. See 41–48 for general discussion of the French presence in the Americas. My remarks about the relative absence of a conception of "race" in Iberian America should not be taken to suggest that these societies are "racial democracies," in the slogan that for much of the twentieth century was used to describe Brazil's official self-conception. Recent work has shown that degree of African, indigenous, and European ancestry strongly correlates with socioeconomic position, and that positive value has always attached to lightness of skin color. See for example, Melissa Nobles, *Shades of Citizenship: Race and the Census in Modern Politics* (Stanford, 2000), 85–129, 146–62, and Anthony Marx, *Making Race and Nation: A Comparison of the United States, South Africa, and Brazil* (Cambridge, U.K., 1997), esp. 250–63. In Brazil there has been a movement to claim a "black" identity, partly in order to gain recognition of the discriminatory character of Brazilian society, and partly to appropriate an African origins identity as a source or pride rather than disvalue. Nobles notes that this *"movimento negro"* has been small and fragile in part because of the fluidity of color categories in Brazil (146), which is to say, the absence of anything like a fully developed notion of race in the North American sense.

17. Suzanne Miers and Igor Kopytoff (eds.), *Slavery in Africa: Historical and Anthropological Perspectives* (Madison, Wisc., 1977); Orlando Patterson, *Slavery and Social Death* (Cambridge, Mass., 1982); O. E. Uya, *African Diaspora and the Black Experience in New World Slavery* (Lagos, Nigeria, 1992).

18. Williams, *Shame and Necessity,* 112.

19. Aristotle's discussion implies that some thinkers were lodging a challenge to the rightness and necessity of slavery, and that he was replying to them. So some Greeks must have been questioning it ethically, and not accepting its necessity.

20. Smedley, *Race in North America*, 99. On black families that became relatively wealthy, respected landowners in the Virginia colony, see T. H. Breen and Stephen Innes, *"Myne Own Ground": Race and Freedom on Virginia's Eastern Shore, 1640–1676* (New York, 1980), and Ira Berlin, *Many Thousands Gone: The First Two Centuries of Slavery in North America* (Cambridge, Mass., 1998), 29–46.

21. Berlin documents the fall in status of persons of African descent in the English colonies with the rise of the plantation system. *Many Thousands Gone*, esp. 15–177.

22. Cited in Nancy Shoemaker, "How Indians Got to Be Red," *American Historical Review* 102, no. 3 (June 1997): 631.

23. The "curse of Ham," the fact that ancient Hebrews owned slaves, and the fact that Jesus never condemned slavery were all used as scriptural rationalizations for slavery by southern Christians. Peter Kolchin, *American Slavery, 1619–1877* (New York, 1993), 192.

24. Racist ideologies also accommodated themselves, though not without some contention, to the eventual Christianization of most slaves. Most colonies passed laws declaring that baptism was not incompatible with slavery. See ibid., 15.

25. See ibid. 3–27, for a detailed account of the complex but almost wholly nonracial factors that led to the gradual imposition of slavery on Africans and their descendants in preference to other groups.

26. Slave owners, especially those in the lower southern colonies, were therefore particularly dismayed and horrified by the Stono Uprising in South Carolina in 1739, in which escaping slaves used drumming and dancing to communicate with co-conspirators. Nearly successful, these slaves had intended to escape English control by reaching the Spanish colony at St. Augustine, Florida. Nathan Irvin Huggins, *Black Odyssey: The African-American Ordeal in Slavery* (New York, 1992), 210–211.

27. Berlin, *Many Thousands Gone*, 109. For other accounts of Bacon's Rebellion, see Smedley, *Race in North America*, 103–04; Theodore W. Allen, *The Invention of the White Race, Volume Two: The Origin of Racial Oppression in Anglo-America* (New York, 1997), 203–22; and Nash, *Red, White, and Black*, 110–14. Berlin comments: "Throughout the seventeenth century, black and white ran away together, joined in petty conspiracies, and, upon occasion, stood shoulder-to-shoulder against the weighty champions of established authority. In 1676, when Nathaniel Bacon's 'Choice and Standing Army' took to the field against forces com-

manded by Virginia's royal governor, it drew on both white and black bondmen in nearly equal proportions" (45).

28. Barbara Fields, however, reminds us in an influential essay that for different economic groups of white Southerners, "race" and "white supremacy" meant very different things. "From the democratic struggles of the Jacksonian era to the disenfranchisement struggles of the Jim Crow era, white supremacy held one meaning for the back-country whites and another for the planters." "Ideology and Race in American History," in *Region, Race, and Reconstruction*, ed. J. M. Kousser and J. M. McPherson (New York: Oxford, 1982), 157.

29. "Massachusetts Slave Petition," in *The Democracy Reader*, ed. Diane Ravitch and Abigail Thernstrom (New York, 1992), 107–8. Benjamin Banneker, a scientist and free black, used a similar argument against slavery in a famous letter to Thomas Jefferson in 1791 (to which Jefferson respectfully replied without acceding to Banneker's argument), in which he argued that blacks should be seen as the equals of whites. See Gary Nash, ed., *Race and Revolution* (Madison, N.J., 1990), 177–81.

30. George Frederickson notes that "the notion that all human beings were equal in some fundamental sense had long been a standard belief of Western Europeans. But before the eighteenth century, universalistic affirmations of equality existed only in forms that had no clear application to the organization of human society. Equality in the eyes of God—an essential Christian belief—was usually seen as no impediment to a hierarchical order in human affairs." *White Supremacy: A Comparative Study in American and South African History* (New York, 1981), 141. For the impact of egalitarian ideals on slavery and movements to abolish it, see David Brion Davis, *The Problem of Slavery in Western Culture* (New York, 1966).

31. George Frederickson, *The Black Image in the White Mind: The Debate on Afro-American Character and Destiny, 1817–1914* (New York, 1971), 2.

32. Ibid., 3.

33. On Abolitionism in the United States and England, see Davis, *Problem of Slavery*; and David Brion Davis, *Slavery and Human Progress* (New York, 1984).

34. In both North and South, free African Americans could not carry firearms, could not purchase slaves, and were liable to the criminal penalties meted out to slaves. They could not testify against whites, hold office, vote, or serve on juries or in the militia. Free African Americans in northern cities faced residential segregation, pervasive job discrimination, segregated public schools, and daily affronts such as exclusion from public concerts, lectures, and libraries, and segregation or exclusion from public transportation. See Ira Berlin, *Slaves without Masters: The Free Negro in the Antebellum South* (New York, 1992), and Melissa Nobles, *Shades of Citizenship: Race and the Census in Modern Politics* (Stanford, Calif., 2000), 29.

35. Jonathan Marks, *Human Biodiversity: Genes, Race, and History* (Hawthorne, N.Y., 1995), 52. In 1962 Sherwood Washburn, president of the American Anthropological Association, called for physical anthropology to take a new approach to the study of race that deemphasized classificatory aspects and focused on the historical study of different human groups and the processes that generated them. Ibid., 59.

36. Ibid., 55.

37. Smedley, *Race in North America*, 160; Marks, *Human Biodiversity*, 50.

38. Stephen Jay Gould argues that because Linnaeus's typical way of ordering the four groups—Americanus (indigenous Americans), Europaeus, Asiaticus, and Africanus—did not correspond to the value ranking of racist thought (since Europeans were not at the top), it should be taken as indicating that Linnaeus was much more focused on a geographical than a value-based order. Stephen Jay Gould, "The Geometer of Race," *Discover*, Nov. 1994, 67, and *The Mismeasure of Man*, rev. and enl. ed. (New York, 1996).

39. Smedley, *Race in North America*, 165. Buffon by no means avoided Eurocentrism in his judgments of other peoples; but he did not build these judgments into his scientific categories. In addition, he condemned in the harshest terms slavery and justifications for it that implied that Africans were suited to such a state: "It is said that they tolerate hunger easily; that they can live for three days on a portion of a European meal; that however little they eat

or sleep, they are always equally tough, equally strong, equally fit for labor. How can men in whom there rests any feeling for humanity adopt such views? How do they presume to legitimize by such reasoning those excesses which originate solely from their thirst for gold?" Count de Buffon, "Varieties of the Human Species," in *Natural History, General and Particular,* trans. William Smellie (London, 1812 [1749]), 394.

40. Marks, *Human Biodiversity,* 152.

41. Frederickson, *Black Image,* 84–90.

42. Despite the use of his view by defenders, Agassiz himself was an opponent of slavery. But the idea of race was used against black people much more broadly than in defending slavery, as we have seen above. There was a large space for rationalizing many forms of discrimination on the basis of African inferiority, such as the denial of the right to vote in most northern states through the Civil War period. Ibid., 183.

43. Darwin's use of the term "race" here hearkens back to the older meaning applying to animal and plant groupings.

44. See Appiah, "Race, Culture, Identity," 66ff.

45. Darwin, *Descent of Man* (London, 1901 [1871]), 276, 278, cited in Ashley Montagu's commentary on UNESCO Statement on Race, 1950, in Montagu, *Statement on Race* (New York, 1972), 23–24. Carl Degler writes that "Darwin's principal reason for rejecting the idea that the races were different species was that he could not figure out how natural selection could have separated the races. The physical differences between races, Darwin thought, could not be accounted for by natural selection, because 'none of the differences between the races are of any direct or special service to him.' He even sought to prove that there was no connection between climate and dark skin color." *In Search of Human Nature: The Decline and Revival of Darwinism in American Social Thought* (New York, 1991), 15.

46. "At some future period, not very distant as measured by centuries, the civilized races of man will almost certainly exterminate and replace the savage races throughout the world." Cited in Frederickson, *Black Image,* 230, drawn from Gertrude Himmelfarb, *Darwin and the Darwinian Revolution* (London, 1959), 343, citing Darwin's *Descent of Man.* See also Degler, *In Search of Human Nature,* 8, 15.

47. At the same time, in his 1871 *Descent of Man* Darwin questioned the value of the concept of race, "observing that the experts classified humans in as few as two and as many as sixty-three separate races." Daniel Blackburn, "Why Race Is Not a Biological Concept," in *Race and Racism in Theory and Practice,* ed. Berel Lang (Lanham, Md., 2000), 4.

48. Spencer wrote several works over the course of his life that defined his philosophy, which became more evolutionist with the rise of Darwinism (although Spencer was an advocate of evolution prior to Darwin)—for example, *The Study of Sociology,* 2d ed. (London, 1874). Spencer coined the term "survival of the fittest," which makes no appearance in Darwin, and which served as a shorthand for the vindication of existing race and class hierarchies. Degler points out that Darwin later accepted this phrase as "a kind of shorthand for natural selection." *In Search of Human Nature,* 11. For Spencer's influence on American racial thought, see Lee Baker, *From Savage to Negro: Anthropology and the Construction of Race, 1896–1954* (Berkeley, Calif., 1998), 29–30.

49. Jacobson, *Whiteness of a Different Color,* 25.

50. Ronald Takaki, "The Heathen Chinee," in *Strangers From a Different Shore: A History of Asian-Americans* (Boston, 1989), 99–112.

51. On the general issue of race and naturalization, see Jacobson, *Whiteness of a Different Color;* Ian Haney-Lopez, *White by Law: The Legal Construction of Race* (New York, 1996); and Rogers Smith, *Civic Ideals: Conflicting Images of Citizenship in U.S. History* (New Haven, Conn., 1997).

52. Frederickson, *Black Image,* 165–197. For an excellent account of Reconstruction, its effects both on blacks and citizenship, its demise, and its legacy, see Smith, *Civic Ideals,* 70–86.

53. The 1873 "slaughterhouse cases," *U.S. v. Reese* (1876) and *U.S. v. Cruikshank* (1876),

and the 1883 civil rights cases restricted federal protection of black civil rights that the Reconstruction Amendments intended to guarantee, and opened the door to disenfranchising black voters in the South through poll taxes and property requirements. Eric Foner, *Reconstruction: America's Unfinished Revolution, 1863–1877* (New York, 1988).

54. Baker, *From Savage to Negro*, 33.

55. Quoted in ibid., 27.

56. Kant's contribution to racial thought has not been generally recognized in contemporary philosophy. His key work is "Of the Different Human Races," from 1777 (reprinted in *The Idea of Race*, ed. Robert Bernasconi and Tommy L. Lott [Indianapolis, 2000], 8–22), but he continued to explore the issue in the better-known *Anthropology from a Pragmatic Point of View* in 1798. Bernasconi and Lott credit Kant with "a clear and consistent terminological distinction between race and species that was lacking in his predecessors but also an insistence on the permanence of racial characteristics across the generations." "Introduction," *Idea of Race*, viii.

Though Herder was a proto-racialist, he did not (in contrast to Hegel and racial thought more generally) see different *Volksgeisten* as ranked in a hierarchy, and he opposed slavery and other attempts by one people to dominate another. He thought each people had a distinct spirit with its own value that was neither better nor worse than any other. See J. G. von Herder, *Reflections on the Philosophy of the History of Mankind*, abr., intro. by Frank E. Manuel (Chicago, 1968 [1791]). In this regard Herder influenced Du Bois (who studied Herder's thought during his two years in Berlin in the 1890s); Du Bois proposed a similar egalitarian, racialist view of the spirit of the white, the black, and other races, in "The Conservation of Races" (1897) and *The Souls of Black Folk*, ed. David Blight and Robert Gooding-Williams (Boston, 1997 [1903]). (This edition of *Souls* includes several other essays including "Conservation.") In these respects both Herder and Du Bois were early theorists of what we now know as "multiculturalism," or egalitarian cultural pluralism. In his influential essay, Appiah cites Herder's views as crucial background to Matthew Arnold, whom Appiah regards as having articulated an important version of literary racialism. Herder, like Arnold, saw the spirit of a people as primarily expressed in its language and literature. Appiah, "Race, Culture, Identity," 52–64.

57. Possibly the most influential European racial theorist, Comte Joseph-Arthur de Gobineau (1816–82) combines the phenotypist and the national-spirit forms of racism. See discussion of de Gobineau, and European racism more generally, in George L. Mosse, *Toward the Final Solution: A History of European Racism* (Madison, Wisc., 1985), Ivan Hannaford, *Race: The History of an Idea in the West* (Washington, D.C., 1996), and Tzvetan Todorov, *On Human Diversity: Nationalism, Racism, and Exoticism in French Thought*, trans. Catherine Porter (Cambridge, Mass., 1993).

58. For the post–World War II period, when the two forms especially begin to converge and intermingle, see Miles, *Racism*. At the same time, European hostility is often more directed toward cultures and religions (often Islam) than toward a racialized conception of somatic characteristics; cultural incompatibility with an alleged national culture (defined as implicitly or explicitly "white"), rather than straightforward inferiorizing, has been the central theme. See Tariq Modood, "'Difference,' Cultural Racism, and Anti-racism," in Werbner and Modood, *Debating Cultural Hybridity*. This phenomenon has been called "cultural racism." Although this label seems partially justified to me, to some extent it too is conceptually inflated. Some elements of what is called "cultural racism" seem more accurately called "nativism"—a hostility to the foreign. In addition, unless "culture" is employed as a veiled way of talking about race, it can not be assumed that cultural animosity is racial. Modood himself guards against this inflation by requiring the cultural hostility to complement an already present racialization. (See chapter 8.)

59. Robert Miles usefully refers to classic race theory as "scientific racism," as distinct from contemporary forms (primarily in United Kingdom) that involve many of the same elements but without the authority of science, which has since abandoned them. See chapter 7.

60. See Appiah, "Race, Culture, Identity," 55. In chapter 7, note 21, I explain why I do not retain this use of "essence" for psychological, mental, and temperamental characteristics alleged to inhere in racial groups.

61. The mechanism of this generational transfer of racial characteristics was not understood or even postulated in the nineteenth century. When races were conceived of as timeless subspecies created as such by God, the need for such a mechanism was obviated. In light of evolution, opinion differed as to whether cultural characteristics could be inherited, with Darwinists denying and Lamarckians affirming it. But in neither case was a genuine biological mechanism of inheritance postulated. In its absence, the idea of "blood" was employed as a kind of place-holder. As the historian of anthropology George Stocking remarks, "'Blood' was for many a solvent in which all problems were dissolved and all processes commingled." George W. Stocking Jr., "The Turn-of-the-Century Concept of Race," in *MODERNISM\modernity* 1, no. 1 (1993): 6. Stocking continues, "Those of us today who are sophisticated in the concepts of the behavioral sciences have lost the richly connotative nineteenth-century sense of 'race' as accumulated cultural differences carried somehow in the blood."

62. The European view agrees on the innateness but is less definitive about the biology.

63. Fields, "Ideology and Race," 147.

64. See Gould, *Mismeasure of Man*, esp. 192, and Diane B. Paul, *Controlling Human Heredity: 1865 to the Present* (Amherst, N.Y., 1998). Eugenics was a movement to breed more "desirable" human beings, through encouragement of positive traits and discouragement of negative ones. The movement presupposed a belief shared by most scientists in the last decades of the nineteenth century and the first decades of the twentieth that these traits were largely genetically determined. Most eugenicists believed that racial groups (defined by the conventions of the time) differed substantially in their possession of desirable and undesirable traits; in this regard most eugenicists were racists, and the converse was true as well (almost by definition, as genetics became the form in which biological innatism came to be understood in racial thought). E. A. Hooton, however, a prominent physical anthropologist of the 1920s, was a nonracist eugenicist. He believed that all races contain a relatively equal proportion of "desirable" and "undesirable" genetically determined characteristics. See Marks, *Human Biodiversity*, 99–101. Paul points out that Francis Galton, the father of eugenics, and his biometrician followers initially thought that Mendelian laws of inheritance applied only to uninteresting characteristics (like seed color in garden peas), and doubted their applicability to humans, but later accepted the Mendelian innatist explanations of all human characteristics (46–48).

65. As we will see in chapter 7, a genetic perspective properly understood undermines rather than supports racial thought.

66. Alfred Binet, a French scientist, developed the test that, in altered form, would become the American IQ test; Binet did not see it as measuring innate ability. For a detailed critique of the American IQ school, see Gould, *Mismeasure*, 176–263, and Paul, *Controlling Human Heredity*, 50–71.

67. Smedley, *Race in North America*, 308–9.

68. Previously, for several decades after the 1840s, the Irish had undergone a similar racialization driven in part by the partly racialized conflict between the English and the Irish of several centuries' standing. See Smedley, *Race in North America*. The racialization of Irish Americans has been extensively documented in recent historical studies: Allen, *Invention of the White Race*, vol. 1: *Racial Oppression and Social Control*; Ignatiev, *How the Irish Became White*; Roediger, *Wages of Whiteness*, 133–163; and Jacobson, *Whiteness*. For a period in the mid-nineteenth century, racial Anglo-Saxonism, drawing some of its ideas from European national-character racialism, was influential in the United States. See Reginald Horsman, *Race and Manifest Destiny: The Origins of American Racial Anglo-Saxonism* (Cambridge, Mass., 1981).

Shifting understandings of who counted as "white" are reflected as well in a series of court cases from the late nineteenth century through the 1920s involving a variety of groups—Japanese, Syrian, Indian—attempting to claim naturalized citizenship under the "free white persons" designation in the 1790 statute. See Haney-Lopez, *White By Law*. Haney-Lopez demonstrates that the courts were never able to find a consistent definition or basis for classifying persons as white. He plausibly suggests that this difficulty is a sign both of the unscientific character of that designation and of a constancy in its meaning—that it always signified privilege and superiority.

69. This racializing of groups that later became unequivocally "white" is akin to the more national, less phenotypist European version of racialism, though in Jacobson's account there is little direct influence of European racial thought on the proliferation of "white races" in the United States.

70. The 1924 Act limited yearly immigration to 2 percent of a national group's percentage in the 1890 census. Jacobson documents the strong influence of prominent racists and eugenicists, such as Lothrop Stoddard, Harry Laughlin, and Madison Grant, on the congressional debate regarding the Act; the 2-percent formula originally emerged in the Report of the Eugenics Committee of the United States Committee on Selective Immigration. Jacobson, *Whiteness of a Different Color*, 81–89.

Hostility to immigrants as such is not racism but what is generally known as "nativism." In the case at hand, however, the eugenicists objected not to all immigrants (for example, not to "Nordics"), but only to certain groups, regarded as racially distinct.

71. This claim of marginality applies only to geneticist racism, not to geneticism more generally. As we will see in chapter 7, developments in understanding the human genome have spurred a general "geneticization" of human characteristics. These developments have not, however, generally attached themselves to racial thought, though some commentators worry, with some reason, that any form of geneticism and hereditarianism lends aid and comfort to racial thinking. Rothman, *The Book of Life*.

72. Richard J. Herrnstein and Charles Murray, the authors of *The Bell Curve: Intelligence and Class Structure in American Life* (New York, 1994), go to great lengths to attempt to distance themselves from various positions that they are concerned could be taken as racist. Their lack of success in doing so has been pointed out by the book's many critics. See especially Steven Fraser, ed., *The Bell Curve Wars: Race, Intelligence, and the Future of America* (New York, 1995), and Bernie Devlin, Stephen Fienberg, Daniel Resnick, and Kathryn Roeder, eds., *Intelligence, Genes, and Success: Scientists Respond to "The Bell Curve"* (New York, 1997).

Chapter 7. Do Races Exist?

1. We will see in chapter 8 that racial groups can share some commonalities of experience that do provide a common bond. Racial thought, however, implies something different—that the groups are bound together by inherent nature. This is the "falsely grounded" sense of commonality I refer to in the text.

2. "Current ways of talking about race are the residue, the detritus, so to speak, of earlier ways of thinking about race; so that it turns out to be easiest to understand contemporary talk about 'race' as the pale reflection of a more full-blooded race discourse that flourished in the last century." Appiah "Race, Culture, Identity," 38.

3. Mills, *Racial Contract*, 23.

4. I am not able to accord the issue of stereotyping attention within the confines of this book. Here is a brief summary of what I take to be the moral harms of all stereotyping, whether the content of the stereotyping is in some way flattering or (as is usually the case) primarily negative: stereotypes always involve false conceptions of groups, thus generating unwarranted and constricting expectations of individual members; stereotyping involves not seeing the internal diversity of a group; it discourages seeing members of groups as individuals; it invites members of the target group to internalize the stereotype, leading to various sorts of psychic damage and restriction. Nor are all racial stereotypes racist. A racist stereo-

type is one that portrays the stereotyped group as humanly inferior or deficient, or in a hateful, evil, demeaning, or degrading manner. Thus the stereotype of blacks as being innately musical is not a racist stereotype, but the stereotype of blacks as lazy is; the latter but not the former is a demeaning stereotype, and involves a significant deficiency. To say that a stereotype is not racist is not to say that it is therefore morally all right, as I argued in more general terms in chapter 1. All stereotyping is bad. In addition, depending on their content and the social and historical context, some stereotypes can be more damaging than others, inviting various forms of mistreatment and misrecognition. These points are explored in detail in L. Blum, "Racial and Ethnic Stereotyping," presentation to the Hoffberger Center for Professional Ethics, University of Baltimore, October 25, 1995.

5. For a sophisticated account of a conception of race that places hierarchy at the center of racialization, see Sally Haslanger, "Gender and Race: (What) Are They? (What) Do We Want Them to Be?" *Noûs*, Mar. 2000, 31–55.

6. The relation between what a group or individual is by nature and what they are "stuck with" is by no means as simple as racial thought implies. I might have poor eyesight by nature, but I can wear glasses. On the other hand, if I am born deaf, the sort of accommodation my society makes to deaf people will very much determine the degree to which my life is restricted by this condition.

7. We saw in chapter 6 that the popularity of *The Bell Curve* suggests at least some continuing vitality of biologistic inherentism, even though the book remains a minority voice within both science and the general culture, where biologistic racism is seen with general disfavor.

8. The internally racist self-attributions on the part of black and Hispanic students cited in chapter 1, note 38, appear also to be inherentist: "Everyone knows that black people are bad. That's just the way we are." "Black people don't like to work hard." "Blacks are poor and stay poor because they're dumber than whites (and Asians)." Minow, *Not Only for Myself*, 149.

9. In chapter 5 I make a more general version of this point—that characteristics can be attributed to a racial group in a way that implies inescapability, or does not. Here I am applying this point specifically to the use of culture in such attribution.

10. William E. Cross Jr., "Oppositional Identity and African American Youth: Issues and Prospects," in *Toward a Common Destiny: Improving Race and Ethnic Relations in America*, ed. Willis D. Hawley and Anthony W. Jackson, 185–204 (San Francisco, 1995).

11. Sally Haslanger suggests a view that lies somewhere between cultural and biological inherentism—that a racial group's cultural practices might affect their biological properties which in turn affect their inherent psychological propensities. The idea that because Asians eat little red meat (a practice partly cultural in character) they lack a competitive nature is an example. (This view is fully inherentist only if the cultural characteristics are regarded as inherent, which they may well not be.) (Personal communication.)

12. For example: "Since World War II, and especially in the past fifteen or twenty years, the cultural conception of race has tended to eclipse all others. It has become paradigmatic." David Theo Goldberg, *Racist Culture* (London, 1993), 71. Michel Wieviorka reports, although he does not endorse, "an image of racial difference [invoked by the idea of 'cultural racism'] which is not natural or biological but contained in language, religion, tradition, national origin." "Is It So Difficult to Be an Anti-racist?" in Werbner and Modood, *Debating Cultural Hybridity*, 141–42.

13. Thus I agree with the Parekh report (with one qualification) when it states, "Academic theory distinguishes between biological racism, which typically uses skin color as a marker of difference . . . and cultural racism, which focuses primarily on supposed differences of culture. Either way, the variations among human beings are imagined to be fixed and final, something determined by nature and unchangeable." Commission on the Future of Multi-ethnic Britain (chair: Bhikhu Parekh), *The Future of Multi-ethnic Britain* (London, 2000), 60. The qualification is that talking of "skin color as a marker of difference" as a way

to define racism is a bit misleading. As we saw in chapter 4, someone who prefers one skin shade to another, and discriminates on that basis, is not necessarily racist. It is only when skin color is taken, not only as a marker of difference, but as signifying inherent mental or temperamental characteristics that constitute such difference, that we have a case of racial discrimination. Indeed, taking skin color as the primary external marker of these characteristics is not essential to racism, or Jews could not be targets of racism.

14. In fact, many theorists who have posited a cultural turn in contemporary understandings of race do say that for a culturalist discourse to be racial, it must be inherentist. An influential case in point is the theory of "new racism" advanced in Britain in the early 1980s to explain the continuing advocacy of excluding Asians and West Indians as immigrants despite abandonment of theories of biological inferiority. Tariq Modood, a British political theorist, describes this development: "What had emerged was a racism based upon cultural differences, upon the 'natural' preference of human beings for their own cultural group [which was understood to coincide with a racial group as conventionally understood], and the incompatibility between different cultures, the mixing or coexistence of which in one country, it was alleged, was bound to lead to violent social conflict and the dissolution of social bonds." "'Difference,' Cultural Racism, and Anti-racism," in Werbner and Modood, *Debating Cultural Hybridity*, 154. Martin Barker, a key figure in analyzing the new racism, shows that the theories in question postulate an evolutionary and genetically based propensity to favor one's own cultural or racial kind. So the new racism, though at least overtly abandoning a theory of racial hierarchy, did not even attempt to abandon biologism and inherentism. Martin Barker, "Biology and the New Racism," in *Anatomy of Racism*, ed. David Theo Goldberg, 18–37 (Minneapolis, 1990).

Modood's own reason for retaining a conception of race within the cultural turn differs from Barker's; but it too recognizes that exclusion or devaluing based *purely* on cultural difference is insufficient to constitute a valid use of race. Modood says that "cultural racism" adds to an already existing racial understanding of the target groups "a further discourse which evokes cultural differences from an alleged British or 'civilised' norm to vilify, marginalise or demand cultural assimilation from groups who also suffer from biological racism." Modood, "'Difference,'" 155. Modood is particularly concerned to conceptualize the distinct form of victimization suffered by south Asian Muslims in Britain.

Both Barker and Modood assume that reference to biology ("instinct," phenotype) is what makes a conception of a group racial. In a sense my own requirement of inherentism is actually weaker than this; for I allow nonbiologistic forms of inherentism. To be sure, cultural inherentism is not a coherent form of inherentism; I agree with the tacit implication of Barker, Modood, and other commentators that biological inherentism is the only intellectually sound form of inherentism. (I argue below, however, that the form of biological inherentism required to provide a sound and rational basis for the contemporary notion of race runs afoul of the findings of modern genetics.) But I am interested in the actual employment of race in popular usage; for that, only intelligibility is necessary, not coherence. Since people are quite capable of holding genuinely contradictory beliefs (as Barbara Fields notes with respect to whites' views of blacks in the United States, discussed in chapter 6), they are certainly capable of holding incoherent ones. If I am right that many people are (generally tacit, but occasionally explicit) "cultural inherentists," then, I am suggesting, they can operate with an intelligible, if incoherent, conception of race.

15. Modood notes with approval that in 1998 the British government introduced "perceived religion" as a ground for protections accorded racial groups under law. Modood, "Liberal Multiculturalism and Real-World Multiculturalism," presentation to the Institute for the Study of Race and Social Division, Boston University, April 25, 2001, 9. Muslim identity in Britain generally takes the form of a communal, ethnic identity more than one based on personal faith; and anti-Muslim prejudice has a corresponding character as more like a racial prejudice than a religious one. So the law that Modood approves of may come close to capturing the specific character of anti-Muslim prejudice. Nevertheless, on a more general

level, it seems to me to come at the cost of clearly distinguishing between *religious* and *racial* bigotry and victimization. If a Bosnian Muslim is demonized for his religious practice by a white Britisher who views him as of the same race as herself, will this count as racism in the terms of the legislation in question? What about the victimization of a Pakistani of Muslim ancestry who has converted to Christianity (and known to have done so by the victimizer) and who is harassed as a "Paki"? Why not protect both racial and religious groups separately, allowing a clear recognition that some persons will suffer from both forms of victimization, while others may suffer only one?

16. Will Kymlicka, *Liberalism, Community, and Culture* (Oxford, 1989), 167. As mentioned earlier, ethnic groups can be thought of as possessing inherent characteristics; their cultures can be thought of as inherent rather than changeable. This would be a case of racialized ethnicity, an ethnic group thought of as more like a racial group.

17. The idea and terminology of "metaphysical inherentism" comes from Sally Haslanger. Berel Lang uses the related term "metaphysical racism" in his insightful essay "Metaphysical Racism (or: Biological Warfare by Other Means)," in *Race/Sex: Their Sameness, Difference, and Interplay*, ed. Naomi Zack, 17–28 (New York, 1997). Lang defines metaphysical racism by saying that it "asserts a basis for group difference . . . in essential . . . features of a group" (24). He seems to mean by this, however, something more fundamental than cultural or biological racism; metaphysical racism underlies both. By contrast, I see metaphysical inherentism as an *alternative* to cultural or biological inherentism. I would also suggest that Lang is unclear as to whether he wants "metaphysical racism" to mean "metaphysical inherentism" or "uncommitted inherentism" (which I discuss below).

18. Although I am talking about racial inherentism here, uncommitted inherentism can attach to all sorts of groups—ethnic, professional, regional, and so on.

19. Pressed on his views of the group in question, Miguel might back off from the generalization entirely, not only from the implication of inherency. "All I can really say is that the people I have encountered from this group are lazy, and other people say they are lazy; but I can't really say the group as a whole is lazy."

20. The ways that stereotypes shape the perceptions on which people often allegedly base racial generalizations are dramatically illustrated in an experiment by B. L. Duncan. A group of persons viewed a videotape of a heated exchange, in which one person mildly shoved a second. The parties to the exchange were varied with regard to race (white shoved black, black shoved black, and so on) for different audiences. The audiences were asked to say whether they saw the exchange as violent. A white audience, in the case of a black shoving a white, saw the act as "violent" 75 percent of the time, but when a white shoved a black, the percentage was only 17 percent. Reported in Walter Stephan and David Rosenfield, "Racial and Ethnic Stereotypes," in *In the Eye of the Beholder: Contemporary Issues in Stereotyping*, ed. Arthur G. Miller, 3–4 (New York, 1982). Stephan and Rosenfield report similar experiments with black audiences that yield the same perception of blacks as more violent than whites.

21. What I have called "inherentism" is sometimes referred to as "essentialism" and is almost uniformly rejected. I have avoided "essence" terminology because the complex philosophical history of this term provides meanings according to which races would have essences. For instance, a thing is sometimes spoken of as having an essence when it possesses nontrivial defining features. On this definition, phenotypic, ancestral, and geographical origin criteria could be used to sort people into traditional racial groups; races would then have essences, independent of whether the groups thus defined possessed further psychological or behavioral characteristics. A second familiar use of "essentialism"—solely as a term of criticism—is to refer to overgeneralization about group characteristics (often, tacitly, on the basis of characteristics of the overgeneralizer's group, for example, generalizing about all women on the basis of the experience of white women); this use does not require that the alleged characteristics be thought of as inherent, and thus, on my view, is not appropriately called "racial." To avoid the possible confusions of these two other familiar understandings

of "essentialism," I have eschewed this term in favor of "inherentism." (I am grateful to Sally Haslanger for clarification of essentialism.)

22. Cf. Tatum, *Why Are All the Black Kids,* 168: "Most biologists and physical anthropologists tell us that there is no such thing as a 'pure' race. All human populations are 'mixed' populations."

23. "The very notion of hybrid or mixed races is based on the false assumption that 'African' and 'Caucasian' are pure racial types available for hybridization." Blackburn, "Why Race," 8.

24. The one-drop rule is an instance of a more general rule of racial classification called "hypodescent," according to which the offspring of parents of two racial groups is assigned to the lower in social status of the two groups. Gloria Marshall, "Racial Classifications: Popular and Scientific," in *Science and the Concept of Race,* ed. Margaret Mead, Theodosius Dobzhansky, Ethel Tobach, and Robert E. Light (New York, 1969), reprinted in *The "Racial" Economy of Science: Toward a Democratic Future,* ed. Sandra Harding, 118 (Bloomington, Ind., 1993). The adoption of the one-drop rule in the United States was prompted primarily by slave owners' desire to maximize the slave population when the supply was not being replenished by importation from Africa, especially after the banning of the slave trade in 1808. See Albert Mosley, "Negritude, Nationalism, and Nativism: Racists or Racialists?" in *Racism,* ed. Leonard Harris (Amherst, N.Y., 1999), 81.

25. Just as blacks have passed, so some who think of themselves and are taken by others as white have some African ancestry and would not be counted as white if all the facts about their ancestry were known.

26. This situation seems less paradoxical once we distinguish races from racialized groups (see chapter 8). Blacks have the least somatic uniformity required to be a race, yet are the most racialized of all groups.

27. I am grateful to Diane Paul for feedback on an earlier draft of the remainder of this chapter, and for sources on material regarding genetics and race.

28. Richard Lewontin, *Human Diversity* (New York, 1995), 123; Joann C. Gutin, "End of the Rainbow," *Discover,* Nov. 1994, 72. The remaining 8–9 percent of total variation is accounted for by differences between ethnic or tribal groups within the same race. In a careful study, Guido Barbujani and his colleagues analyzed molecular diversity at 109 DNA markers in sixteen populations which differed greatly in geographical location, origin, and somatic and cultural characteristics, including Mbuti pygmies from Zaire, Cambodians (sampled in the San Francisco area), northern Italians, Mayans in Yucatan, white Australians, and New Guineans. The authors conclude, "We found that differences between members of the same population accounts for 84.4% of the total, which is in excellent agreement with estimates based on allele frequencies of classic, protein polymorphisms [the basis for Lewontin and Gutin's estimates]." Guido Barbujani, Arianna Magagni, Eric Minch, and L. Luca Cavalli-Sforza, "An Apportionment of Human DNA Diversity," *Proceedings of the National Academy of Sciences* 94 (Apr. 1997): 4516–19 (quote from 4516).

29. Blackburn, "Why Race," 14, citing L. L. Cavalli-Sforza, P. Menozzi, and A. Piazza, *The History and Geography of Human Genes* (Princeton, 1994). Lewontin makes a similar point: "If, after a great cataclysm, only Africans were left alive, the human species would have retained 93% of its total genetic variation." *Human Diversity,* 123.

30. Gutin, "End of the Rainbow," 72; Paul Hoffman, "The Science of Race," *Discover,* Nov. 1994, 4.

31. Figures and general discussion from Lewontin, *Human Diversity,* 29, 117, 119, 120.

32. For multifaceted critiques of *The Bell Curve,* see the essays collected in Devlin et al., *Intelligence, Genes, and Success: Scientists Respond to "The Bell Curve"* (New York, 1997).

33. Lewontin, *Human Diversity,* 29; Jared Diamond, "Race without Color," *Discover,* Nov. 1994, 86. Natural selection and adaptation are not the only possible explanations of genetic differences among populations. Another is the so-called founder effect, in which an "unusual condition in a population can be traced to a founding ancestor who happened to carry

a novel mutation into the region." The founder effect explains the high incidence of Huntington's disease in the Lake Maracaibo region of Venezuela and of Tay-Sachs disease among Ashkenazi Jews. Natalie Angier, "Do Races Differ? Not Really, Genes Show," *New York Times*, Aug. 22, 2000, 6.

34. Jared Diamond points out that southern European whites (for example, Greeks and Italians) carry another antimalarial gene that does not cause sickle-cell anemia. So, if one were grouping according to the possession of antimalarial genes, some whites and many blacks would be in one group, while other whites, some blacks, and some Asians and Arabs would be in another. "Race without Color," 86.

35. James Shreeve, "Terms of Estrangement," *Discover*, Nov. 1994, 63. Hypertension is a particularly complex example, because if one were to think consistently about a truly racial explanation, one would have to look at hypertension also among Africans—which turns out to be quite low—as well as among white groups, where it turns out, for example, that Finns and Russians have high rates. Ibid. In other words, here a consistently and comprehensively racial view would lead to jettisoning a race-based generalization about hypertension.

36. See Abby Lippman, "Prenatal Genetic Testing and Screening: Constructing Needs and Reinforcing Inequities," *American Journal of Law and Medicine* 17, nos. 1–2 (1991): 15–50. "Geneticization refers to an ongoing process by which differences between individuals are reduced to their DNA codes, with most disorders, behaviors, and physiological variations defined, at least in part, as genetic in origin" (19). Lippman's concept of "geneticization" has come into wide use among those involved in genetics-related social controversies. Diane Paul, personal communication, Nov. 12, 2000. But Lippman's qualification, "in part," muddies the waters a bit. I would prefer to define geneticization as "conferring a substantially greater significance on genetic factors than evidence warrants." Geneticization is not "genetic determinism" if that means that important human characteristics are *fully determined* by genetic structure. "Geneticization" makes a somewhat weaker claim of genetic determination.

37. Angier, "Do Races Differ?" 6.

38. The article's use of the word "shaped" is sufficiently ambiguous, I suppose, to be consistent with a view that the expression of such traits as "intelligence" and "artistic talent" is almost wholly due to cultural, familial, and other environmental factors, with genetics providing only the biological potentialities. But, in context, the use of "shaped" seems to me much more naturally read as implying a strong genetic component to the actual expression of such traits.

A similar implication of geneticization appears in a health newsletter of Johns Hopkins University. "In less than a decade [researchers] identified approximately 50,000 human genes—segments of DNA that influence behavior, physical appearance, vulnerability to illness, and virtually every other human characteristic. This information was compiled to create the genome map." "What the Human Genome Means to You," *Johns Hopkins Medical Letter, Health after 50* 12, no. 10: 6. "Influence" might be a bit weaker than "shaped," but the context strongly suggests that mapping the human genome has significantly advanced our understanding of what causes individuals to manifest particular traits, or at least what causes human beings in general to do so. In fact, the human genome has done nothing of the sort. Richard Lewontin's prefatory remarks to the 1998 edition of *Human Diversity* are pertinent here: "The most important result of studying DNA has been that although there is much more genetic variation than we could have detected from the study of proteins alone, there have been no major changes in our picture of the pattern and origin of human diversity. . . . The study of DNA has not resulted in the discovery of genes for intelligence, aggressiveness, or the ability to play the viola. The very aspects of human diversity that fascinate us the most remain outside the domain of genetics."

39. Smedley, *Race in North America*, 305, lists several such definitions, some drawn from respected textbooks.

40. Ibid., 306.

41. Ibid., 307–8. The genes that determine human skin color vary independently of other genes. There are evolutionary or other explanations of skin color; evidence points to the protection that melanin provides against ultraviolet solar radiation as an explanation for why sub-Saharan Africans, Australian aboriginals, and Indians have dark skin. The reasons why some people have lighter skin and others darker do not carry over to other genetically determined characteristics. Blackburn, "Why Race?" 8, 9. Blackburn points out that there is less scientific consensus on an evolutionary explanation for light skin color, for example in northern Europeans (9–10). Whites do have melanin-producing genes, as do blacks (and all other groups); but other genetic factors "more or less turn off melanin production" in whites. Rothman, *Book of Life*, 69.

42. Diamond, "Race without Color," 86.

43. Smedley, *Race in North America*, 306–7.

44. Cf. Appiah, "Race, Culture, Identity," 73. The distinguished population geneticist L. L. Cavalli-Sforza claims that there is an irreducible arbitrariness in the level of taxonomic classification one chooses to define "races" in the biological sciences: "The classification into races has proved to be a futile exercise for reasons that were already clear to Darwin. Human races are still extremely unstable entities in the hands of modern taxonomists, who define from 3 to 60 or more races. . . . Although there is no doubt that there is only one human species, there are clearly no objective reasons for stopping at any particular level of taxonomic splitting. In fact, the analysis we carry out in chapter 2 for purposes of evolutionary study shows that the level at which we stop our classifications is completely arbitrary. . . . All populations or population clusters overlap when single genes are considered, and in almost all populations, all alleles are present but in different frequencies. No single gene is therefore sufficient for classifying human populations into systematic categories." Cavalli-Sforza, Menozzi, and Piazza, *History and Geography of Human Genes*, 19. Despite this arbitrariness regarding scientific classifications of race, I think Michael Root is correct to say that even though there are no races in the popular meaning of the term, there *could have been* races in that sense. If different population groups had developed in different parts of the world in such a way that they were radically different genetically, phenotypically, culturally, and psychologically, these groups would have a claim to being the fundamental biological divisions of humankind that people wrongly think the groups we currently call races are. Michael Root, "Racial Realism," in *Philosophical Research on African-American Social Inequality*, ed. Tommy Lee Lott (Lanham, Md., 2001).

45. Smedley, *Race in North America*, 305.

46. Some interesting philosophical defenses of the legitimacy of the concept of race seem to me to founder on this confusion between specialized scientific definitions of race and ordinary understandings of it. For example, Albert Mosley deploys a population geneticist account of race (drawn from one of its early proponents, Theodosius Dobzhansky) to defend a belief in race against Anthony Appiah's critique. Appiah, "Race, Culture, Identity"; and *In My Father's House*, chap. 1; Mosley, "Negritude, Nationalism, and Nativism," 74–86. Appiah's critique, however, is meant to apply to the popular understanding of race, and Mosley does not clearly link his defense of the population genetics account to this popular understanding. Mosley also takes issue with Appiah's claim that race is a useless and indeed destructive idea for understanding and mobilizing constructive action around problems facing Africa; but Mosley's pertinent and interesting arguments on this issue of the strategic uses of racial identification seem to me only tangentially related to his defense of Dobzhansky's account of race.

Philip Kitcher defends a more complex and qualified form of the "reproductive isolation" account of race. If I have understood him correctly (and I am not certain that I have), his argument still renders the relation between our current racial categories and his proposed conception of race problematic, tendentious, or unclear. For example, Kitcher says that racial divisions are sustained by "patterns of mating" that fall along racial lines, a practice he allegedly regards as "natural." We should not infer from the role of genetics in calling into question inherent differences among "racial" groups that the idea of race is itself a genetic concept. Genetic differences unconnected to psychological traits have little relevance to the commonsense idea of race. Yet when Kitcher goes on to explain why American blacks and whites intermarry at a low rate, he (correctly) cites primarily social and historical reasons (although the rate of *increase* over the past thirty years is quite substantial), rather than anything that could be considered biological, or inherent in the racial character of the groups in question. It is not clear, therefore, how what Kitcher calls "race" bears on what we ordinarily understand by that term. Philip Kitcher, "Race, Ethnicity, Biology, Culture," in Harris, *Racism,* 87–117, esp. 106, 107–8.

47. Barkan, *Retreat of Scientific Racism.* Smedley also describes the antiracist efforts of the pioneering German American anthropologist Franz Boas. Smedley, *Race in North America,* 297–300. Boas is discussed more fully in Vernon J. Williams Jr., *Rethinking Race: Franz Boas and His Contemporaries* (Lexington, Ky., 1996), and Baker, *From Savage to Negro.*

48. See Smedley, *Race in North America,* 311: "With very few exceptions, contemporary scientists deplore racism as an abominable by-product of the layperson's confused misconception of the 'true' or 'real' meaning of race. They believe that if people were only made cognizant of the actual scientific understandings of biological differences, then the irrational prejudice upholding racism would disappear."

49. Diamond, "Race without Color," 89.

Chapter 8: Racialized Groups and Social Constructions

1. In *Racism* (73–77), Miles usefully discusses different ways the concept of "racialization" has been used in literature on race. Miles's own definition involves attaching social meaning to somatic characteristics in a way that defines collectivities. As he points out, this definition does not require a concept of race to have been developed in relation to such collectivities; somatic characteristics only have to be noted, and taken to define a significant social identity, as in ancient Greece. My own definition is more limited, to such collectivities as distinctly racial attributes are attributed (inherent mental and psychological traits, radical difference between races, and so on).

2. Haney-Lopez, *White by Law.*

3. Cheryl Harris, "Whiteness as Property," in *Black on White: Black Writers on What It Means to Be White,* ed. David Roediger (New York, 1998), 102–18. Mills states this very well: "In a racially structured polity, the only people who can find it psychologically possible to deny the centrality of race are those who are racially privileged, for whom race is invisible precisely because the world is structured around them, whiteness as the ground against which the figures of other races—those who, unlike us, are raced—appear." Mills, *Racial Contract,* 76.

4. Mary Waters argues that ethnicity in the 1980s provided whites with a form of identity that masked their racial privilege and the racial disadvantages of nonwhites. *Ethnic Options: Choosing Identities in America* (Berkeley, Calif., 1990), 147–68.

5. What I call "racialization" others have called (the process of being) "raced." (This locution is used more in relation to individuals than is my use of "racialization," which I apply primarily to groups.) Lucius Outlaw's use of the similar expression "raciation" is quite interesting. In the introduction to his exceptionally illuminating discussions of race and ethnicity in *On Race and Philosophy* (New York, 1996), Outlaw introduces the concepts of "raciation" and "ethnicization" as "the complicated processes (biological, socio-cultural, historical) by which such populations and population subgroups are formed and maintained" (5). Outlaw's descriptions of these processes seem to me to support the idea that the groups we call races are not *actually* races. But Outlaw talks about races in a way that implies that they are real biological and social divisions. For instance: "Raciation and ethnicization develop as responses to the need for life-sustaining and meaningfully acceptable *order* of various kinds

(conceptual, social, political)" (8). He may or may not be right about ethnicity, but in my view ethnicities are real whereas races are not. I agree that racialized identity can provide a source of order in people's lives; but I think the human species would have been a lot better off without races, and the idea of races. Racialized identities provide personal order only in response to an oppressive and stratified society. Ethnicity, by contrast, is typically not developed as a response to oppression; although political processes are involved in the creation of ethnic identities, the cultural groupings that form the basis for most ethnicities are more like natural responses to the meaning-seeking proclivities that Outlaw is pointing to.

6. The more general idea of a "pan" identity is of a larger group consisting of distinct subgroups, often national in character, such as "pan-Slav," "pan-Arab," and "pan-African." In many cases the "pan" identity takes a *political* form, although it implies, independent of empirical foundation, a cultural or linguistic commonality.

7. An excellent treatment of panethnicity in general—and Asian American panethnicity in particular—to which my account is indebted, is Espiritu, *Asian American Panethnicity*.

8. For discussion of the Vincent Chin case, see ibid., 141–55.

9. Indeed the framing of the Census question—and this is true of the 1970 and 1980 Censuses also—weakly implies that each of these separate ethnicities is itself a race. This may in part reflect an earlier twentieth-century understanding of Chinese, Japanese, Filipino, and others as distinct races.

10. Eric Liu, *The Accidental Asian: Notes of a Native Speaker* (New York, 1998), 63–64. Liu feels that his Chinese American identity, by contrast, has real substance. At the same time he recognizes that "Asian American" can be a very personally meaningful identity, even if it is not to him. Liu's discussion of these matters is extremely illuminating.

11. See Waters, *Ethnic Options*.

12. After a lobbying effort, Asian Indians were included in the Asian/Pacific Islander portion of the Census, and are now therefore eligible to seek minority status protection, access to affirmative action status, and the capacity to participate in many federal programs. Espiritu, *Asian American Panethnicity*, 125.

13. Hollinger, *PostEthnic America*, esp. chap. 1. It is not clear that the "African American" designation is parallel to the others. This label is, I believe, generally understood to apply to black Americans whose ancestry lies in slavery within the United States; thus it does not include Caribbean Americans and recent African immigrants. There may be no label other than "black" to perform this "pan" function for persons of African ancestry, though we have seen that this seemingly purely racial designation tends in the United States to carry ethnocultural associations as well. It is worth noting that for the first generation of slaves, "African American" was a genuinely panethnic designation, since the slaves came from very distinct cultures in Africa.

14. See note 2. There can be disagreement about the criteria for assigning persons to a race—what counts for being "white"—and also disagreement as to whether a particular person meets those criteria.

15. The "Hispanic origins" category was invented in 1977 by the Office of Management and Budget in its guidelines for federal racial classifications (the so-called Directive No. 15) and was first used on the federal Census in 1980; the same category appeared on the 1990 Census. The 2000 Census wording is "Hispanic or Latino." Nobles, *Shades of Citizenship: Race and the Census in Modern Politics*, 80–83.

16. The census question reads: "Is person 1 Spanish/Hispanic/Latino?" If the answer to this question is "Yes," four further choices are provided: "Mexican, Mexican American, Chicano," "Puerto Rican," "Cuban," and "other Spanish/Hispanic/Latino." If the latter, the subject is to specify which group.

17. Jorge J. E. Gracia (not to be confused with Jorge L. A. Garcia, whose work is discussed elsewhere in this book) discusses the concept of *mestizaje* in some detail. He claims that it is distinct from amalgamation, in which the component elements lose their distinctive character entirely and become a wholly new entity. In *mestizaje*, the indigenous, the Spanish (or

Iberian), and the African elements continue to be recognizable, but they modify each other both physically and culturally, as well as producing new elements through the mix. Jorge J. E. Gracia, *Hispanic/Latino Identity: A Philosophical Perspective* (Malden, Mass., 2000), 108–21, esp. 111. I have the impression that mestizo and mestiza identity is sometimes understood to emphasize the indigenous and European elements of the mix, leaving the African element in the shadows.

18. Nevertheless, prior to the 1930 Census, Mexican Americans were scored as "white," with their Spanish descent in mind. With the influx of larger numbers of immigrants, they were more distinctly viewed in racial terms, reflected in this instruction to the 1930 Census enumerators: "Practically all Mexican laborers are of a racial mixture difficult to classify, though usually well recognized in the localities in which they are found." Nobles, *Shades of Citizenship*, 189, 72–74.

19. Puerto Ricans, Dominicans, and Cubans have a much greater degree of African ancestry in their national mixes than do Mexicans.

20. Nobles, *Shades of Citizenship*, 87, and passim.

21. Rebecca Blank, "An Overview of Trends in Social and Economic Well-being, by Race," in *America Becoming: Racial Trends and Their Consequences*, vol. 1, ed. Neil Smelser, William Julius Wilson, and Faith Mitchell (Washington, D.C., 2001).

22. Mary C. Waters, "Explaining the Comfort Factor: West Indian Immigrants Confront American Race Relations," in *The Cultural Territories of Race: Of Black and White Boundaries*, ed. Michele Lamont (Chicago, 1999), 85, 71. Waters is addressing the question why whites are more comfortable with Caribbean blacks than with African Americans. Some of the factors she cites do not appear to bear directly on an actual deracializing of Caribbean blacks—for example, the perception that Caribbeans are more accepting of white people, especially as having authority over them in jobs, than are African Americans (85).

23. Although Caribbean immigrants can be seen as more welcomed, and less racialized, than native blacks, they can also be the target of nativist hostility—that is, hostility to foreigners or immigrants—that is not directed toward American natives. Nativism is not intrinsically race-based. In its first incarnation in the nineteenth century it was directed primarily against Catholics. Its conceptual target is the "foreign," not the "racial other." Blacks can direct nativist hostility toward other persons of color, including other blacks. Latinos who have been in the United States for several generations may direct nativist hostility toward newly arrived Latinos; here the hostility may not be pure nativism, but, to some extent, a not-yet-fully accepted group wishing to distance themselves from a group to which they are ethnically linked yet who are *more* marginalized and who therefore may taint them by association. This would perhaps be a derivative nativism. See Arian Campo-Flores, " 'Mexicano' Against 'Chicano,' " *Newsweek*, Sept. 18, 2000, 49, 51. Here "Chicano" refers to Mexican Americans who have been in the United States for several generations, and "Mexicano" to new immigrants.

As the vast majority of post-1965 immigrants to the United States are people of color, and most "nativism" is expressed by whites, it has become difficult to disentangle the racial from the purely nativist strands in anti-immigrant hostility, which intensified (though irregularly) throughout the 1990s. See Juan F. Perea, ed., *Immigrants Out! The New Nativism and the Anti-immigrant Impulse in the United States* (New York, 1997).

24. Mary Waters demonstrates this ethnic masking of race in *Ethnic Options*, 147–68.

25. The cover of *Newsweek* for Sept. 18, 2000, boldly announces a special report, "Redefining Race in America." The introductory remarks in the table of contents to the ten articles on this subject suggest that the increase in racial intermarriage, the greater visibility and self-claimed identity of people of mixed race, and the influx of immigrants of many different nonblack, nonwhite groups means that "the old labels of black and white can't begin to capture the subtleties of blood and identity" (p. 3). In itself this is quite true, but this framing of the articles, and occasional elements of the articles themselves, suggest that the new complexity of the racial landscape is rendering racial categories and antiblack racism

increasingly obsolescent, if not obsolete. But the substance of most of the articles does not support this view. Continuing black disadvantage, though downplayed, is occasionally acknowledged. No evidence of any substantial deracializing of whites and blacks is presented.

These articles also share a tendency in contemporary American culture and media to identify the problematizing of racial categories with the mitigating of racism. Though these two things are not entirely unconnected, current personal and societal racism and legacies of historical racism and injustice can outlast a weakening of racial consciousness. Indeed, as we will see in chapter 9, certain forms of nonconsciousness of race actually support racial inequality.

None of this is to deny that some of the developments documented in the articles—a movement in Birmingham, Alabama, to renounce racial prejudice, and the general increase in interracial marriages—are quite hopeful developments.

26. I am indebted to Jorge L. A. Garcia and Sally Haslanger for several conversations about social construction which have greatly contributed to my understanding.

27. Social construction is a complex and contested idea. I will discuss only certain strands within this general rubric that bear specifically on the issue of race.

28. By "nation" I mean "nation-state." The former word is sometimes used more broadly to include territorially concentrated ethnic groups, such as the Basque, the Kurds, or the Flemings, especially when those groups have a collective identity as distinct from their host nation-states.

29. Benedict Anderson, *Imagined Communities,* rev. ed. (New York, 1993).

30. Being treated as members of a race gives those in a racialized group a basis for a sense of shared fate, that "we are all in this together." But the idea of a shared destiny carries a further implication of a divinity or world spirit (as in Hegel) or some sort of cosmic ordering within which a self-existing collectivity (not a mere social creation) is accorded a role. This is why I say that racialized groups can not have shared destinies. W. E. B. Du Bois's early views on race had something of this "shared destiny" flavor, which accompanied his belief that races were real, a view he began to abandon in the early twentieth century. See "Conservation of Races."

31. Walter Benn Michaels suggests that on a constructivist account of race, it is incoherent to speak of a black person "passing" as white (see discussion in chapters 5 and 7), since an individual could not be "really" black apart from being identified by the wider society as black. "The No-Drop Rule," *Critical Inquiry* 20 (Summer 1994): 90. In an insightful discussion of this article, Robert Gooding-Williams notes that social construction regarding race does not mean that people are simply what they are visually taken to be. Rather, the rules of racial designation provide for descent-based criteria as well, and these override somatic criteria; someone passes if her parents are black but she "looks white" (and her ancestry is not known to those to whom she is passing). "Race, Multiculturalism, and Democracy," *Constellations* 5, no. 1 (1998): 18–41, esp. 19–22. That having been said, a clearer distinction between races and racialized groups would obviate Michaels's somewhat understandable response to the idea that races are not real but only social constructs—how, then, could someone be "really" black? The answer is that the complex rules of racial designation apply to racialized groups, not real races; it is racialized groups that are real.

32. *Malone V. Haley* No. 88–339, Sp. Jud. Ct. Suffolk County, Mass., July 25, 1989. The case is discussed in Christopher Ford, "Administering Identity: The Determination of 'Race' in Race-conscious Law," *California Law Review* 82, no. 5 (Oct. 1994): 1231–1285.

33. The court used as evidence somatic features associated with race ("fair skin, fair hair coloring"), birth certificate reporting "white" identifications for the previous three generations, the way the Malone brothers appeared to present themselves socially, and their self-identification on a previous civil service exam. Ibid., 1233.

34. In his essay "Race, Culture, Identity," which has served as a springboard for my own arguments for the nonreality of races in chapter 7, Anthony Appiah draws on Ian Hacking's idea that the labels we apply to people can serve as a basis for meaningful collective identi-

ties. Appiah says that racial identities are created when people shape their life projects by reference to the racial labels that have been ascribed to them, in a process Appiah calls "identification" (78). Appiah is concerned to show how race can continue to be an important social and personal identity even if there are no races and even if people abandon central tenets of a racial outlook, such as that groups defined by phenotype also possess distinctive mental and psychological characteristics (or "racial essence").

What exactly is a "racial identity," on Appiah's account? At the ascriptive level, it involves ancestry and phenotype. "Identification" involves acknowledgment of these ascriptive criteria, but also recognition of the history of attributing racial essences to the groups that are somatically and ancestrally defined, although the identifier need not himself believe in such "essences." Appiah goes on to propose healthy and appropriate forms of racial, and specifically black American, identification—for example, that it not be too "tightly scripted" (implying a plethora of constricting norms about how blacks ought to behave), that it not be confused with a cultural identity, and that it not be allowed to "imperialize" other important social and personal identities (a fault I have called "moral racialism" in chapter 3).

In this discussion of racial identity, Appiah seems to me to have lost sight of his earlier powerful critique of "race." His reliance on Hacking seems to have led him to make too much of the fact that we possess socially agreed-upon criteria for racial identities, and to pay too little attention to the moral baggage that normally accompanies racial categorization; that is, he tends to reduce the meaning of race to mere racial classification.

Appiah's discussion of racial identity does not follow through on the distinction that his previous critique of race should have led him to draw, between a racialized identity and a genuinely racial identity. On Appiah's account, does the individual who adopts a "black" racial identity recognize that races do not exist? That is, does he reject (doctrinal) racialism? If so, he is more likely to avoid the pitfalls of racial identity that Appiah mentions (too-tight scripting, confusion with cultural identity, imperialization). Such an individual is also, as I have argued, more likely to avoid the other divisive associations with race that I have been concerned to emphasize (radical "otherizing," moral distance, and so on)—features which Appiah somewhat implies in his critique of race earlier in the article but does not explicitly state, and does not carry over to the discussion of racial identity in the latter part of the article. On the other hand, if this individual views his identity as based on real racial divisions, he is quite likely to fall into the traps Appiah mentions, as well as those he implies earlier. Appiah does not clarify which sort of "racial identity" this individual possesses.

Appiah does recognize that racial identification takes on a feature of race beyond ascription according to standard somatic/ancestral criteria—the history of ascribing racial essences. But he does not explain the implications of this recognition for current racial identifications, and identities. Could not someone recognize that history but regard it as having no bearing on what racial identities *currently* signify? Might she not say, for example, that people formerly believed that blacks, whites, Asians, and so on possessed certain distinct mental and temperamental characteristics, but that aside from a small minority, such beliefs have been abandoned?

Yet if current racial meanings go beyond ascriptive criteria for categorization, perhaps plus a recognition of certain historical features attributed to races, Appiah has not explained what those meanings are. More specifically, he does not, in this section, acknowledge the inherently divisive character of racial identity—its baggage of false homogeneity, exaggerated differentness among races, inherency and unchangeability of characteristics, and the like.

And so, to summarize, I think a major reason for Appiah's failure to carry his argument against race into his discussion of "racial identity" is his reliance on Hacking's "labelizing" understanding of social construction in the article on which Appiah draws. See Ian Hacking, "Making Up People," in *Reconstructing Individualism: Autonomy, Individuality, and the Self in Western Thought*, ed. Thomas Heller, Morton Sosna, and David Wellbery (Stanford, Calif., 1986). Hacking may well have changed or amplified that understanding in his book-length treatment of this issue, *The Social Construction of What?* (Cambridge, Mass., 1999).

35. Rainier Spencer decries this familiar move undertaken in the name of social construction: "In an effort to distance the acceptance of race from biologistic notions, race is recast as a social construction, suggesting—wrongly—that as such it is independent of and not informed by an underlying belief in biological race. This appears to give race a legitimacy. The false consciousness should not be referred to as a 'social reality.' " Spencer, *Spurious Issues*, 39. Orlando Patterson sees a similar pattern in certain contemporary writing about race: "Having demolished and condemned as racist the idea that observed group differences have any objective, biological foundation, the liberal intellectual community has revived the 'race' concept as an essential category of human experience with as much ontological validity as the discarded racist notion of biologically distinct groups." Patterson, *The Ordeal of Integration: Progress and Resentment in America's "Racial" Crisis* (Washington, D.C., 1997), 72.

36. *Boys on the Side*. Dir. Herbert Ross. Alcor Films, 1995.

37. I draw the idea of scalarity from Anthony Skillen, "Racism: Flew's Three Concepts of Racism," *Journal of Applied Philosophy* 10, no. 1 (1993): 78.

38. Donna Reed, Robert Redford, Barbara Streisand, and the film *The Way We Were* (dir. Sydney Pollack. Columbia Pictures, 1973) are all used as "white" cultural markers in relation to Robin.

39. Harlon Dalton, discussing the issue of scalar race in relation to culture and identity, writes: "What really matters is not whether a black person talks, acts, or performs White, but whether it appears that she would prefer to *be* White." *Racial Healing*, 89.

40. Stephen Carter, "The Black Table, the Empty Seat, and the Tie," in Early, *Lure and Loathing*.

41. To be more precise, Carter is distrustful of setting standards for how one manifests attachment to or love for black people; but he does not really raise the question whether "love for black people" is an appropriate norm for black persons. Anthony Appiah is more clearly concerned with the ways constricting standards can get built into what it means to be "black." Appiah, "Identity, Authenticity, and Survival," and "Race, Culture, Identity."

42. In his study of ethnoracial groups at the University of California at Berkeley, Troy Duster reports that "Native American students express the highest levels of internal tension and conflict between the demands of assimilation and accommodation to new cultural and social skills required for success in the university setting and maintaining the integrity of their cultural roots and connections." Duster, *Diversity Project*, 19.

Chapter 9. Should We Try to Give Up Race?

1. Glenn Loury makes this point well: "Many proponents of color-blindness as the primary moral ideal come close to equating the use of racial information in administrative practices with the continued awareness of racial identity in the broad society . . . The implicit assumption of color-blind advocates is that, if we would just stop putting people into these boxes, they would oblige us by not thinking of themselves in these terms. But, this assumption is patently false." Loury, *Shape of the River*, xxviii.

2. There is evidence that white workers are especially harmed by not recognizing their commonality of interest with minority, especially black, workers. One study found that 59 percent of blacks, compared to 28 percent of nonblacks, would vote for a union if given a chance. Cited in Richard D. Kahlenberg, "Unionization as a Civil Right," *American Prospect*, Sept. 11, 2000, 14. Gerald Torres and Lani Guinier plausibly argue that racial minority workers are often the most militant and the least prone to buy into ruling elites' mystifications of their interests; and that white workers can and do benefit from following the lead of such workers. *The Miner's Canary* (Cambridge, Mass., 2002).

3. I am grateful to Melissa Nobles for assistance with this section.

4. Nobles, *Shades of Citizenship*.

5. "Mulatto" was understood as someone with approximately half "black African" ancestry and half white; "quadroon" one-fourth black; and "octoroon" one-eighth black.

6. "The mulatto category was a qualifier of the 'negro' category, not a wholly independent category." Nobles, *Shades of Citizenship*, 82. The elimination of the "mulatto" category from the 1930 Census signaled the ascendancy of the "one-drop" rule. See further discussion below.

7. The designing of racial categories for the Census from 1980 on has an interesting history, recounted in Nobles. The categories were the product of a committee representing a range of federal agencies concerned with collecting racial and ethnic data. The basic structure of categories for all federal agencies was laid out in the so-called Directive No. 15 of the Office of Management and Budget in 1977. This document has remained the basis of Census categorization; but the input of different ethnic and racial groups, often directly sought by the federal government, which has appointed Asian Pacific, black, Hispanic, American Indian, and Alaskan Native advisory committees, has resulted in some changes in the 1990 and 2000 censuses.

8. Nobles, *Shades of Citizenship*, 80.

9. In contrast to the others, the "Asian/Pacific Islander/Native Hawaiian" category is not accorded a panethnic designation on the census; instead, ethnic subdivisions of that category are listed—Chinese, Filipino, Native Hawaiian, Samoan, Vietnamese, and so on—as discussed in the previous chapter.

10. Nobles points out that civil rights groups did not themselves explicitly take up the matter of "race" itself, but were concerned only with attacking racial discrimination. Nobles, *Shades of Citizenship*, 75–77. Challenging discrimination and its moral foundation without challenging the full notion of "race" is one reason racial identity remains regarded as largely unproblematic by many American blacks. See chaps 5 and 6.

11. In its preamble, the OMB Directive no. 15 takes a baby step in the direction of rejecting racialism: "These classifications should not be interpreted as being scientific or anthropological in nature." The directive does not give any instruction as to a clear alternative way of thinking about the meaning of these categories (e.g., as referring to racialized groups); nor does it suggest what might be the consequences of jettisoning a scientific or anthropological understanding of them.

12. Patterson makes this argument in *Ordeal of Integration*, 72–77. He also offered the proposal specifically in relation to the then upcoming decennial Census in "The Race Trap," *New York Times* (date unknown, but almost certainly 1996 or 1997, as those were the years of public debate about categories to appear on the 2000 Census). The same proposal was made by the American Anthropological Association, and was also made in the 1950 UNESCO statement on race, written by a distinguished group of scientists that was dominated by anthropologists: "Because serious errors . . . are habitually committed when the term 'race' is used in popular parlance, it would be better when speaking of human races to drop the term 'race' altogether and speak of ethnic groups." Montagu, *Statement on Race*, 13.

13. Patterson, *Ordeal of Integration*, 74.

14. Ibid., 76.

15. In his thoughtful account of contemporary usage of "racism" as a category of historical analysis, the historian George Frederickson analyzes it as a form of assertion of ethnic group status based on ancestry. "Understanding Racism: Reflections of a Comparative Historian," in Frederickson, *The Comparative Imagination* (Berkeley Calif., 1999), esp. 84–86. One virtue Frederickson sees in this analysis is his claim (drawn from Donald Horowitz) that "designation of people by skin color and the mistreatment of them on that basis has no special features that would distinguish it in any definitive way from group domination based on religion, culture, or the simple belief that some people have defective ancestry" (84). See Donald Horowitz, *Ethnic Groups in Conflict* (Berkeley, Calif., 1985), esp. 64–83. Frederickson's purposes are analytical rather than normative, and his account of racism may well possess some virtues for those purposes. But the statement quoted above does not seem true. As

a comparison of Irish and black Americans suggests, race is not the same as ethnicity, even if both involve some tie to ancestry. Nor is race equivalent to "designation of people by skin color." The ancient Greeks designated people by skin color but lacked a notion of race. Race is not simply seeing skin color as conferring a social identity. It brings the full baggage of implication of unequal worth, inherent mental and psychological characteristics, and moral division. In addition, "ethnicity" really means one thing in the United States—where it is explicitly *contrasted* with "race"—and another in other parts of the world. Serbs and Croats, Tutsis and Hutus exemplify a form of what amounts to "racialized ethnicity" in which the groups are thought of as having something like different natures and are experienced as radically "other" in the manner characteristic of race. (This kind of ethnicity is akin to the early twentieth-century view of southern and eastern European immigrants that Patterson mentions, and, in that regard, also more akin to the European strand of nineteenth-century racial thought discussed in chapter 6). Horowitz's work mostly concerns ethnic groups in Asia, Africa, and the Caribbean, so his notion of ethnicity is closer to this racialized form than to the American version. Regarding the United States, Frederickson and Horowitz's view overlooks the fact that ethnicity is, in large measure, a less morally troubling form of distinction among persons than race.

16. Cross, "Oppositional Identity," 198.

17. Norimitsu Onishi, "New Sense of Race Arises among Asian-Americans," *New York Times*, May 30, 1996, A1, B6.

18. Ibid., B6.

19. Ibid.

20. Du Bois, *Souls of Black Folk*, 38.

21. This is true as well of Du Bois, though when he wrote *Souls* he still believed in races in the classic sense. He abandoned this belief in the early decades of the twentieth-century.

22. Appiah, "Race, Culture, Identity," 89–90.

23. Liu, *Accidental Asian*, 79.

24. On the exploitation of black music particularly in the 1950s, see Reebee Garofalo, *Rockin' Out: Popular Music in the USA* (Boston, 1997).

25. Nobles, *Shades of Citizenship*, 35–69. See also note 6. But opposition to interracial marriage and a view of biracial persons as defective have by no means disappeared from American life. In 1994 a school principal in Alabama forbade racially mixed couples from attending the prom, and told a mixed-race student who protested the policy that the rule was aimed at preventing "mistakes" like her. Carlos A. Fernández, "Government Classification of Multiracial/Multiethnic People," in *The Multiracial Experience: Racial Borders as the New Frontier*, ed. Maria P. P. Root (Thousand Oaks, Calif., 1996), 32–33.

26. Maria P. P. Root, "The Multiracial Experience: Racial Borders as a Significant Frontier in Race Relations," in *Multiracial Experience*, xv.

27. Eric Schmitt, "For 7 Million People, One Race Category Isn't Enough," *The New York Times on the Web*, Mar. 13, 2001, http://nytimes.qpass.com/qpass-archives.

28. Shipler, *Country of Strangers*, 117.

29. As of 1997, the few states that had defined "multiracial" for the purposes of state record-keeping had defined it as "biracial." California, however, defines a "multiracial" person as "an individual whose biological parents, grandparents, or great-grandparents are of more than one race." Nobles, *Shades of Citizenship*, 139. This definition is a step toward the idea of thinking of oneself as possessing a mix of racial ancestry without tying that mix to specific persons in that ancestry; this is what I mean by "multiracial." Maria Root suggests that "biracial" itself can be employed with a similar connotation, "when . . . there is racial mixing in the family history that is important to the individual." "Glossary," in Root, *Multiracial Experience*, ix.

30. Cynthia Nakashima, "Voices from the Movement: Approaches to Multiraciality," in Root, *Multiracial Experience*, 82.

31. Among those claiming dual or multiple racial communities, some may wish the com-

munity to accept them *as multiracial* (as well as "black," "white," or "Latino"). Others may be indifferent to this sort of acknowledgment, or even prefer to be thought of as "just like everyone else" in the group.

32. Nakashima, "Voices from the Movement," 81. Since each racial group has a distinct identity and faces distinct racial issues, some multiracial or biracial people seek community only with those of the same "mix" as themselves, not with all other multiracials.

33. The two major organizations are "Project RACE" ("Reclassify All Children Equally"), and the Association for Multiethnic Americans (AMEA). The former's mission is to advocate for a multiracial classification on all official forms asking for racial data. The latter's is to promote a positive awareness of interracial and multi-ethnic identity; this group was supportive of the Census Bureau's ultimate decision to allow respondents to check "all that apply" without providing a distinct "multiracial" category, while Project RACE was not. See discussion of the philosophies and political initiatives regarding identity recognition and the Census in Nobles, *Shades of Citizenship*, 130–45.

34. Joel Perlmann points out that the separate category "multiracial" conveys no new information about an individual who provides "her component races" but "it sends the message that somehow something more is being communicated, that multiraciality is somehow equivalent to a new racial status." "Reflecting the Changing Face of America: Multiracials, Racial Classification, and American Intermarriage," in *Black-White Intermarriage in American History, Literature, and Law,* ed. Werner Sollors (New York, 2000), 516.

35. The methods by which the Census is tabulated also affect the visibility of multiracials. The Census Bureau could simply report the number of all persons who availed themselves of more than one racial designation in the "check all that apply" option. Or they could report how many persons checked each category, thus in a sense double-counting multiracial individuals but not tabulating them as a distinct group. Or, somewhat against the spirit of the new option but in line with the concern to monitor civil rights compliance and to gain an accurate count of racial minorities who might be the target of discrimination or who are entitled to various programs (as a proportion of the actual population), multiracials who are partly white could be counted only in their nonwhite category. These options are not mutually exclusive; different tabulations could be used for different purposes. For a discussion of tabulation options, see Nobles, *Shades of Citizenship*, 164–69. As of this writing (May 2001), the Bureau had begun to avail itself of some of these options. See Schmitt, "For 7 Million."

36. Nakshima, "Voices from the Movement," 81. Naomi Zack, a mixed-race philosopher, articulates such a humanistic, antirace position, though one that could be adopted by monoracial as well as multiracial people: "The concept of race is an oppressive cultural invention and convention, and I refuse to have anything to do with it. . . . Therefore I have no racial affiliation and will accept no racial designations." "An Autobiographical View of Mixed-Race Deracination," *American Philosophical Association Newsletter on Philosophy and the Black Experience* 91, no. 1 (spring 1992): 6–10. Cited in Nakashima, *Voices from the Movement,* 89.

37. The *Newsweek* issue discussed in note 25, chap. 8, partakes to some degree in both these developments—a shift in interest from racism to multiracial people, and a conflating of questioning race with undermining racial injustice.

38. Although how the individual is viewed racially by others is the primary desideratum, the Census no longer gathers such information by having its own enumerators identify a subject's race. Since 1970 the Census has operated only by self-designation. If the Census allows only the standard racial designations as options, however, it probably presumes that, on the whole, self-designation corresponds to the way the individual is viewed by the wider society. Only if "multiracial" is offered as an option might these two views begin to diverge in significant numbers.

39. Regarding the possible tension between civil rights and individual identity recognition, it is worth noting that Republicans tended to support the addition of a "multiracial" category (through the "Tiger Woods" bill, introduced in 1997), whereas the Democrats opposed it. Nobles comments: "Republicans were attracted to the idea that 'multiracial' fur-

ther complicated the country's already complex and highly charged racial politics. Democrats, in contrast, dared not risk alienating their key constituencies, and they remained committed, on some level, to monitoring civil rights violations and enforcing of civil rights legislation." *Shades of Citizenship*, 141

40. It is worthy of note, however, that at least some mixed-race persons opted for only "black" and not also "white" on the 2000 Census, with its instruction to "check all that apply." "Many people, indeed most, who could claim more than one race are not expected to do so, demographers and census officials say." Diana Jean Schemo, "Despite Options on Census Many to Check 'Black' Only," *New York Times*, Feb. 12, 2000, A1, A9.

I have been able only to skim the surface of the many complex issues regarding mixed-race identity and its significance for race, racial injustice and racism, and harmony among racial groups. These issues are explored in a burgeoning literature, sometimes in the form of collections of personal testimonies of those claiming mixed-race or biracial identity. For some representative examples, see Maria P. P. Root, ed., *Racially Mixed People in America* (Newbury Park, Calif., 1992); Root *The Multiracial Experience*; Naomi Zack, *American Mixed Race: The Culture of Microdiversity* (Lanham, Md., 1995); Lisa Funderburg (ed.), *Black White Other: Biracial Americans Talk about Race and Identity* (New York, 1994); and Sollors *Black-White Intermarriage*.

Bibliography

Adarand Constructors, Inc., v. Pena, 515 U.S. 200 (1995).

Alcoff, Linda. "Mestizo Identity." In *American Mixed Race,* edited by Naomi Zack. Lanham, Md., 1995.

Allen, Theodore W. *The Invention of the White Race,* vol. 1: *Racial Oppression and Social Control.* London, 1994.

———. *The Invention of the White Race,* vol. 2: *The Origin of Racial Oppression in Anglo-America.* London, 1997.

Allport, Gordon. *The Nature of Prejudice.* Reading, Mass., 1988 [1954].

Andersen, Margaret L., and Patricia Hill Collins, eds. *Race, Class, and Gender: An Anthology.* Belmont, Calif., 1992.

Anderson, Benedict. *Imagined Communities: Reflections on the Origins and Spread of Nationalism.* Rev. ed. New York, 1993.

Anderson, Elizabeth. "Integration, Compensation, and Affirmative Action." Presentation to Harvard Colloquium on Constitutional Law and Political Theory, November, 2000.

Angier, Natalie. "Do Races Differ? Not Really, Genes Show." *New York Times,* August 22, 2000, 6.

Apache. "Kill d'White People." *Apache Ain't Shit.* Tommy Boy Music, Time Warner, 1993. Cited in "Lyrics by Black or Latin Artists Who Put out Violent Racism and Who Were Either Awarded Grammy's or Were Promoted by Artists Who Won Grammy's," July 26, 1999, at website: http://home.att.net/*~phosphor/introtogrammys.html.

Appiah, Anthony. "Identity, Authenticity, Survival: Multicultural Societies and Cultural Reproduction." In *Multiculturalism,* edited by Amy Gutmann, 149–64. Princeton, N.J., 1994.

————. *In My Father's House: Africa in the Philosophy of Culture.* New York, 1992.

————. "Race, Culture, Identity: Misunderstood Connections." In K. A. Appiah and A. Gutmann, *Color Conscious*, 30–105. Princeton, N.J., 1996.

————. "Racisms." In *Anatomy of Racism*, edited by David Theo Goldberg, 3–17. Minneapolis, 1990.

Appiah K. A., and A. Gutmann. *Color Conscious.* Princeton, N.J., 1996.

Aristotle. *Metaphysics.* Translated by Hugh Lawson-Tancred. London, 1998.

————. *Politics.* Translated by T. A. Sinclair, revised and represented by Trevor J. Saunders. London, 1992.

Armour, Jody David. *Negrophobia and Reasonable Racism: The Hidden Costs of Being Black in America.* New York, 1997.

Armstrong, Robb. "Jump Start" (cartoon). United Feature Syndicate, 1997.

Babbitt, Susan, and Sue Campbell, eds. *Racism and Philosophy.* Ithaca, N.Y., 1999.

Baker, Lee. *From Savage to Negro: Anthropology and the Construction of Race, 1896–1954.* Berkeley, Calif., 1998.

Baldwin, James. *The Fire Next Time.* New York, 1988 [1963].

Banton, Michael. *Racial Theories*, 2d ed. Cambridge, Eng., 1998.

Barbujani, Guido, Arianna Magagni, Eric Minch, and L. Luca Cavalli-Sforza. "An Apportionment of Human DNA Diversity." *Proceedings of the National Academy of Sciences* 94: 4516–19 (April 1997).

Barkan, Elazar. *The Retreat of Scientific Racism: Changing Concepts of Race in Britain and the United States between the World Wars.* Cambridge, Eng., 1992.

Barker, Martin. "Biology and the New Racism." In *Anatomy of Racism*, edited by David Theo Goldberg, 18–37. Minneapolis, 1990.

Barndt, Joseph. *Dismantling Racism: The Continuing Challenge to White America.* Minneapolis, 1991.

Bartolomé, Lilia, and Donaldo Macedo. "Dancing With Bigotry: The Poisoning of Racial and Ethnic Identities." *Harvard Education Review* 67(2): 241–42 (summer 1997).

Bay, Mia. *The White Image in the Black Mind: African-American Ideas about White People, 1830–1925.* New York, 2000.

Belluck, Pam. "A White Supremacist Group Seeks a New Kind of Recruit." *New York Times*, July 7, 1999, A1, A14.

Berlin, Ira. *Many Thousands Gone: The First Two Centuries of Slavery in North America.* Cambridge, Mass., 1998.

Bernasconi, Robert, and Tommy L. Lott. Introduction to *The Idea of Race*, edited by Robert Bernasconi and Tommy L. Lott, vi–xviii. Indianapolis, 2000.

————, eds. *The Idea of Race.* Indianapolis, 2000.

Berry, Mary Frances. "How Percentage Plans Keep Minority Students Out of College." *Chronicle of Higher Education*, August 4, 2000 (on line: http://chronicle.com/weekly/v46/i48/48a0480l.htm).

"Black, White Officers Cited in Noose Incident." *Boston Globe*, April 29, 1999, B1.

Blackburn, Daniel. "Why Race is Not a Biological Concept." In *Race and Racism in Theory and Practice*, edited by Berel Lang, 3–26. Lanham, Md., 2000.

Blank, Rebecca. "An Overview of Trends in Social and Economic Well-Being, by Race." In *America Becoming: Racial Trends and Their Consequences*, vol. 1, edited by Neil Smelser, William Julius Wilson, and Faith Mitchell. Washington, D.C., 2001.

Blauner, Bob. "Talking Past Each Other: Black and White Languages of Race." In *Race and Ethnic Conflict: Contending Views on Prejudice, Discrimination, and Ethnoviolence*, edited by Fred L. Pincus and Howard J. Ehrlich, 18–28. Boulder, Colo., 1994.

Blight, David, and Robert Gooding-Williams, eds. *The Souls of Black Folk*, by W. E. B. Du Bois. Boston, 1997.

Blum, Lawrence. "Antiracism, Multiculturalism, and Interracial Community: Three Educational Values for a Multicultural Society." Office of Graduate Study and Research, University of Massachusetts, Boston, 1992.

——. "Ethnicity, Identity, Community." In *Justice and Caring: The Search for Common Ground in Education*, edited by Michael Katz, Nel Noddings, and Kenneth Strike, 127–45. New York, 1999.

——. "Moral Asymmetries in Racism." In *Racism and Philosophy*, edited by Susan Babbitt and Sue Campbell, 79–97. Ithaca, N.Y., 1999.

——. "Multicultural Education as Values Education." Working paper of Harvard Children's Initiative, 1999.

——. "Multiculturalism, Racial Justice, and Community: Reflections on Charles Taylor's 'The Politics of Recognition.'" In *Defending Diversity: Contemporary Philosophical Perspectives on Pluralism and Multiculturalism*, edited by L. Foster and P. Herzog, 175–206. Amherst, Mass., 1994.

——. "Racial Integration in a Multicultural Age." In *NOMOS*, edited by Stephen Macedo and Yael Tamir. New York, 2001.

——. "Recognition, Value, and Equality: A Critique of Charles Taylor's and Nancy Fraser's Accounts of Multiculturalism." In *Theorizing Multiculturalism: A Guide to the Current Debate*, edited by Cynthia Willett, 73–99. London, 1998.

——. "What is 'Racism' in Antiracist Education?" *Teachers College Record* 100(4): 860–80 (Summer 1999).

Bobo, Lawrence. "Racial Attitudes and Relations at the Close of the Twentieth Century." In *America Becoming: Racial Trends and Their Consequences*, vol. 1, edited by Neil Smelser, William Julius Wilson, and Faith Mitchell, 264–301. Washington, D.C., 2001.

Bowen, William G., and Derek Bok. *The Shape of the River: Long-term Consequences of Considering Race in College and University Admissions*, with new introduction. Princeton, N.J., 2000.

Bowser, Benjamin, ed. *Racism and Anti-racism in World Perspective*. London, 1995.

Boxill, Bernard. *Blacks and Social Justice*. Rev. ed. Lanham, Md., 1992.

Boys on the Side. Directed by Herbert Ross. Alcor Films, 1995.

Bradley, Michael. *The Iceman Inheritance: Prehistoric Sources of Western Man's Racism, Sexism, and Aggression*. Toronto, Ont., 1978.

Breen, T. H., and Stephen Innes. *"Myne Own Ground": Race and Freedom on Virginia's Eastern Shore, 1640–1676*. New York, 1980.

Brooke, James. "Killing Wasn't Much, Skinhead Says." *New York Times*, November 22, 1997, A7.

Buffon, Count Georges-Louis Leclerc de. "Varieties of the Human Species." In *Natural History, General and Particular*, translated by William Smellie. London, 1812 [1749].

Butterfield, Fox. "Racial Disparities Seen as Pervasive in Juvenile Justice." *New York Times*, April 26, 2000.

Byrnes, Deborah. "Addressing Race, Ethnicity, and Culture in the Classroom." In *Common Bonds: Anti-bias Teaching in a Diverse Society*, edited by Deborah Byrnes and Gary Kiger, 11–22. Wheaton, Md., 1992.

Byrnes, Deborah, and Gary Kiger, eds. *Common Bonds: Anti-bias Teaching in a Diverse Society*. Wheaton, Md., 1992.

Campo-Flores, Arian. "'Mexicano' Against 'Chicano.'" *Newsweek*, September 18, 2000, 49, 51.

Carter, Stephen. "The Black Table, the Empty Seat, and the Tie." In *Lure and Loathing: Essays on Race, Identity, and the Ambivalence of Assimilation*, edited by Gerald Early, 55–79. New York, 1994.

Cavalli-Sforza, L. Luca, Paolo Menozzi, and Alberto Piazza. *The History and Geography of Human Genes*. Princeton, N.J., 1994.

Chadwick, Ruth, ed. *Encyclopedia of Applied Ethics*. San Diego, Calif., 1998.

Ciccone, John. Letter to *Boston Globe*, November 12, 1998.

City of Richmond v. J. A. Croson Co., 488 U.S. 469 (1989).

Cleburne v. Cleburne Living Center, Inc., 473 U.S. 432 (1985).

Clegg, Roger. "Photographs and Fraud over Race." *Chronicle of Higher Education*, November 24, 2000, B17.

Cohen, M., T. Nagel, and T. M. Scanlon, eds. *Equality and Preferential Treatment*. Princeton, N. J., 1977.

Commission on the Future of Multi-ethnic Britain. *The Future of Multi-ethnic Britain* (*The Parekh Report*). London: Profile Books, 2000.

Cox, Oliver Cromwell. *Class, Caste, and Race: A Study in Social Dynamics*. New York, 1948.

Cross, William E., Jr. "Oppositional Identity and African American Youth: Issues and Prospects." In *Toward a Common Destiny: Improving Race and Ethnic Relations in America*, edited by Willis D. Hawley and Anthony W. Jackson, 185–204. San Francisco, 1995.

——. *Shades of Black: Diversity in African-American Identity*. Philadelphia, 1991.

Dalton, Harlon. *Racial Healing: Confronting the Fear Between Blacks and Whites*. New York, 1996.

Daniels, Roger. *Coming to America: A History of Immigration and Ethnicity in American Life*. New York, 1990.

Darley, John, and Bibb Latane. "When Will People Help?" *Psychology Today* 2(7), 1968.

Darwin, Charles. *Descent of Man*. London, 1901 [1871].

Davidson, Basil. *The Search for Africa: History, Culture, Politics*. New York, 1994.

Davidson, Florence H., and Miriam M. Davidson. *Changing Childhood Prejudice: The Caring Work of the Schools*. Westport, Conn., 1995.

Davis, David Brion. *The Problem of Slavery in Western Culture.* New York, 1966.
———. *Slavery and Human Progress.* New York, 1984.
Davis, F. James. *Who is Black? One Nation's Definition.* University Park, Pa., 1991.
Degler, Carl. *In Search of Human Nature: The Decline and Revival of Darwinism in American Social Thought.* New York, 1991.
Derman-Sparks, Louise, and Carol Brunson Phillips. *Teaching/Learning Anti-racism.* New York, 1997.
Devlin, Bernie, Stephen E. Fienberg, Daniel P. Resnick, and Kathryn Roeder, eds. *Intelligence, Genes, and Success: Scientists Respond to "The Bell Curve."* New York, 1997.
Diamond, Jared. "Race Without Color." *Discover,* November 1994, 82–89.
Dikötter, Frank. "The Idea of Race in Modern China." In *Ethnicity,* edited by John Hutchinson and Anthony Smith. Oxford, 1996.
Directive No. 15. U.S. Office of Management and Budget (guidelines for federal racial classifications). Washington, D.C., 1977.
Du Bois, W. E. B. "The Conservation of Races." In *The Souls of Black Folk,* edited by David Blight and Robert Gooding-Williams, 228–238. Boston, 1997.
Do the Right Thing. Directed by Spike Lee. 40 Acres and a Mule Filmworks, 1987.
D'Souza, Dinesh. *The End of Racism: Principles for a Multiracial Society.* New York, 1995.
———. *Illiberal Education: The Politics of Race and Sex on Campus.* New York, 1991.
Duster, Troy, and Institute for the Study of Social Change at the University of California, Berkeley. *The Diversity Project, Final Report.* Berkeley, Calif., 1991.
Early, Gerald, ed. *Lure and Loathing: Essays on Race, Identity, and the Ambivalence of Assimilation.* New York, 1993.
Elrich, Mark. "The Stereotype Within: Why Students Don't Buy Black History Month." *Washington Post,* February 13, 1994, C1.
Encyclopedia Britannica OnLine. 1999. http://search.eb.com/bol/topic?map_id+172664000&tmap_typ+dx#index.
Espiritu, Yen Le. *Asian American Panethnicity: Bridging Institutions and Identities.* Philadelphia, 1992.
Extra! 9(2): 18 (March/April 1996).
Ezorsky, Gertrude. *Racism and Justice: The Case for Affirmative Action.* Ithaca, N.Y., 1991.
Feagin, Joe R., and Hernan Vera. *White Racism.* New York, 1995.
Fields, Barbara J. "Ideology and Race in American History." In *Region, Race, and Reconstruction,* edited by J. M. Kousser and J. M. McPherson, 143–77. New York, 1982.
Fine, Michelle, Lois Weis, Linda C. Powell, and L. Mun Wong, eds. *Off White: Readings on Race, Power, and Society.* New York, 1997.
Fischer, Claude, Michael Hout, Martín Sanchez Jankowski, Samuel R. Lucas, Ann Swidler, and Kim Voss. *Inequality by Design: Cracking the Bell Curve Myth.* Princeton, N.J., 1996.
Fiss, Owen. "Groups and the Equal Protection Clause." In *Equality and Preferential Treatment,* edited by M. Cohen, T. Nagel, and T. M. Scanlon, 84–154. Princeton, N.J., 1977.

Flanagan, Owen, and Amélie O. Rorty, eds. *Identity, Character, and Morality: Essays in Moral Psychology.* Cambridge, Mass., 1990.

Flew, A. G. N. "Three Concepts of Racism." *Encounter* 73 (1990).

Foner, Eric. *Reconstruction: America's Unfinished Revolution, 1863–1877.* New York, 1988.

"For the Record." *The Southern Poverty Law Center's Intelligence Report,* spring 1997.

Ford, Christopher. "Administering Identity: The Determination of 'Race' in Race-conscious Law." *California Law Review* 82(5): 1231–85 (October 1994).

Foster, L., and P. Herzog, eds. *Defending Diversity: Contemporary Philosophical Perspectives on Pluralism and Multiculturalism.* Amherst, Mass., 1994.

Fraser, Steven, ed. *The Bell Curve Wars: Race, Intelligence, and the Future of America.* New York, 1995.

Frederickson, George. *The Black Image in the White Mind: The Debate on Afro-American Character and Destiny, 1817–1914.* New York, 1971.

———. *The Comparative Imagination.* Berkeley, Calif., 1999.

———. *White Supremacy: A Comparative Study in American and South African History.* New York, 1981.

French, Howard. "Forever Korean: Once Scorned, Always Scorned." *New York Times,* November 20, 2000, A4.

Friedman, Marilyn. "Racism: Paradigms and Moral Appraisal (a Response to Blum)." In *Racism and Philosophy,* edited by Susan E. Babbitt and Sue Campbell, 98–107. Ithaca, N.Y., 1999.

"Friends Helped Labor Nominee Move Up, Then Almost Brought Her Down." *New York Times,* March 12, 1997.

Frontiero v. Richardson, 411 U.S. 677, 686 (1973).

Funderberg, Lisa. *Black White Other: Biracial Americans Talk about Race and Identity.* New York, 1994.

———, eds. *Prejudice, Discrimination, and Racism.* Orlando, Fla., 1986.

Gaertner, Samuel, and John F. Dovidio. "The Aversive Form of Racism." In *Prejudice, Discrimination, and Racism,* edited by Samuel Gaertner and John F. Dovidio, 61–89. San Diego, Calif., 1986.

Gaertner, Samuel L., John F. Dovidio, Brenda S. Banker, Mary C. Rust, Jason A. Nier, Gary R. Mottola, and Christine M. Ward. "Does White Racism Necessarily Mean Antiblackness? Aversive Racism and Pro-whiteness." In *Off White: Readings on Race, Power, and Society,* edited by Michelle Fine, Lois Weis, Linda C. Powell, and L. Mun Wong, 167–78. New York, 1997.

Garcia, Jorge L. A. "Current Conceptions of Racism: A Critical Examination of Some Recent Social Philosophy." *Journal of Social Philosophy* 28(2): 5–42 (fall 1997).

———. "The Heart of Racism." *Journal of Social Philosophy* 27(2): 5–45 (fall 1996).

———. "Philosophical Analysis and the Moral Concept of Racism." *Philosophy and Social Criticism* 25(5): 1–32 (1999).

Garofalo, Reebee. *Rockin' Out: Popular Music in the USA.* Boston, 1997.

Gaston County v. the United States, 395 U.S. 285 (1969).

Gilroy, Paul. *Between Camps: Nations, Cultures, and the Allure of Race.* London, 2000.

Gioseffi, Daniela, ed. *On Prejudice: A Global Perspective.* New York, 1993.

Goffman, Erving. *Stigma: Notes on the Management of Spoiled Identity*. New York, 1986.

Golda, Ted. "A Megastar Long Buried under a Layer of Blackface." *New York Times*, October 22, 2000, Arts & Lesire 1, 34.

Goldberg, Carey. "Fat People Say an Intolerant World Condemns Them on First Sight." *New York Times*, November 5, 2000, 28.

Goldberg, David Theo. *Racist Culture: Philosophy and the Politics of Meaning*. London, 1993.

Gooding-Williams, R. "Race, Multiculturalism, and Democracy." *Constellations*, 5(1): 18–41 (1998).

Gossett, Thomas. *Race: The History of an Idea in America*. New York, 1963.

Gould, Stephen Jay. "The Geometer of Race." *Discover*, November 1994, 65–69.

Gracia, Jorge J. E. *Hispanic/Latino Identity: A Philosophical Perspective*. Malden, Mass., 2000.

Griffin, John Howard. *Black Like Me*. New York, 1976 [1960].

Guinier, Lani, and Gerald Torres. *The Miner's Canary*. Cambridge, Mass., 2001.

Gutin, Joann C. "End of the Rainbow." *Discover*, November 1994, 71–75.

Gutmann, Amy, ed. *Multiculturalism*. Princeton, N.J., 1994.

Hacker, Andrew. *Two Nations: Black and White, Separate, Hostile, Unequal*. Rev. ed. New York, 1995.

Hacking, Ian. "Making Up People." In *Reconstructing Individualism: Autonomy, Individuality, and the Self in Western Thought*, edited by Thomas Heller, Morton Sosna, and David Wellbery, 222–36. Stanford, Calif., 1986.

———. *The Social Construction of What?* Cambridge, Mass., 1999.

Hage, Ghassan. *White Nation: Fantasies of White Supremacy in a Multicultural Society*. Annandale, Australia, 1998.

Hale, Grace Elizabeth. *Making Whiteness: The Culture of Segregation in the South, 1890–1940*. New York, 1999.

Haney-Lopez, Ian. *White by Law: The Legal Construction of Race*. New York, 1996.

Hannaford, Ivan. *Race: The History of an Idea in the West*. Washington, D.C., 1996.

Harding, Sandra, ed. *The "Racial" Economy of Science: Toward a Democratic Future*. Bloomington, Ind., 1993.

Harris, Cheryl. "Whiteness as Property." In *Black on White: Black Writers on What It Means to Be White*, edited by David R. Roediger, 103–19. New York, 1998.

Harris, Leonard, ed. *Racism*. Amherst, N.Y., 1999.

Haslanger, Sally. "Gender and Race: (What) Are They? (What) Do We Want Them to Be?" *Noûs* 34(1): 31–55 (March 2000).

———. "Ontology and Social Construction." *Philosophical Topics* 23(2): 95–125 (Fall 1995).

Hawley, Willis D., and Anthony W. Jackson, eds. *Toward a Common Destiny: Improving Race and Ethnic Relations in America*. San Francisco, 1995.

Healy, Patrick. "Civil Rights Office Questions Legality of College's Use of Standardized Tests." *Chronicle of Higher Education*, May 28, 1999, A28.

Heller, Thomas, Morton Sosna, and David Wellbery, eds. *Reconstructing Individualism: Autonomy, Individuality, and the Self in Western Thought*. Stanford, Calif., 1986.

Herrnstein, Richard, and Charles Murray. *The Bell Curve: Intelligence and Class Structure in American Life.* New York, 1994.

Hidalgo, Nitza, Emilie Siddle, and Ceasar McDowell, eds. *Facing Racism in Education.* Cambridge, Mass., 1990.

Higham, John. *Strangers in the Land: Patterns of American Nativism, 1860–1925.* 2d ed. New Brunswick, N. J., 1988.

Himmelfarb, Gertrude. *Darwin and the Darwinian Revolution.* London, 1959.

Hirschfeld, Magnus. *Racism.* Translated and edited by Eden and Cedar Paul. London, 1938; reissued Port Washington, N.Y., 1973 (originally published in German in 1933).

Hitt, Jack. "Confederate Chic." *Gentleman's Quarterly,* November 1997, 261, 264–69.

Hochschild, Jennifer. *Facing Up to the American Dream: Race, Class, and the Soul of the Nation.* Rev. ed. Princeton, N.J., 1996.

Hodes, Martha, ed. *Sex, Love, Race: Crossing Boundaries in North American History.* New York, 1999.

Hoffman, Paul. "The Science of Race." *Discover,* November 1994, 4.

Hollinger, David. *PostEthnic America: Beyond Multiculturalism.* New York, 1995.

Hopwood v. State of Texas, 78 F. 3d 932 (5th Cir. 1996).

Horowitz, Donald. *Ethnic Groups in Conflict.* Berkeley, Calif., 1985.

———. "Immigration and Group Relations in France and America." In *Immigrants in Two Democracies,* edited by Donald Horowitz and Gerard Noriel, 3–35. New York, 1992.

Horowitz, Donald, and Gerard Noriel, eds. *Immigrants in Two Democracies.* New York, 1992.

Horsman, Reginald. *Race and Manifest Destiny: The Origins of American Racial Anglo-Saxonism.* Cambridge, Mass., 1981.

Huggins, Nathan Irvin. *Black Odyssey: The African-American Ordeal in Slavery.* Revised ed. New York, 1992.

Hutchinson, John, and Anthony D. Smith. "Introduction." In *Ethnicity,* edited by John Hutchinson and Anthony D. Smith. Oxford, 1996.

———, eds. *Ethnicity.* Oxford, 1996.

Ignatiev, Noel. *How the Irish Became White.* New York, 1995.

"Insurer to Pay Back $206 Million." *Boston Globe,* June 22, 2000, D2.

Jacobson, Matthew Frye. *Whiteness of a Different Color: European Immigrants and the Alchemy of Race.* Cambridge, Mass., 1998.

Jordan, Winthrop D. *White over Black: American Attitudes toward the Negro, 1550–1812.* Chapel Hill, N.C., 1969.

Jung, Patricia Beattie, and Ralph F. Smith. *Heterosexism: An Ethical Challenge.* Albany, N.Y., 1993.

Kahlenberg, Richard D. "Unionization as a Civil Right." *The American Prospect,* September 11, 2000, 14.

Kaplan, Fred. "Meter is Running on Giuliani's Crackdown on Cabbies." *Boston Globe,* November 12, 1999, A3.

Katz, Michael, Nel Noddings, and Kenneth Strike, eds. *Justice and Caring: The Search for Common Ground in Education.* New York, 1999.

Kennedy, Randall. "My Race Problem—and Ours." *Atlantic Monthly*, May 1997, 55–66.

——. "Who Can Say 'Nigger' . . . and Other Related Questions." Tanner Lectures, Stanford University, 1999.

Kinder, Donald R., and Lynn M. Sanders. *Divided By Color: Racial Politics and Democratic Ideals.* Chicago, 1996.

King, Martin Luther, Jr. "I Have a Dream." In *Testament of Hope: The Essential Writings and Speeches of Martin Luther King Jr.*, edited by James M. Washington, 217–21. New York, 1991.

Kitcher, Philip. "Race, Ethnicity, Biology, Culture." In *Racism*, edited by Leonard Harris, 87–117. Amherst, N.Y., 1999.

Kolchin, Peter. *American Slavery, 1619–1877.* New York, 1993.

Koppelman, Andrew. *Antidiscrimination Law and Social Equality.* New Haven, Conn., 1996.

Kousser, J. M., and J. M. McPherson, eds. *Region, Race, and Reconstruction.* New York, 1982.

Kovel, Joel. *White Racism: A Psychohistory.* New York, 1971.

Kymlicka, Will. *Liberalism, Community, and Culture.* Oxford, 1989.

Lamont, Michele, ed. *The Cultural Territories of Race: Of Black and White Boundaries.* Chicago, 1999.

Lang, Berel. "Metaphysical Racism (or: Biological Warfare by Other Means)." In *Race/Sex: Their Sameness, Difference, and Interplay*, edited by Naomi Zack, 17–28. New York, 1997.

Levinson, Sanford. "They Whisper: Reflections on Flags, Monuments, and State Holidays, and the Construction of Social Meaning in a Multicultural Society." *Chicago-Kent Law Review* 70(3): 1079–1119 (1995).

Lewin, Tamar. "Growing Up, Growing Apart." *New York Times,* June 25, 2000, 12.

Lewontin, Richard. *Human Diversity.* New York, 1995.

Lhamon, W. T., Jr., *Raising Cain: Blackface Performance from Jim Crow to Hip Hop.* Cambridge, Mass., 1998.

Lippman, Abby. "Prenatal Genetic Testing and Screening: Constructing Needs and Reinforcing Inequities." *American Journal of Law and Medicine* 17(1–2): 15–50 (1991).

Lipsitz, George. "'Swing Low, Sweet Cadillac': White Supremacy, Antiblack Racism, and the New Historicism." *American Literary History* 7(4): 700–725 (1995).

Liu, Eric. *The Accidental Asian: Notes of a Native Speaker.* New York, 1998.

Lott, Eric. *Love and Theft: Blackface Minstrelsy and the American Working Class.* New York, 1993.

Lott, Tommy Lee, ed. *Philosophical Research on African-American Social Inequality.* Lanham, Md., 2001.

Loury, Glenn. *The Anatomy of Racial Inequality:* Cambridge, Mass., 2002.

——. "Foreword." In *The Shape of the River: Long-term Consequences of Considering Race in College and University Admissions*, by William G. Bowen and Derek Bok (with new introduction), xxi–xxx. Princeton, N.J., 2000.

Malone v. Haley No. 88–339 (Sp. Jud. Ct. Suffolk County, Mass. July 25, 1989).

Margalit, Avishai. *The Decent Society.* Cambridge, Mass., 1996.

Marks, Jonathan. *Human Biodiversity: Genes, Race, and History.* Hawthorne, N.Y., 1995.

Marshall, Gloria. "Racial Classifications: Popular and Scientific." In *The "Racial" Economy of Science: Toward a Democratic Future,* edited by Sandra Harding, 116–27. Bloomington, Ind., 1993.

Marx, Anthony W. *Making Race and Nation: A Comparison of the United States, South Africa, and Brazil.* Cambridge, Eng., 1997.

"Massachusetts Slave Petition." In *The Democracy Reader,* edited by Diane Ravitch and Abigail Thernstrom, 107–8. New York, 1992.

McCall, Nathan. *Makes Me Wanna Holler.* New York, 1994.

McConahay, John B. "Modern Racism, Ambivalence, and the Modern Racism Scale." In *Prejudice, Discrimination, and Racism,* edited by Samuel Gaertner and John F. Dovidio, 91–125. Orlando, Fla., 1986.

McIntosh, Peggy. "White Privilege and Male Privilege: A Personal Account of Coming to See Correspondences through Work in Women's Studies." In *Race, Class, and Gender: An Anthology,* edited by Margaret L. Andersen and Patricia Hill Collins, 70–82. Belmont, Calif., 1992.

Michaels, Walter Benn. "The No-Drop Rule." *Critical Inquiry* 20 (summer 1994): 758–769.

Miers, Suzanne, and Igor Kopytoff, eds. *Slavery in Africa: Historical and Anthropological Perspectives.* Madison, Wisc., 1977.

Miles, Robert. *Racism.* London, 1989.

Miller, Arthur G., ed. *In the Eye of the Beholder: Contemporary Issues in Stereotyping.* New York, 1982.

Mills, Charles. *The Racial Contract.* Ithaca, N.Y., 1997.

Minow, Martha. *Not Only for Myself: Identity, Politics, and the Law.* New York, 1997.

Modood, Tariq, "'Difference,' Cultural Racism, and Anti-racism." In *Debating Cultural Hybridity,* edited by Pnina Werbner and Tariq Modood, 154–72. London, 1997.

——. "Liberal Multiculturalism and Real-world Multiculturalism." Presentation to the Institute for the Study of Race and Social Division, Boston University, April 25, 2001.

Montagu, Ashley. *Man's Most Dangerous Myth: The Fallacy of Race.* Cleveland, Ohio, 1964 [1942].

——. *Statement on Race.* New York, 1972.

Monteiro v. Tempe Union High School District, 158 F. 3d 1022 (CA 9 1998).

Morgan, Edmund. *American Slavery, American Freedom.* New York, 1975.

Morgan, Thomas. "The World Ahead: Black Parents Prepare Their Children for Pride and Prejudice." *New York Times,* October 27, 1985 32.

Morrow, Lance. *Time,* December 5, 1994. Cited in *Extra!* 9(2): 18 (March/April 1996).

Mosley, Albert. "Negritude, Nationalism, and Nativism: Racists or Racialists?" In *Racism,* edited by Leonard Harris, 74–86. Amherst, N.Y., 1999.

Mosse, George. *Toward the Final Solution: A History of European Racism.* Madison, Wisc., 1985.

Myrdal, Gunnar. *An American Dilemma.* New York, 1964.

Nakashima, Cynthia L., "Voices from the Movement: Approaches to Multiraciality." In *The Multiracial Experience: Racial Borders as the New Frontier,* edited by Maria P. P. Root, 79–97. Thousand Oaks, Calif., 1996.

Nash, Gary B. "The Hidden History of Mestizo America." In *Sex, Love, Race: Crossing Boundaries in North American History,* edited by Martha Hodes, 10–32. New York, 1999.

———. *Race and Revolution.* Madison, N. J., 1990.

———. *Red, White, and Black: The Peoples of Early North America.* 4th ed. Upper Saddle River, N.J., 2000.

Nathanson, Stephen. "Is Patriotism Like Racism?" *American Philosophical Association Newsletter on Philosophy and the Black Experience* 91(2): 9–11 (1992).

Navarette, Ruben, Jr. *A Darker Shade of Crimson.* New York, 1993.

Nixon, Ron. "Letter from South Carolina." *Nation,* May 15, 2000, 21–23.

Njeri, Itabari. "Sushi and Grits." In *Lure and Loathing: Essays on Race and Identity, and the Ambivalence of Assimilation,* edited by Gerald Early, 13–40. New York, 1993.

Nobles, Melissa. *Shades of Citizenship: Race and the Census in Modern Politics.* Stanford, Calif., 2000.

Nuechterlein, James. "First Things." *Chronicle of Higher Education,* September 6, 1996, B9.

Ojito, Mirta. "Best of Friends, Worlds Apart." *New York Times,* June 5, 2000, A1, A16–17.

Oliver, Melvin, and Thomas Shapiro. *Black Wealth/White Wealth: A New Perspective on Racial Inequality.* New York, 1997.

Omi, Michael, and Howard Winant. *Racial Formation in the United States: From the 1960s to the 1990s,* 2d ed. New York, 1994.

Onishi, Norimitsu. "New Sense of Race Arises among Asian-Americans." *New York Times,* May 30, 1996, A1, B6.

Outhwaite, William, and Tom Bottomore, eds. *The Blackwell Dictionary of Twentieth-Century Social Thought.* Oxford, Eng., 1994.

Outlaw, Lucius T., Jr. *On Race and Philosophy.* New York, 1996.

Paley, Vivian Gussin. *Kwanzaa and Me.* Cambridge, Mass., 1995.

Pang, Valerie Ooka. "Racial Prejudice: Still Alive and Hurtful." In *Facing Racism in Education,* edited by Nitza Hidalgo, Emilie Siddle, and Ceasar McDowell, 28–32. Cambridge, Mass., 1990.

Patterson, Orlando. *The Ordeal of Integration: Progress and Resentment in America's "Racial" Crisis.* Washington, D.C., 1997.

———. "The Race Trap." *New York Times,* July 11, 1997, A27.

———. *Slavery and Social Death.* Cambridge, Mass., 1982.

———. "Taking Culture Seriously." Presentation to the Institute on Race and Social Division, Boston University, January 2000.

Paul, Diane B. *Controlling Human Heredity, 1865 to the Present.* Amherst, New York, 1998.

Perea, Juan F., ed. *Immigrants Out! The New Nativism and the Anti-immigrant Impulse in the United States*. New York, 1997.

Perlmann, Joel. "Reflecting the Changing Face of America: Multiracials, Racial Classification, and American Intermarriage." In *Black-White Intermarriage in American History, Literature, and Law*, edited by Werner Sollors, 506–33. New York, 2000.

Peters, William. *A Class Divided, Then and Now*. Rev. ed. New Haven, Conn., 1987.

Pincus, Fred L., and Howard J. Ehrlich, eds. *Race and Ethnic Conflict: Contending Views on Prejudice, Discrimination, and Ethnoviolence*. Boulder, Colo., 1994.

Piper, Adrian M. S. "Higher-order Discrimination." In *Identity, Character, and Morality: Essays in Moral Psychology*, edited by Owen Flanagan and Amélie O. Rorty, 285–310. Cambridge, Mass., 1990.

"*Playboy* Interview—Spike Lee—Candid Conversation." *Playboy*, 38: July 1991, 7, 51.

Post, Robert. "Prejudicial Appearances: The Logic of American Antidiscrimination Law." *California Law Review* 8(1): 23 (January, 2000).

Post, Robert, and Michael Rogin, eds. *Race and Representation: Affirmative Action*. New York, 1998.

"Race, the Final Frontier." *Harper's Magazine*, July 2000, 24, 26.

"Rebels with a Cause." *The Southern Poverty Law Center's Intelligence Report* 99: 6–12 (summer 2000).

"Redefining Race in America." *Newsweek*, September 18, 2000, 38–66.

Regents of the University of California v. Bakke, 438 U.S. at 303. 1978.

Reischauer, Edwin O. "Race Prejudice Pervades the World." In *On Prejudice: A Global Perspective*, edited by Daniela Gioseffi, 182–88. New York, 1993.

Remember the Titans. Directed by Boaz Yakin. Walt Disney Productions, 2000.

Report of the National Advisory Commission on Civil Disorders. New York, 1968.

Rex, John. "Racism." In *The Blackwell Dictionary of Twentieth-Century Social Thought*, edited by William Outhwaite and Tom Bottomore, 536–38. Oxford, 1994.

———. "Racism, Institutionalized and Otherwise." In *Racism*, edited by Leonard Harris, 141–60. Amherst, N.Y., 1999.

Ridgeway, James. *Blood in the Face: The Ku Klux Klan, Aryan Nations, Nazi Skinheads, and the Rise of a New White Culture*. New York, 1990.

Robertson, Tatsha. "Old Symbols, New Debates." *Boston Globe*, August 7, 1999, B1, B5.

Roediger, David. *The Wages of Whiteness: Race and the Making of the American Working Class*. New York, 1991.

Rogin, Michael. *Blackface, White Noise: Jewish Immigrants in the Hollywood Melting Pot*. Berkeley, Calif., 1996.

Root, Maria P. P. "The Multiracial Experience: Racial Borders as a Significant Frontier in Race Relations." In *The Multiracial Experience: Racial Borders as the New Frontier*, edited by Maria P. P. Root, xv. Thousand Oaks, Calif., 1996.

———, ed. *The Multiracial Experience: Racial Borders as the New Frontier*. Thousand Oaks, Calif., 1996.

———, ed. *Racially Mixed People in America*. Newbury Park, Calif., 1992.

Root, Michael. "Racial Realism." In *Philosophical Research on African-American Social Inequality*, edited by Tommy Lee Lott,. Lanham, Md., 2001.

Rothenberg, Paula, ed. *Racism and Sexism: An Integrated Study*. New York, 1988.

Rothman, Barbara Katz. *The Book of Life: A Personal and Ethical Guide to Race, Normality, and the Implications of the Human Genome Project.* Boston, 1998.

Royko, Mike. "Time to Be Color Blind to All Words of Hatred." *Chicago Tribune,* February 9, 1994, 3.

Rubin, Lillian. *Families on the Fault Line: America's Working Class Speaking about the Family, the Economy, Race, and Ethnicity.* New York, 1994.

Russell, Kathy, Midge Wilson, and Ronald Hall, *The Color Complex: The Politics of Skin Color among African Americans.* New York, 1993.

Sagar, H. Andrew, and Janet Ward Schofield. "Integrating the Desegregated School: Problems and Possibilities." In *Advances in Motivation and Achievement: A Research Annual,* ed. M. Maehr and D. Bartz. Greenwich, Conn., 1984.

Sauer, Carl. *Sixteenth-Century North America.* Berkeley, Calif., 1971.

Schemo, Diana Jean. "Despite Options on Census Many to Check 'Black' Only." *New York Times,* February 12, 2000, A1, A9.

Schneller, Johanna. "Drama Queen." *Premier,* August 2000, 57–62.

Schofield, Janet Ward. *Black and White in School: Trust Tension or Tolerance?* New York, 1989.

Schuman, Howard, Charlotte Steeh, Lawrence Bobo, and Maria Krysan. *Racial Attitudes in America: Trends and Interpretation.* Rev. ed. Cambridge, Mass., 1997.

Sears, David O., Jim Sidanius, and Lawrence Bobo, eds. *Racialized Politics: The Debate about Racism in America.* Chicago, 2000.

Sears, David, John Hetts, Jim Sidanius, and Lawrence Bobo, "Race in American Politics." In *Racialized Politics: The Debate about Racism in America,* edited by David O. Sears, Jim Sidanius, and Lawrence Bobo, 1–43. Chicago, 2000.

Shanklin, Eugenia. *Anthropology and Race.* Belmont, Calif., 1994.

Shipler, David K. *A Country of Strangers: Blacks and Whites in America.* New York, 1997.

Shoemaker, Nancy. "How Indians Got to Be Red." *American Historical Review,* 102(3): 631 (June 1997).

Shreeve, James. "Terms of Estrangement." *Discover,* November 1994, 56–63.

Siegel, Reva. "The Racial Rhetorics of Colorblind Constitutionalism: The Case of *Hopwood v. Texas.*" In *Race and Representation: Affirmative Action,* edited by Robert Post and Michael Rogin, 29–72. New York, 1998.

Skillen, Anthony. "Racism." In *Encyclopedia of Applied Ethics,* vol. 3, edited by Ruth Chadwick, 777–789. San Diego, Calif., 1998.

———. "Racism: Flew's Concepts of Racism." *Journal of Applied Philosophy,* 10: 73–89 (1993).

Skin Deep. Directed by Frances Reid. Iris Films, 1991.

Sleeper, Jim. *Liberal Racism.* New York, 1997.

Smedley, Audrey. *Race in North America: Origin and Evolution of a Worldview.* 2d ed. Boulder, Colo., 1993.

Smith, Robert C. *Racism in the Post Civil Rights Era: Now You See It, Now You Don't.* Albany, NY., 1996.

Sniderman, Paul M., and Edward G. Carmines. *Reaching Beyond Race.* Cambridge, Mass., 1997.

Sniderman, Paul M., and Thomas Piazza. *The Scar of Race.* Cambridge, Mass., 1993.

Snowden, Frank M. *Before Color Prejudice: The Ancient View of Blacks.* Cambridge, Mass., 1983.

Snowden, Frank. "Europe's Oldest Chapter in the History of Black-White Relations." In *Racism and Anti-racism in World Perspective,* edited by Benjamin Bowser, 3–26. London, 1995.

A Soldier's Story. Written by Charles Fuller, directed by Norman Jewison. Columbia Pictures, 1984.

Sollors, Werner. "Foreword: Theories of American Ethnicity." In *Theories of Ethnicity: A Classical Reader,* edited by Werner Sollors, x–xi. New York, 1996.

———, ed. *Interracialism: Black-White Intermarriage in American History, Literature, and the Law.* New York, 2000.

———, ed. *Theories of Ethnicity: A Classical Reader.* New York, 1996.

Spencer, Rainier. *Spurious Issues: Race and Multiracial Identity Politics in the United States.* Boulder, Colo., 1999.

Stephan, Walter. *Reducing Prejudice and Stereotyping in Schools.* New York, 1999.

Stephan, Walter, and David Rosenfield. "Racial and Ethnic Stereotypes." In *In the Eye of the Beholder: Contemporary Issues in Stereotyping,* edited by Arthur G. Miller, 92–136. New York, 1982.

Stocking, George W. Jr. "The Turn-of-the-Century Concept of Race." *MODERNISM\modernity* 1(1) (1993): 4–16.

Sturm, Susan, and Lani Guinier. "The Future of Affirmative Action: Reclaiming the Innovative Ideal." *California Law Review* 84(4): 953–1036 (July 1996).

Suskind, Ron. *A Hope in the Unseen: An American Odyssey from the Inner City to the Ivy League.* New York, 1998.

Takaki, Ronald. "The Heathen Chinee." In *Strangers from a Different Shore: A History of Asian-Americans,* 99–112. Boston, 1989.

Tatum, Beverly. *"Why Are All the Black Kids Sitting Together in the Cafeteria?" and Other Conversations about Race.* Rev. ed. New York, 1997.

Taylor, Charles. "The Politics of Recognition." In *Multiculturalism,* edited by Amy Gutmann, 25–74. Princeton, N.J., 1994.

———. *Sources of the Self: The Making of Modern Identity.* Cambridge, Mass., 1989.

Terkel, Studs. *American Dreams: Lost and Found.* (New York, 1980).

———. *Race: How Blacks and Whites Think and Feel about the American Obsession.* New York, 1992.

Thomas, Laurence. "Moral Deference." In *African-American Perspectives and Philosophical Traditions,* edited by John P. Pittman. New York, 1997.

Tirrell, Lynne. "Derogatory Terms: Racism, Sexism, and the Inferential Role Theory of Meaning." In *Language and Liberation,* edited by Christina Hendricks and Kelly Oliver, 41–79. Albany, N.Y., 1999.

Tizon, Alex. "Whale Killing Uncovers Anti-Indian Hatred." *Boston Globe,* May 30, 1999.

Todorov, Tzvetan. *On Human Diversity: Nationalism, Racism, and Exoticism in French Thought.* Translated by Catherine Porter. Cambridge, Mass., 1993.

Tribe, Laurence. *Constitutional Choices.* Cambridge, Mass., 1985.

Trow, Martin. "California After Racial Preferences." *Public Interest,* spring 1999, 64–85.

Uya, O. E. *African Diaspora and the Black Experience in New World Slavery*. Lagos, Nigeria, 1992.

Vasquez, Daniel, and Stephen Kurkjian. "Probe Finds No Racism in Noose." *Boston Globe*, May 5, 1999, A1, A23.

Vaughan, Alden. *Roots of American Racism: Essays on the Colonial Experience*. New York, 1995.

von Herder, J. G. *Reflections on the Philosophy of the History of Mankind*. Abridged and with Introduction by Frank E. Manuel. Chicago, 1968.

Wasserman, David. "Discrimination, Concept of." In *Encyclopedia of Applied Ethics* vol. 1, edited by Ruth Chadwick, 805–814. San Diego, Calif., 1998.

Waters, Mary. *Ethnic Options: Choosing Identities in America*. Berkeley, Calif., 1990.

——. "Explaining the Comfort Factor: West Indian Immigrants Confront American Race Relations." In *The Cultural Territories of Race: Of Black and White Boundaries*, edited by Michele Lamont, 63–96. Chicago, 1999.

The Way We Were. Directed by Sydney Pollack. Alcor Films, 1973.

Weberman, David, and Yolanda Howze. "On Racial Kinship." *Social Theory and Practice* 27, no. 3 (July 2001).

Weinraub, Bernard. "Stung by Criticism of Fall Shows, TV Networks Add Minority Roles." *New York Times*, September 20, 1999, A1, A14.

Wellman, David T. *Portraits of White Racism*, 2d ed. Cambridge, Eng., 1993.

Wessmann v. Gittens, 160 F. 3d 790 (U.S. Court of Appeals 1st Cir. 1998).

"What the Human Genome Means to You." *Johns Hopkins Medical Letter, Health After 50* 12 (10): 6 (December 2000).

Wieviorka, Michel. "Is It So Difficult to Be an Anti-racist?" In *Debating Cultural Hybridity: Multi-cultural Identities and the Politics of Anti-racism*, edited by Pnina Werbner and Tariq Modood. London, 1997.

Wilkins, David. "Introduction: The Context of Race." In *Color Conscious*, edited by K. A. Appiah and A. Gutmann, 3–29. Princeton, N.J., 1996.

Willett, Cynthia, ed. *Theorizing Multiculturalism: A Guide to the Current Debate*. London, 1998.

Williams, Bernard. *Shame and Necessity*. Berkeley, Calif., 1993.

Williams, Patricia. *The Rooster's Egg: On the Persistence of Prejudice*. Cambridge, Mass., 1995.

Williams, Vernon J., Jr. *Rethinking Race: Franz Boas and His Contemporaries*. Lexington, Ky., 1996.

Wilson, William Julius. *The Truly Disadvantaged: The Inner City, the Underclass, and Public Policy*. Chicago, 1987.

——. *When Work Disappears: The World of the New Urban Poor*. New York, 1996.

Winter, Greg. "Coca-Cola Settles Racial Bias Case." *New York Times*, November 17, 2000, A1, C6.

Wygant v. Jackson Board of Education, 106 S. Ct. 1842 (1986).

Zack, Naomi. "An Autobiographical View of Mixed Race and Deracination." *American Philosophical Association Newsletter on Philosophy and the Black Experience* 91 (1): 6–10 (spring 1992).

——, ed. *American Mixed Race: The Culture of Microdiversity*. Lanham, Md., 1995.

——, ed. *Race/Sex: Their Sameness, Difference, and Interplay*. New York, 1997.

Index